Navigating Stress in the Workplace

Dr. Pauline Belton

ISBN: 979-8-9864216-9-8

Published by: Quill & Company Publishing
thequillandcompany@gmail.com

First edition, 2025
Printed in the United States of America

Contents

Introduction

I didn't even realize my body was shutting down until it screamed loud enough for me to listen.

The first time it happened, I was 24 years old. It was 1994, and my life was a whirlwind of new beginnings. I had just finished my master's degree, started my career as a school counselor, and moved to a new state. One afternoon, I was driving home on a busy stretch of highway in Charlotte, North Carolina, when the traffic lights ahead dissolved into blurry, indistinguishable smudges of light. My world was refusing to come into focus. A cold, sharp panic seized my chest. I was terrified.

That moment was the first sign. The first time my body sent a desperate signal that I didn't know how to read. I was young, ambitious, and grieving the recent loss of my grandmother, one of the biggest fans in my life. I was pressing through, moving through, not paying attention to my body because I thought I could handle it all. After doctors misdiagnosed the incident as a detached retina, I spent three months unable to work, resting my body while my mind raced with fear. My sight eventually returned, however, the message was clear, even if I didn't fully hear it then. I didn't do stress well.

Seventeen years later, my body screamed again. By 2011, my life was fuller and more complex. I was a mother, a wife, a school administrator, and my private practice was growing. I was doing probably way too much, and in the midst of navigating personal instability and the lingering grief from my mother's passing, it happened again. Driving home on a busy highway, my vision blurred, and the world went out of focus. This time, I learned the truth. I had a rare condition, affecting less than 1% of the population, where acute stress causes physical trauma in the retina. I had abandoned all the routines and systems I'd put in place to keep myself aligned. My body was simply reacting to neglect.

That should have been the final wake-up call. However, it wasn't.

The final call came in the form of 18 months of painful, inexplicable hives. Doctors ran every test imaginable. Nothing made sense. I was still showing up, as an assistant principal, a leadership consultant, and a clinical therapist, smiling through the chaos because I didn't know what else to do. Finally, an allergist at Johns Hopkins University discovered the truth: my histamine system had collapsed under chronic stress.

It wasn't a food allergy. It wasn't an autoimmune disorder. It was burnout. The invisible kind. My body simply couldn't take it anymore. That was my true wake-up call. I didn't need another prescription. I needed a full body reset. I needed a way to heal without quitting my career or sacrificing my sanity. I had to learn what was missing. I was pushing through instead of building resilience. I was ignoring the signs, my body was screaming at me.

And that's when everything changed.

This book is for the high-achievers, the leaders, and the dedicated professionals who feel the weight of expectation and are tired of paying the high cost of success. It is for anyone who has been told that burnout is just the price of ambition but refuses to accept that premise. This is for you if you are ready to build a different way forward. This realization led me to deconstruct everything I thought I knew and build a new way forward. Not just about coping but about reclaiming your energy, your calm, and your ability to thrive. Because here's what I discovered lying on that examination table at Johns Hopkins, covered in hives and finally willing to hear the truth: **the problem wasn't that I couldn't handle stress. The problem was that no one had ever taught me how to build real resilience.**

Not the Instagram version. Not the "just breathe and it'll be fine" version. But the kind of resilience that catches you before the crash, that rebuilds you stronger after the breakdown, that transforms your relationship with stress from something that destroys you into something that develops you.

So if you're pushing through the pain, convincing yourself you're fine, and ignoring the whispers your body is already shouting, let this be your wake-up call. Don't wait until your body forces you to stop. Say yes to your reset. Say yes to a new way of living that could shift your entire life.

Say yes to the 3 A's of Resilience.

The Framework Born from Rock Bottom

Here's what I learned from my body's rebellion: **coping isn't the same as thriving.** And resilience isn't something you're born with, it's something you build, deliberately and daily.

After that final breakdown, I didn't just want to "manage" my stress. I wanted to understand why I kept ignoring every warning sign until my body had no choice but to shut me down. I needed a system that would catch me *before* the crash, not after. Something practical. Something I could actually use in the middle of a chaotic workday when the pressure was mounting, and the old patterns were screaming at me to just push through.

That's when the 3 A's Resilience Framework was born not from a textbook or a weekend retreat, but from 18 months of hives, two vision crises, and the humbling realization that everything I'd been taught about handling stress was fundamentally broken.

The 3 A's aren't theory. They're survival to thriving.

Awareness: You can't change what you can't see. For years, I missed every single signal my body sent because I was too busy performing productivity. Awareness taught me to catch the whispers before they became screams, to notice the tension in my jaw during meetings, the shallow breathing when my calendar was overbooked, the irritability that had nothing to do with my team and everything to do with my neglected needs. This is where resilience begins: recognizing your stress signals before your body forces a shutdown.

Action: Awareness without action is just expensive self-awareness. Action is where the reset happens. It's the boundary you finally set. The meeting you decline. The morning routine you protect like your life depends on it, because it does. Action is choosing resilience over performance, over and over again, even when everything in your environment rewards the opposite. It's not about grand gestures. It's about the small, consistent choices that honor what your body is telling you.

Adaptation: Here's what no one tells you about resilience: it's not about bouncing back to who you were before the crisis. It's about evolving into someone who doesn't break the same way twice. Adaptation means learning from every breakdown, recalibrating your systems, and building flexibility into your life so you can bend without shattering. It's the difference between surviving stress and leveraging it for growth. You don't just recover. You become more resilient than you were before.

This framework saved my life. Now it's saving my clients' lives too.

Because here's the truth most workplace wellness programs won't tell you: **stress doesn't care about your meditation app or your standing desk.** Real resilience isn't built in a yoga class or a mindfulness retreat. It's built in the moment you're about to say yes when you need to say no. It's built when you choose to honor what your body is telling you instead of pushing through one more time. It's built when you use every challenge as data for becoming stronger, smarter, and more sustainable.

The workplace isn't going to get less demanding. The deadlines aren't going to disappear. The pressure isn't going to ease up. But you can change how you navigate it. You can build a life where success doesn't require burnout as the entry fee. You can develop the kind of resilience that doesn't just help you survive. It helps you thrive.

That's what this book is about giving you the framework I wish I'd had at 24, at 41, and every overwhelmed moment in between. Not theory. Not platitudes. Just the truth about what actually works when your body is screaming and your career is demanding and you refuse to choose between your health and your ambitions.

You don't have to wait for your wake-up call. This is it.

Let's do this together.

Chapter 1
The Anatomy of Stress

Let me tell you about a client I'll call David. When he first walked into my office, he looked like the quintessential high-achiever. Sharp suit, firm handshake, a résumé that read like a highlight reel of corporate success. He was a vice president at a competitive tech firm, a man paid to solve complex problems and lead teams through high-stakes product launches. He came to me not because he thought he was "stressed". Rather, his doctor, after a series of tests for chronic migraines, had given him an ultimatum: "Figure out your stress, or you'll be on medication for the rest of your life."

"I'm not stressed," David insisted, sitting stiffly on the edge of the couch. "I thrive on pressure. The deadlines, the competition... that's just the cost of doing business. My problem is these headaches. My sleep. I haven't had a decent night's sleep in months. And maybe," he conceded, his voice dropping, "I've been a little short with my team. And my wife."

David's story is one I've heard a hundred times in a hundred different forms. He was a man at war with a phantom enemy. He was fighting his migraines, his insomnia, and his irritability. However, he completely failed to recognize the unifying force behind them all. He was suffering from one of the most profound and common misconceptions of our time: he believed stress was an external event, a series of difficult circumstances to be powered through. He couldn't see that stress wasn't the demanding boss, the impossible deadline, or the market pressure. Those were just the triggers. The stress was what was happening *inside* him. It was the frantic, silent alarm ringing erratically through his nervous system, an alarm he had become so accustomed to hearing that he no longer recognized it as a warning.

Before we can even begin to navigate stress, we have to learn to define it correctly. We have to stop looking outside of ourselves and start looking within. This is where the first "A" of resilience, **Awareness**, becomes non-negotiable.

The Great Misconception: Stress vs. Stressors

In my workshops, I often start with a simple question: "What is stress?" The answers come flying back at me: "My boss." "My commute." "My inbox." "My kids' school schedule." "The looming recession."

I listen patiently and then I gently correct them. "Those aren't stress," I explain. "Those are **stressors**."

This is the single most important distinction you must understand if you want to reclaim how you show up in your life. **A stressor is any external person, place, thing, or situation that places a weighted demand on you.** It's the trigger. **Stress, on the other hand, is your body's internal response to that trigger.** It is the cascade of physiological and psychological events that happen inside you when your brain perceives a threat, a challenge, or a demand.

Here's the truth most workplace wellness programs won't tell you: **you can't control the stressors, but you can absolutely transform your stress response.** This is the foundation of everything we'll build together in this book.

The False Alarm Economy: Why Your Body Keeps Screaming

Think of stress like a building's emergency system. The stressor is the actual emergency, the smoke, the fire, the break-in. Your stress response is the alarm system designed to alert you and mobilize action.

But here's where it gets complicated for high-functioning professionals like David: **most of us are living in what I call the False Alarm Economy.** We've trained our internal alarm systems to treat every email like a five-alarm fire. Every meeting becomes a four-alarm emergency. Every deadline triggers a three-alarm response. Your system is so flooded with false alarms that you can no longer distinguish between a genuine crisis and Tuesday.

The result? You stop trusting your own internal signals. You override them. You silence them. You convince yourself that the constant ringing is just "the sound of success" or "the price of ambition." And your body, brilliant, resilient, but not invincible, starts breaking down in creative and alarming ways.

This is the False Alarm Economy: a state where your nervous system is perpetually in emergency mode, responding to perceived threats with the same intensity it would respond to actual danger. It's expensive. The currency isn't money. It's your health, your relationships, your decision-making capacity, and eventually, your career.

David was bankrupt in this economy. His body had been screaming for months, but he'd learned to ignore the alarm so completely that he needed a doctor's ultimatum to even consider that something was wrong.

The Two Faces of Stress: Growth Pressure vs. Breaking Pressure

Further complicating our relationship with stress is the fact that not all stress is created equal. Your body's alarm can ring for different reasons, some of which actually indicate growth and expansion, while others signal genuine danger and depletion. I call these **Growth Pressure and Break-ing Pressure.**

Growth Pressure is the productive stress that stretches your capacity without snapping it. It's the stress that feels exciting, motivating, and energizing. It sharpens your focus and pushes you toward a bigger version of yourself. Think of the internal state you experience in these workplace scenarios:

> **The Big Promotion:** You've just been offered the leadership position you've been working toward for years. It comes with a new title, a bigger salary, and a team to lead. The demands are immense. You feel a jolt of nervous energy, your heart beats a little faster when you think about the responsibility, and you might have a few sleepless nights anticipating the challenge. This is Growth Pressure. Your body is preparing you to expand into a larger professional identity. The stress is a byproduct of evolution, not destruction.

> **A High-Stakes Presentation:** You're about to present your team's project to the executive board. You've prepared for weeks. In the moments before you speak, your palms might be sweaty, and your stomach might be doing flips. This is your body's way of preparing you for peak performance. It's flooding your system with the right chemicals at the right time to make you sharp, focused, and articulate. This is Growth Pressure in action. It enhances your capabilities when you need them most.

Launching a New Venture: You're leading a team on a new, innovative project that could redefine the company's future. The timeline is aggressive, the budget is tight, and the outcome is uncertain. The pressure is on. However, the work is meaningful, and your team is buzzing with creative energy. The stress you feel is tied to a sense of purpose and possibility. It fuels late-night breakthroughs and collaborative innovation.

Breaking Pressure is the destructive stress that feels depleting, demoralizing, and overwhelming. It's the kind of stress that dismantles you piece by piece, chipping away at your confidence, your health, and your sense of professional identity. Breaking Pressure is what leads to the breakdowns I see in my practice. Consider these all-too-common workplace examples:

The Toxic Boss: Your supervisor is a micromanager who communicates exclusively through criticism and condescension. Every interaction with them leaves you feeling small, anxious, and defensive. You dread going to work. Your stomach clenches every time you see their name pop up in your inbox. This is Breaking Pressure. It's a chronic, corrosive stress that erodes your sense of psychological safety and self-worth. There is **no growth here, only survival.**

Impossible Workload: Your company has gone through layoffs, and you've inherited the responsibilities of two former colleagues. You're working 12-hour days just to keep your head above water. However, you're constantly falling behind. The feeling is not one of exciting challenge, but of hopeless, relentless overwhelm. You're exhausted, you're making mistakes, and you see no end in sight. This is Breaking Pressure, **stress without meaning, effort without impact.**

A Project Failure: A major project you were leading has failed publicly. You're facing criticism from leadership and you're filled with a sense of shame and professional dread. The stress you're feeling is tied to a fear of consequences and a loss of identity. It keeps you up at night, replaying every misstep and catastrophizing about your future. This is Breaking Pressure **masquerading as accountability.**

Here's what makes this distinction so crucial: **on a purely physiological level, your body's initial response to Growth Pressure and Breaking Pressure can look remarkably similar.** The jolt of getting a promotion and the jolt of a critical email from your boss can both trigger the same stress hormones. Your heart rate can spike in both scenarios.

The critical difference lies in three factors: **context, duration, and recovery.** Growth Pressure is typically short-term, manageable, and followed by periods of rest and integration. It's perceived as a challenge you can meet with your current or slightly stretched resources. Breaking Pressure is often long-term, unmanageable, and offers no recovery time. It's perceived as a threat you cannot handle, no matter what you do.

Without the tools to manage your internal state, without the **Awareness** to distinguish between these two types of pressure, your body defaults to treating everything like Breaking Pressure. You get stuck in the False Alarm Economy, unable to differentiate between a thrilling challenge and a debilitating threat.

The Timeline of Stress: Flash Fires vs. Slow Burns

The impact of stress on our lives is also profoundly shaped by its duration. We must learn to distinguish between a stressful moment and a stressful life. This is the difference between what I call **Flash Fire stress and Slow Burn stress.**

Flash Fire stress is your body's immediate reaction to a sudden, unexpected challenge. It's intense, dramatic, and short-lived. It is the classic survival response in its purest form, your body preparing you to handle an immediate threat with maximum resources.

Imagine you're in a big meeting with senior leadership. You think you're just there to observe. However, suddenly, the CEO turns to you and says, "What's your take on the Q3 numbers?"

In that instant, your Flash Fire response ignites. Your adrenal glands dump stress hormones into your bloodstream. Your heart rate skyrockets. Your breathing becomes shallow and rapid. Your pupils dilate. Your mind races through every data point you can remember. This is your body preparing you to handle a sudden, high-stakes moment. You deliver your answer, the moment passes, and within an hour, your system returns to baseline. You might feel a little drained, like you just sprinted up a flight of stairs, but you recover. Flash Fire stress is a normal, and often helpful, part of professional life.

Slow Burn stress is a different beast entirely. It is the chronic, relentless, low-grade state of being perpetually on alert. If Flash Fire stress is a sudden explosion, Slow Burn stress is the coal mine fire that smolders underground for years, invisible but devastating. It occurs when the stressors in our lives are constant and we feel we have no power to change them.

It's the toxic boss you have to face every single day. It's the financial pressure that never lets up. It is the feeling of being perpetually behind at work, no matter how many hours you put in. It's the dysfunctional team dynamic that drains your energy in every meeting. It's the organizational chaos that makes even simple tasks feel like navigating a minefield.

For high-functioning professionals, Slow Burn stress is the silent epidemic. It doesn't always look like a dramatic breakdown. More often, it manifests as a slow erosion of who you used to be. It looks like:

Decision fatigue: The inability to make simple choices at the end of the day because your executive function is depleted.

Emotional numbness: A feeling of being disconnected from your work, your family, and yourself. You're going through the motions, but you're not actually present.

Cynicism and irritability: A negative outlook and a short fuse become your new default. You barely recognize yourself.

Procrastination and avoidance: You dodge important tasks not because you're lazy, but because you subconsciously know you lack the mental and emotional energy to engage with them effectively.

Physical breakdown: Chronic headaches, digestive issues, insomnia, frequent illness, your body waving every red flag it has.

This was the state my client Jason was in when he was referred to me by his company's HR department.

On paper, Jason was a corporate dream. A mid-level manager in a large corporation, he was consistently hitting his numbers, staying late, and was known as the "go-to" guy when projects derailed. His superiors saw him as a rising star, the epitome of a reliable and committed leader.

The story Jason revealed in our sessions was starkly different, however. He was living in a full-blown Slow Burn. He was waking up at 3:00 AM, his mind already racing, to check emails from overseas clients. He would lie in the dark, the blue light of his phone illuminating a face tight with anxiety, his heart pounding in response to a minor query that could have easily waited until morning. He was drinking two energy drinks just to push through the afternoon slump, leaving him feeling wired but utterly exhausted. At home, he was a ghost, physically present but mentally absent. He would snap at his children for minor infractions, like spilling a glass of milk, and then be consumed by a wave of guilt and shame.

"I don't understand," he told me in our first session, his voice carrying equal parts confusion and desperation. "I've always been able to handle pressure. I don't know what's wrong with me."

Nothing was "wrong" with Jason. His body was doing exactly what it was designed to do: sending increasingly urgent signals that he was operating in an unsustainable way. The problem was that Jason had become fluent in the language of productivity but completely illiterate in the language of his own nervous system.

The turning point came when I taught him the first "A" of The 3 A's Framework™: **Awareness.** Instead of dismissing his headaches and irritability as "normal" for a man in his position, I had him start tracking his stress signals. He kept a small journal for one week, noting only three things:

Physical signals: What was his body doing? (tight chest, shallow breathing, clenched jaw, etc.)

Emotional signals: What was he feeling? (anxious, irritable, numb, overwhelmed)

Situational triggers: What was happening right before these signals appeared?

He was stunned when we reviewed his notes together. "I had no idea," he told me, looking at the patterns with genuine disbelief. "I thought I was fine until I was yelling at my kid. But my body was telling me I was in trouble hours, sometimes even days, before I snapped. I just wasn't listening."

By building this **Awareness**, the first critical A of resilience, Jason could finally see the alarm system that had been blaring in the background of his life. He wasn't broken. He wasn't weak. He was simply living in the False Alarm Economy, treating every workday like an emergency, and his body was paying the price.

Once Jason could see the patterns, we moved to the second A: **Action.** He began to pause. He replaced his automatic reactivity to tense emails with a 30-second breathing reset before responding. He started taking a five-minute walk before his weekly team meetings to clear his system. He set a hard boundary on checking work emails after 8:00 PM.

His stress didn't disappear. The stressors were still there. The demanding job, the global clients, the high expectations. However, he stopped letting his stress response control his leadership style. Within a few months, Jason went from being a stressed manager to becoming an intentional leader, modeling a sense of regulated calm that began to permeate his entire team's culture.

The third A, **Adaptation**, came naturally after that. Jason learned to use every stressful situation as data, constantly refining what worked and what didn't. He became more resilient not by eliminating stress, but by transforming his relationship with it.

The Takeover: When Your Brain Goes Offline

To understand why Jason's small pauses had such a profound impact, we need to understand what I call **The Takeover**, the moment when your emotional brain commandeers your rational thinking and you lose access to your best judgment.

Deep within your temporal lobes are two small, almond-shaped structures called the amygdala. Think of the amygdala as your brain's threat detection system, constantly scanning your environment for signs of danger. When it detects a threat, whether it's a real physical danger like a speeding car or a perceived professional danger like a critical email from your boss, it initiates what I call **The Takeover.**

During a Takeover, your amygdala sends an emergency signal to your hypothalamus, your brain's command center. This command center immediately communicates with the rest of your body through your nervous system. In milliseconds, you're in survival mode. Stress hormones flood your system. Your heart pounds, your breath quickens, and your muscles tense.

Here's the critical part: **during a Takeover, the signal from your amygdala is so strong and so fast that it bypasses your prefrontal cortex**, the part of your brain right behind your forehead that handles rational thought, strategic planning, and impulse control. Your thinking brain is essentially taken offline. Your emotional, survival-focused brain is now driving the car.

This is a brilliant system for surviving an actual physical threat. If a car is speeding toward you, you don't need a committee meeting to decide whether to jump out of the way. You need immediate action.

However, it's a terrible system for navigating the nuanced, complex situations of modern professional life. **The Takeover doesn't distinguish between a physical threat and a perceived threat to your ego, your status, or your competence.** To your amygdala, a critical email and a charging bear trigger the same emergency response.

Let's walk through a scenario I see constantly with my corporate clients.

I call it **The Friday Takeover.**

It's 4:45 PM on a Friday. You're trying to wrap up your work and get home to your family. An email lands in your inbox. The subject line is from a senior leader: "Problem with the Q3 report."

Phase 1: The Trigger (0-2 seconds)

Your eyes scan the words. Before your conscious mind has even processed the content, your amygdala has already detected a potential threat. The smoke detector goes off. **The Takeover begins.**

Phase 2: The Mental Takeover (2-30 seconds)

With your prefrontal cortex offline, your thinking becomes catastrophic and binary. Your internal narrative might spiral: "I'm going to get fired. This is all my fault. I knew that data was shaky. My career is over. Everyone must think I'm incompetent. How am I going to explain this to my spouse? What if I can't find another job? What if..."
Notice what's missing here: nuance, perspective, curiosity, rational problem-solving. There is only the perceived certainty of doom. This is what thinking looks like when your emotional brain is in charge.

Phase 3: The Physical Takeover (Simultaneous with Mental)

Before you've even had a fully formed thought, your body reacts:

Jolt of adrenaline in your stomach

Heart rate instantly accelerates

Hot flush creeping up your neck or sudden coldness in your hands

Breathing becomes shallow and rapid, confined to your upper chest

Jaw clenches, shoulders rise toward your ears

Muscles tense as if preparing for physical combat

You are now, physiologically, in survival mode, primed to fight, flee, or freeze.

Phase 4: The Reactive Behavior (30 seconds - 5 minutes)
Driven by this Takeover state, you react. You might:

Immediately fire off a defensive, emotionally charged email, CC'ing a dozen people to protect yourself

Storm over to a colleague's desk and blame them for the error

Spiral into panicked paralysis, staring at the screen, unable to think or act

Call your spouse and unload your anxiety, ruining their evening too

Pour yourself a drink the moment you get home, trying to chemically override the alarm that's still screaming

This entire sequence, from email notification to reactive behavior, can unfold in less than sixty seconds. And for many high-functioning professionals, the workday is a series of these **micro-Takeovers**, leaving you drained, reactive, and making decisions you'll regret by Monday morning.

This is why the 30-second pause that Jason implemented was so transformative. **That pause was just long enough to interrupt The Takeover before it reached Phase 4.** It created a precious window of time for blood flow to return to his prefrontal cortex, allowing his rational brain to come back online and choose a regulated, strategic response instead of a reactive one.

The pause didn't eliminate his stress. It gave him **Awareness** of what was happening in his body. And that Awareness created the space for **Action**, a different choice than the one his hijacked brain was screaming at him to make.

This is the foundation of navigating stress in the workplace: learning to recognize The Takeover the moment it begins, and having the tools to interrupt it before it interrupts your career, your relationships, and your health.

The Stress Signature: Your Unique Warning System

Here's something crucial that most stress management programs miss: **your body's stress response is as unique as your fingerprint.** I call this your **Stress Signature**, the specific, predictable pattern of physical and emotional signals your body sends when you're entering the False Alarm Economy.

Some people's Stress Signature shows up as:

Tension headaches or migraines

Digestive issues (stomach pain, nausea, IBS symptoms)

Jaw clenching or teeth grinding

Shallow, rapid breathing or chest tightness

Insomnia or disrupted sleep

Skin issues (breakouts, hives, eczema flare-ups)

Increased irritability or emotional volatility

Brain fog or difficulty concentrating

Procrastination or avoidance behaviors

Changes in appetite (eating too much or too little)

My Stress Signature included vision problems and hives. Jason's was 3:00 AM anxiety spirals and jaw tension. David's was chronic migraines and insomnia.

Learning to read your Stress Signature is the foundation of Awareness, the first A of the 3 A's Framework. Once you can identify your unique warning system, you can catch yourself in the early stages of stress escalation instead of waiting until your body forces a shutdown.

This is what I taught Jason to do with his one-week tracking journal. He wasn't documenting every stressor, that would be overwhelming. He was learning to read his own Stress Signature, to become fluent in the language his body was already speaking.

Stress Across Sectors: The Same Body, Different Battles

While the internal mechanics of stress are universal, we all have the same basic nervous system, the same Takeover response, the same capacity for both Growth Pressure and Breaking Pressure. The specific stressors that trigger these responses look very different depending on your professional environment.

In my work across government agencies, academic institutions, and corporate teams, I've identified what I call **The Stress Landscape**, the unique terrain of pressure points and challenges that define each sector. Understanding your specific landscape is crucial because the intervention strategies that work brilliantly in one environment might be completely ineffective in another.

Primary Stressors: Rigid bureaucracy, limited resources, public accountability, slow-moving systems, political pressures

The Breaking Pressure Pattern: The stress here often manifests as a chronic sense of futility and powerlessness. You might have a brilliant idea for improving a critical system, but you know it will take two years and fifteen committees to get it approved, if it gets approved at all. The distress comes from feeling trapped in a web of red tape where your best efforts seem to disappear into a bureaucratic void.

Common Stress Signature: Cynicism, emotional exhaustion, disengagement, feeling "checked out" while still showing up

Navigation Strategy: Focus on radical acceptance of what you cannot control, identify your sphere of influence (what you can impact), and build strong boundaries to protect against the exhaustion of fighting immovable systems. The key is finding meaning in incremental progress rather than waiting for systemic transformation.

Primary Stressors: The "three-legged stool" of competing demands (teaching, research, service), publish-or-perish culture, emotional labor of mentoring, endless committee meetings, limited institutional support

The Breaking Pressure Pattern: The stress is one of fragmentation being pulled in a dozen directions simultaneously, unable to give any area the depth of focus it deserves. For students, it's the dual pressure of newfound independence combined with intense performance expectations.

Common Stress Signature: Mental exhaustion, feeling perpetually behind, guilt about "not doing enough," resentment toward activities that feel like they "don't count" toward advancement

Navigation Strategy: Ruthless prioritization, building micro-resets between classes or meetings, seeking institutional support for emotional labor, and creating clear boundaries around which demands you'll meet and which you'll strategically decline.

Primary Stressors: Profit-driven pressure, aggressive deadlines, competitive culture, constant evaluation, unclear communication, blurred work-life boundaries

The Breaking Pressure Pattern: The distress here is one of constant evaluation and the fear of falling behind. It's the 9:00 PM email from a director that, even if it says "respond in the morning," sets your entire nervous system on high alert. It's the feeling that if you're not always available, always performing, always exceeding expectations, you're somehow failing.

Common Stress Signature: Sunday evening dread, difficulty disconnecting from work, checking emails compulsively, irritability at home, sacrificing health and relationships for performance metrics

Navigation Strategy: Establish firm boundaries around availability, create clear communication protocols with your team, build performance resilience that allows for both ambition and recovery, and redefine success to include sustainability alongside achievement.

The Universal Truth

No matter which landscape you're navigating, the underlying truth remains the same: **un-navigated stress is expensive.** It costs you your health, your relationships, your creativity, your decision-making capacity, and ultimately, your career longevity.

The first step to reclaiming these things is to understand the true anatomy of stress, to see it not as an external enemy to be conquered, but as an internal signal to be understood, respected, and navigated with intention.

Reflection Questions for Chapter 1

Self-Assessment Question: Think about the last time you felt "stressed." Can you separate the **stressor** (the external event) from your **stress response** (your internal reaction)? What physical or emotional signals did your body send you that you might have ignored or minimized?

Pattern Recognition Question: Can you identify one example of **Growth Pressure** and one example of **Breaking Pressure** in your work life over the past month? Where in your body do you feel the difference? Are there patterns you've been dismissing as "normal" that might actually be your body's early warning system?

Application Question: Describe a recent experience where you felt emotionally hijacked at work. Looking back with the framework of **The Takeover**, what is one small thing you could do differently at the Intervention Point, before the reactive behavior begins?

Accountability Question: How will you track your progress in building **Awareness** this week? Commit to logging at least one instance of your **Stress Signature** each day in a journal or a note on your phone to begin building the habit of noticing.

Future-Focused Question: What becomes possible for you if you master the ability to distinguish between stressors and your stress response? What would change in your career and life if you could catch **The Takeover** before it takes complete control?

Chapter 2
THE COST OF CARRYING STRESS

I want to introduce you to a woman I'll call Sarah. When she first came to me, she was the picture of dedication. A veteran high school English teacher, she was adored by her students and respected by her colleagues. She was the one who stayed late to help students with their college essays, the one who chaperoned every dance, the one whose classroom was a safe haven for kids who felt lost in the sprawling, impersonal hallways of the school. Sarah didn't just teach literature, she taught life. She believed, with every fiber of her being, that this was her calling.

She sought me out not for burnout, a term she associated with younger, less committed teachers, but for what she described as a persistent "brain fog" and a troubling lack of patience with her husband. "I just feel... flat," she explained, her hands resting limply in her lap. "I go to school, I perform, I'm 'On.' I'm the energetic, inspiring Mrs. Davidson my students need me to be. The moment I get into my car to go home, however, it's like a switch flips. All the color drains out of the world. I have nothing left. My husband asks me about my day, and I feel a surge of irrational anger. All I want is silence."

Sarah was paying a heavy price for her dedication, a tax she didn't even know was being levied. It was the cost of carrying unmanaged stress, a cost that is often invisible, unacknowledged, and profoundly damaging. She was a master of a skill that is both highly valued and incredibly dangerous in today's workplace: **The Performance Tax**, the exhausting work of regulating your emotions to meet everyone else's needs while completely neglecting your own.

The costs of unmanaged stress aren't found on a balance sheet or in a performance review, at least not at first. They are hidden costs, accumulating silently in the background, like a debt gathering compound interest. They are paid in the currency of our health, our relationships, our creativity, and our very sense of self. Eventually, that debt always comes due. And when it does, the bill is astronomical.

The Performance Tax: The Invisible Cost of Showing Up

The Performance Tax is what I call the exhausting, often uncompensated work of managing your internal emotional state to create a desired effect in others. It's not just about "faking a smile," though that's certainly part of it. It's the constant, conscious effort to project calm in the middle of chaos, to manufacture empathy when you feel drained, and to perform patience in the face of frustration. It is a low-level, continuous performance that most people don't even realize they're giving until they're completely depleted.

The Performance Tax is levied every single day in workplaces across every sector. And like any tax, it extracts a cost from your finite resources. The problem is that most of us don't track what we're paying, so we're shocked when we discover we're bankrupt.

Think about the different forms this Performance Tax takes in the workplace:

> **The Empathetic Leader:** A team leader has to announce a round of layoffs. Privately, she is heartbroken and anxious about her own job security. In the meeting, however, she must project an aura of steady, compassionate authority to

manage the fear and grief of her team. She absorbs their anger and their sadness, holding a space for them that no one is holding for her. She pays the Performance Tax in full while her own emotional needs remain completely unfunded.

The HR Manager: An HR professional spends their day listening to a litany of employee grievances, from claims of harassment to the raw pain of a recent death in a colleague's family. They must remain neutral, supportive, and professional, acting as a container for the organization's collective trauma, all while suppressing their own emotional responses. The Performance Tax here is enormous. They're expected to be emotionally available to everyone while remaining emotionally invisible themselves.

The ER Nurse: An emergency room nurse works a 12-hour shift filled with tragedy and high-stakes medical crises. He must deliver devastating news to a family with calm compassion, then immediately pivot to handle a new trauma patient with focused, life-saving urgency, suppressing his own feelings of grief or overwhelm. The Performance Tax is extracted shift after shift, with little time for emotional recovery between withdrawals.

The Call Center Representative: A customer service agent is verbally abused by a frustrated customer. Her job requires her to remain polite, helpful, and apologetic, even as her nervous system is screaming that she is under attack. She has to swallow her own defensive anger and guide the conversation to a calm resolution. The Performance Tax here is particularly brutal because it requires her to betray her own self-protective instincts in real-time.

For my client Sarah, the Performance Tax was immense. She was a daily emotional shock absorber for 150 teenagers. She absorbed their academic pressures, their social dramas, their fears about the future, and sometimes, the trauma of their unstable home lives. Her job required her to be a beacon of stability, enthusiasm, and endless patience, day after day, period after period, year after year.

The critical thing to understand about the Performance Tax is this: **it's not free. Every withdrawal has a cost.** And if you're making constant withdrawals without any deposits, you will eventually overdraw your account.

The Resilience Budget: Your Daily Emotional Economy

To understand why the Performance Tax is so devastating, you need to understand what I call **The Resilience Budget**, your daily allotment of emotional, mental, and physical resources.

Imagine you wake up each morning with a specific budget of resilience points. Let's say it's 100 points. These points represent your capacity to handle stress, regulate emotions, make decisions, show up with patience and presence, and perform at your best. Everything you do throughout the day either makes a withdrawal from this budget or, in rare cases, makes a deposit.

Here's what a typical day might look like:

Morning:

Wake up after poor sleep due to work stress: Start day at 85 points (already depleted)

Skip breakfast to answer urgent emails: -5 points (no fuel, heightened stress)

Difficult commute with traffic: -10 points

Arrive at work already at 70 points

Workday:

Back-to-back meetings with no breaks: -15 points

Difficult conversation with underperforming team member (Performance Tax): -20 points

Urgent request from senior leadership requiring immediate attention: -15 points

Skip lunch to meet deadline: -10 points

By 3 PM, you're at 10 points

Late Afternoon/Evening:

One more "quick" meeting added to your calendar: -5 points

Critical email arrives at 4:45 PM (triggers The Takeover): -10 points

Now in negative balance: -5 points

Drive home in survival mode, completely depleted

Husband asks "How was your day?" and you snap at him

This is exactly what was happening to Sarah. By the time she got into her car, her Resilience Budget wasn't just depleted. It was deeply overdrawn. The anger she felt toward her husband wasn't really about him. It was her system's desperate attempt to protect what little energy she had left.

The critical insight: Most high-functioning professionals are operating in deficit spending every single day. They're making massive withdrawals to meet the demands of their jobs without making any meaningful deposits through rest, joy, authentic connection, or recovery. This chronic deficit spending is what leads to the next devastating cost: **The Ghost in the Chair.**

The Ghost in the Chair: The Hidden Cost of Physical Presence

When you're constantly operating in Resilience Budget deficit, it leads to what I call **The Ghost in the Chair** phenomenon. This is my term for what organizational psychologists call "presenteeism," but that sterile, academic term doesn't capture the haunting reality of what's actually happening.

The Ghost in the Chair is when your body shows up to work, but your mind, your spirit, and your capacity have already left the building. You're physically present, sitting in meetings, responding to emails, going through the motions, but you are not *there*. Not really. Your capacity to focus, to create, to problem-solve, to connect authentically, and to perform at even a fraction of your potential has been hollowed out by unmanaged stress.

This is the quiet, invisible middle stage of burnout, and it is devastatingly costly for both individuals and organizations. The Ghost in the Chair can cut individual productivity by one-third or more, and it's a major source of workplace errors, missed opportunities, and team dysfunction. Yet because the person is physically present, leadership often doesn't see the problem until it becomes catastrophic.

Here are some of the high-performers I've worked with who were unknowingly operating as Ghosts in the Chair:

Mark, the Meticulous Analyst: The Precision Ghost

Mark was a financial analyst known for his laser focus and attention to detail. His spreadsheets were legendary for their accuracy. He was the person leadership turned to when they needed numbers they could trust.

Over a period of six months, however, something shifted. Mark started making small, uncharacteristic errors, a misplaced decimal here, a miscalculated formula there. They were minor enough to go unnoticed at first. However, one of them eventually contributed to an inaccurate quarterly forecast, a significant problem for his company that affected major strategic decisions.

The warning signs had been there for anyone trained to see them. Mark had stopped participating in team meetings, staring blankly during discussions as if he were watching a movie with the sound off. His colleagues noticed he looked perpetually exhausted, his eyes flat and distant. He was physically at his desk for ten hours a day. However, his sharp, analytical mind was only truly online for three or four of them. The rest of the time, he was operating on autopilot, a ghost going through familiar motions in an empty building.

When Mark finally came to work with me, mandated by his concerned manager, he described the experience perfectly: "It's like I'm watching myself work from somewhere outside my body. I can see my hands typing, but I'm not connected to it. I know I'm making mistakes, but I can't seem to care enough to fix them. I'm just... not there."

Maria, the Passionate Project Manager: The Innovation Ghost

Maria was a dynamic project manager who genuinely loved her job. She was known for her creative ideas, her proactive approach to solving problems, and her infectious enthusiasm that energized entire teams. Maria was the kind of leader who made work feel meaningful.

After a grueling year-long project with an incredibly demanding client, constant scope changes, unrealistic deadlines, and zero appreciation for her team's efforts, her colleagues noticed a profound shift. Maria became quiet in brainstorming sessions, the spark completely gone from her eyes. She stopped offering innovative solutions and instead just executed the bare minimum required to move her projects forward. She was still technically competent, she never missed a deadline, but her discretionary effort, the passion, creativity, and strategic thinking that had once made her a star performer, had vanished completely.

Maria had become a Ghost in the Chair. Her body showed up, her hands moved the work forward, but the person who had once brought meaning and innovation to her role was no longer present. She was operating in a state of profound emotional and creative bankruptcy.

The Ghost in the Chair is not laziness. It's not a character flaw. It's not even really a choice. **It's a survival mechanism.**

When your Resilience Budget is chronically depleted, when you're making massive daily withdrawals with no deposits, your nervous system eventually shifts into a low-power conservation mode to protect whatever energy remains. It's the human equivalent of a smartphone switching to low-battery mode: dimming the screen, closing background apps, disabling unnecessary features to preserve core functions.

The "core functions" your system keeps running are basic task execution and physical survival. Everything extra, creativity, innovation, strategic thinking, authentic connection, proactive problem-solving, enthusiasm, gets shut down to conserve energy. You become a ghost of your former professional self, haunting your own workplace.

This is where **Awareness**, the first A of The 3 A's Framework™, becomes absolutely critical. You cannot fix a problem you cannot see. Mark didn't realize he'd become a Ghost until his errors became undeniable. Maria didn't recognize her own absence until a trusted colleague pulled her aside and said, "You're not yourself anymore. What's going on?"

The earlier you can develop Awareness of your Resilience Budget and recognize when you're slipping into deficit spending, the earlier you can take **Action**, the second A, before you become a Ghost in your own professional life.

The Three Faces of Burnout: When the Ghost Becomes Permanent

If the Performance Tax and The Ghost in the Chair are the chronic warning signs, burnout is the acute diagnosis, the moment when your system stops warning you and simply shuts down.

The World Health Organization now officially recognizes burnout as an occupational phenomenon, not a personal failing. It's not "having a bad week" or "just being stressed." **Burnout is a state of profound physical, emotional, and mental exhaustion caused by prolonged and excessive stress.** It's what happens when you ignore your Resilience Budget for so long that your account doesn't just go into deficit. It gets closed entirely.

In my clinical work, I use researcher Christina Maslach's framework as a foundation, but I've reframed it through the lens of what I see in my practice. Understanding these three dimensions of burnout helps my clients see that their experience isn't a personal failure. It's a predictable, patterned response to an unsustainable situation.

The Depletion is the hallmark of burnout, and it's an exhaustion that goes far beyond normal tiredness. This isn't "I need a vacation" tired. This is bone-deep, soul-crushing depletion that sleep doesn't seem to touch.

It's the feeling of waking up in the morning with the same oppressive sense of fatigue you had when you went to bed, as if you never rested at all.

It's physical: chronic headaches, digestive issues, increased susceptibility to illness, a body that feels heavy and uncooperative. It's also emotional and cognitive, a feeling that you simply *cannot* face another day, another meeting, another demand. The very thought of a new task feels like being asked to lift an impossibly heavy weight with arms that have no strength left.

The Depletion is your Resilience Budget at absolute zero. You have nothing left to withdraw. You are running on fumes, and even those are almost gone.

The Disconnection is a powerful, and often subconscious, protective mechanism. When you are deeply depleted and feel you have no control over your workload or environment, your mind creates emotional distance to survive. If you can't leave the situation, you leave *yourself*.

The Disconnection manifests as profound cynicism and depersonalization. It's that protective wall your psyche builds to stop caring so much about things that are breaking you. It's the passionate teacher, like Sarah, who starts referring to her students as "these kids" and feels growing resentment toward their needs. It's the dedicated doctor who starts seeing patients not as people with complex lives, but as a collection of symptoms or a room number. It's the idealistic nonprofit worker who starts making sarcastic, bitter jokes about the very mission they once cherished.

The Disconnection is an attempt to numb the pain of caring deeply when you no longer have the resources to act on that care. It's a tragic sign that a person has become separated from their own sense of purpose and meaning. The work that once felt like a calling now feels like a burden. The people you once served with passion now feel like obstacles. You've disconnected from the very thing that made the work worthwhile.

The Collapse is the final, devastating dimension where The Depletion and The Disconnection converge into a full crisis of professional competence and personal identity.

The exhaustion makes it impossible to perform at your best. The cynicism robs you of your motivation. As a result, your effectiveness declines. You start making mistakes. You fall behind on projects. You struggle with tasks that once came easily. Your performance metrics drop. You see the quality of your work slipping, and you feel powerless to stop it.

This creates a vicious, self-reinforcing cycle. You see your performance declining, which validates the cynical voice in your head that says, "This job is pointless, and I'm not even good at it anyway." It's the feeling that you are no longer making a meaningful contribution. You're not just exhausted and disconnected, you're incompetent. Or at least, that's what it feels like.

For high-achievers, The Collapse is often the most painful dimension of burnout because their professional identity is deeply intertwined with their competence and contribution. When they start to feel ineffective, it doesn't just feel like a work problem, it feels like a fundamental failure of self. This is where imposter syndrome thrives, whispering that you were always a fraud and now everyone can finally see it. This is where people tragically conclude, "I'm the problem. Something is wrong with me."

The truth is: nothing is wrong with you. Everything is wrong with operating chronologically in Resilience Budget deficit while paying exorbitant Performance Tax with no recovery strategy.

The Ripple Effect: The True Cost to Organizations and Lives

The cost of allowing burnout to fester, of ignoring the Performance Tax, dismissing the Ghosts in the Chairs, and failing to address Resilience Budget deficits, is astronomical. The damage doesn't stay contained to individual employees. It creates a devastating ripple effect that touches every aspect of an organization and every corner of a person's life.

For **organizations**, the financial and cultural impact is staggering, though often invisible until it's too late:

The Turnover Tsunami: Burned-out employees leave. And when they do, they take years of institutional knowledge, established client relationships, and hard-won expertise with them. The cost of recruiting, hiring, and training a replacement for a skilled employee can be one to two times their annual salary. Multiply that by every person who quietly resigns or suddenly quits, and you're looking at millions in preventable losses. But the financial cost is only the beginning. The real cost is the destabilization of teams, the loss of trust, and the message sent to those who remain: "You're next."

The Error Epidemic: A depleted, disengaged workforce is a workforce that makes mistakes. These can be as small as a coding bug that takes hours to fix or an accounting error that delays a project. Or they can be catastrophic: a major safety violation, a compliance failure, a medical error that harms a patient. When people are operating as Ghosts in the Chair, physically present but cognitively and emotionally depleted, the margin for error collapses. And in high-stakes environments, that collapse can be deadly.

The Contagion Effect: Burnout is contagious. A single burned-out leader can infect their entire team. Their cynicism, lack of engagement, and reactive behavior lowers morale, stifles creativity, and creates a culture of fear and exhaustion around them. When a manager is operating in The Disconnection, their team picks up on it immediately. Trust erodes. Psychological safety disappears. People stop taking risks, stop speaking up, stop innovating. The cultural damage spreads like wildfire, normalizing exhaustion and making it unsafe for anyone to set boundaries or prioritize wellbeing.

The Innovation Void: Burnout is the enemy of innovation. Creativity, strategic thinking, and breakthrough problem-solving require a surplus of mental and emotional energy, the very things burnout annihilates. A burned-out organization is an organization stuck in survival mode, unable to adapt, evolve, or create its own future. While competitors are innovating, burned-out organizations are just trying to keep the lights on. The opportunity cost is incalculable.

For **individuals**, the cost is even more profound and personal. The person who leaves the office at the end of the day is not the same person who arrived that morning. We bring the depleted, cynical, and ineffective version of ourselves home, and that version infects every other area of our lives.

Relationships Suffer and Fracture: We snap at our partners over minor things. We are disengaged and impatient with our children. We withdraw from our friends because social interaction feels like yet another demand on our overdrawn Resilience Budget. The very relationships that are meant to be a source of resilience and recovery become casualties of our depletion. Instead of being sources of joy, they become additional stressors. This is what was happening to Sarah. Her husband wasn't the problem. Her depleted state made his simple question feel like an attack.

Health Deteriorates Dramatically: Chronic stress is not a benign condition. It's a precursor to a host of serious health problems: cardiovascular disease, diabetes, autoimmune disorders, chronic pain conditions, and depression. The long-term physical cost of operating in constant Resilience Budget deficit can be life-altering, and in some cases, life-ending. Your body keeps the score, and eventually, it presents the bill.

Identity Crumbles: For many of us, our work is a core part of our identity and our sense of purpose in the world. When we burn out, we can experience a profound identity crisis. The dedicated "helper" who no longer has the capacity to help. The brilliant "problem-solver" who now feels incompetent. The passionate "leader" who has become cynical and disconnected. This loss of self can be the most painful and disorienting cost of all, leading to a deep sense of shame, worthlessness, and hopelessness. You no longer recognize yourself. And that's terrifying.

My Wake-Up Call: When the Bill Came Due

I didn't even realize my body was shutting down, until it screamed loud enough for me to listen.

For 18 months, I was covered in painful, inexplicable hives. Doctors ran every test imaginable and still couldn't give me a definitive answer. Nothing made sense. And through all of it, I kept showing up, kept performing, kept paying the Performance Tax. I was working full-time as an assistant principal during the day, running my leadership and organizational consulting practice in the evenings, and maintaining my clinical therapy practice at night. I was the picture of productivity. I was also dying from the inside out.

Here's what they finally discovered at Johns Hopkins: I was part of the 1% of the population whose histamine system collapses under chronic, unmanaged stress.

It wasn't a food allergy. It wasn't an autoimmune disorder. It was burnout, the invisible kind that high-functioning people convince themselves doesn't apply to them. My body couldn't take the chronic Resilience Budget deficit anymore. My Performance Tax bill had come due, and I couldn't pay it.

That was my true wake-up call. I didn't need another prescription or another expert opinion. I needed a full-body, full-life reset. I needed a way to heal, without quitting my career or sacrificing everything I'd built. I had to learn what was missing. I was pushing through instead of building genuine resilience. I was ignoring the signs my body was screaming at me.

That realization led me to deconstruct everything I thought I knew about stress, resilience, and sustainable high performance. It led me to create The 3 A's Framework™, not as an academic exercise, but as a survival strategy. And it's why I'm so passionate about this work. **I know what it costs to ignore the warning signs. I've paid that bill. And I'm here to help you avoid paying it yourself.**

So if you're pushing through the pain, convincing yourself you're fine, ignoring the whispers your body is already shouting, let this be your wake-up call. Don't wait until your body forces you to stop. Don't wait until you become a Ghost in the Chair. Don't wait until the bill comes due and you can't pay it.

Say yes to your reset. Say yes to learning a different way. Say yes to building real resilience instead of just performing competence.

Case Study: Amira—The Silent Burnout of a Helper

Amira was the heart and soul of her pediatric social work unit. She was known for her boundless compassion and her relentless commitment to the vulnerable children on her caseload. When a particularly traumatic case came in, a child from a deeply abusive home situation, it was always Amira who was trusted to handle it. She rarely said no. She couldn't. To her colleagues, she appeared composed, steady, and unbreakable. To herself, she had become indispensable. Her identity was completely fused with her role as the person who could handle anything.

Inwardly, she was unraveling. The descent into burnout was so gradual she didn't recognize it as descent. She thought it was just "the job." It started with skipping lunch to finish paperwork. Then it was the chronic, dull headaches she dismissed as "just stress" and treated as her new normal. Then came the emotional numbness. She would listen to a horrific story of child neglect, and while she performed all the right empathetic responses: the concerned facial expressions, the compassionate tone, the appropriate clinical interventions, she would feel a disturbing sense of detachment on the inside. Nothing touched her anymore. She mistook this numbness for professional composure, necessary armor for doing the work.

She had become a Ghost in the Chair in her own life, showing up physically but completely disconnected from her own humanity.

When she first came to work with me, it was after a full-blown panic attack had left her unable to drive to a client's home. She'd had to pull over on the side of the road, hyperventilating and sobbing, convinced she was having a heart attack. "I feel like I'm carrying everyone's life on my shoulders," she told me in our first session, her voice trembling with exhaustion and confusion, "and I'm disappearing in the process. I don't even know who I am anymore outside of this work."

Our work began with **Awareness**, the first A of The 3 A's Framework™. Amira had been operating in such severe Resilience Budget deficit for so long that she had lost all ability to track her own internal state. She could tell you everything about her clients' stress levels, but nothing about her own.

I had her start a simple tracking practice. Not about her cases, she'd been documenting those meticulously for years. This was about *her*. I asked her to journal about her own internal state using three questions:

Energy Check: On a scale of 1-10, what's your energy level right now? (Not "I should be at a 7," but "I actually am at a 3")

Depletion Mapping: Which specific interactions or tasks today left you feeling depleted versus energized?

Body Signals: What physical sensations are you experiencing? (tension, exhaustion, numbness, pain)

Within one week, Amira was stunned by the patterns that emerged. "I had no idea," she said, looking at her journal with something between disbelief and grief. "I thought the problem was that I couldn't handle the volume of work. But the real pattern is the Performance Tax. The cases that drain me the most aren't the most complex ones. They're the ones where I have to absorb everyone else's emotions while getting zero acknowledgment from my overburdened supervisors. I'm not just tired from the work. I'm exhausted from being invisible."

That **Awareness**, seeing the specific pattern of her depletion instead of just feeling generally overwhelmed, was the turning point. She could finally see where the massive withdrawals from her Resilience Budget were actually happening.

Next, we moved to **Action**, the second A. Instead of continuing to bottle up her overwhelm and say yes to every request, Amira started practicing what we developed together and called **"Boundary Scripts"**, specific, respectful ways to decline or negotiate demands.

When asked to take on another complex case when her plate was already overflowing, she learned to say: "I want to give that child the focus they deserve. Can we look at my current caseload together and prioritize? If this case is urgent, what could we reassign to create capacity?"

This small shift, from automatic "yes" to collaborative negotiation, was revolutionary for Amira. She wasn't being difficult. She wasn't being selfish. She was being strategic about her Resilience Budget so she could actually serve her clients effectively instead of becoming another Ghost in the Chair.

She also implemented what I call **Recovery Routines:** non-negotiable deposits back into her Resilience Budget:

A five-minute reset in her car between client visits where she listened to music and practiced deep breathing

A hard stop at 6:00 PM on Fridays, no exceptions

Weekly supervision sessions where she could process her own emotional responses instead of just reporting case updates

Finally, we focused on **Adaptation**, the third A. Amira began to intentionally rebuild the parts of her life and identity that had nothing to do with work. She started painting again, an old hobby she had abandoned years ago because "there wasn't time." She scheduled weekly walks with a friend where she was explicitly forbidden from talking about work. She rejoined her book club.

Most importantly, she adapted her internal narrative. She stopped seeing boundaries as selfishness and started seeing them as professional necessity. She stopped measuring her worth by how much she could endure and started measuring it by how sustainably she could serve.

Amira's transformation was profound. She shifted from a state of silent burnout to one of sustainable service. She still loved her work deeply. She was still passionate about helping vulnerable children. However, she no longer allowed the work to consume her entire identity. She learned that to truly help others over the long term, she first had to protect her own humanity. **You cannot pour from an empty cup. You can only bleed out.**

The ROI of Resilience: Why This Matters to Organizations

Organizations often hesitate to invest in stress navigation and resilience training because they see it as a "soft" benefit, not a strategic imperative. They think it's about being "nice" or creating a "comfortable" workplace. That fundamentally misunderstands what resilience work actually is.

Resilience work is risk management. It's performance optimization. It's strategic infrastructure building. And the return on investment (ROI) is massive.

After I worked with a regional leadership team at a logistics company, teaching them The 3 A's Framework™ and helping them understand concepts like The Performance Tax and The Resilience Budget, one director pulled me aside three months later. "It's lighter," he said, searching for the right words. "I don't know how else to describe it. Our team meetings are more collaborative. People are speaking up more. We just averted a major scheduling crisis because two different departments were actually talking to each other proactively instead of waiting until things exploded.

And, this is the thing that really got leadership's attention, our employee retention rate improved by 23% in one quarter."

The ROI of addressing the cost of unmanaged stress isn't just about preventing negative outcomes like turnover, errors, and toxic culture. It's about cultivating positive outcomes that directly impact the bottom line:

Higher engagement and discretionary effort: Employees with healthy Resilience Budgets don't just show up, they contribute innovation and creativity

Increased psychological safety: Teams where people aren't operating as Ghosts can actually collaborate effectively

Better decision-making: Leaders who aren't operating in chronic deficit make smarter strategic choices

Reduced healthcare costs: Healthier employees mean lower insurance premiums and fewer sick days

Stronger client relationships: Employees who aren't burned out provide better service

Sustainable high performance: You build a culture that can maintain excellence over years, not just quarters

Investing in your people's resilience isn't a cost. It's the single most effective investment you can make in your organization's long-term viability and competitive advantage. The cost of carrying stress is simply too high to ignore. And the organizations that understand this will be the ones that thrive while their competitors burn out.

Understanding the costs of unmanaged stress is the first step. But awareness alone is not enough. To truly counter The Performance Tax and avoid becoming a Ghost in the Chair, we must move from counting the costs to making strategic deposits. This requires building a life capable of supporting our well-being before the storms arrive. In the next chapter, we will explore the essential, non-negotiable foundations of that resilient lifestyle, preparing the very ground upon which the 3 A's can be practiced.

Reflection Questions for Chapter 2

The Performance Tax: Describe the specific "Performance Tax" required in your role. What emotions are you expected to manage or project that don't match your internal state? Where in your day do you feel the biggest withdrawals from your Resilience Budget? What deposits, if any, are you making?

The Ghost Check: Have you experienced being "The Ghost in the Chair" or witnessed it in a colleague? What were the warning signs? What was the impact on work quality, decision-making, and team dynamics? If you're honest with yourself, what percentage of your workweek are you actually fully present versus just going through the motions?

The Burnout Inventory: Looking at the three dimensions of burnout—The Depletion (exhaustion), The Disconnection (cynicism), and The Collapse (reduced effectiveness)—do you see early signs of any of these in yourself or your workplace culture? Which one resonates most strongly with you right now, and why? What would it cost you to ignore these signs for another six months?

Chapter 3

FOUNDATIONS OF A RESILIENT LIFESTYLE

For most of my life, I treated my body like a machine. A very capable, high-performance machine, but a machine nonetheless. I believed that with enough willpower, enough green tea, and enough sheer determination, I could override its need for rest and recovery. I saw sleep as a necessary inconvenience, nutrition as a matter of fuel efficiency, and a day off as a sign of weakness. I was, like so many of my high-achieving clients, trying to build a skyscraper of success on a foundation of sand. As my personal story shows, that structure is destined to collapse.

Resilience is not an innate character trait you're either born with or you're not. It is not about having a higher pain tolerance or a superhuman capacity to "push through." That is a dangerous myth, a relic of a hustle culture that glorifies burnout as a badge of honor. **True, sustainable resilience is a practice.** It is a dynamic state of well-being that is actively and intentionally cultivated. It is a muscle that must be conditioned daily through a set of foundational practices.

Before we can even begin to apply the powerful framework of The 3 A's Framework™, Awareness, Action, and Adaptation, we must first prepare the soil. We must build a lifestyle that is capable of supporting our well-being, a platform strong enough to hold us when the inevitable storms of life and work arrive. In this chapter, we will explore the non-negotiable pillars of that foundation: a radical redefinition of rest, the strategic protection of your energy, the completion of stress cycles through movement, and the biochemical foundation of stable performance. These are not luxuries or "self-care" add-ons. **They are the architecture of a resilient life.**

Rest as Strategic Infrastructure: The Non-Negotiable Investment

For years, my personal relationship with rest was one of deep conflict and suspicion. In my mind, rest was the antithesis of progress. It was wasted time, a surrender, a luxury I couldn't afford. I would think to myself, "What would my clients do if I don't show up? What would my family do if I'm not constantly managing everything? The world doesn't stop just because I'm tired." I carried this belief like armor, and it justified every late night, every over-scheduled weekend, every ignored sign of exhaustion.

The moment that shattered this illusion came not from a medical journal or a wellness seminar. It came from a conversation with a very good friend during the worst of my health crisis. I was exhausted, resentful, covered in hives that doctors couldn't explain, and I was venting my frustration to her about the crushing pressure to always be "on." I repeated my familiar refrain: "I can't afford to rest. What would my clients do if I don't show up?"

My friend paused, looked me directly in the eyes, and asked a simple question that felt like a physical blow:

"Forget that. What would they do if you *aren't able to show up?*"

It was a gut punch. Her question reframed my entire reality in an instant. She wasn't talking about me choosing to take a day off. She was talking about my body making that choice for me, permanently. She was talking about a catastrophic health event, a complete breakdown, a collapse from which I might not recover. What would my clients do then? What would my family do then? What would happen to everything I'd built if I became completely unable to function?

In that moment, I understood. **Rest was not an act of selfish indulgence. It was the most profound act of leadership and responsibility I could take.** It was strategic infrastructure, not optional maintenance.

My friend's question is now the one I pose to the high-achievers who sit in my office, the CEOs and surgeons and attorneys and executives who tell me they are too important to rest. I tell them: "As good as you are, your family, your team, and your clients need you at your best, not just the exhausted, depleted, Ghost-in-the-Chair version of you. They need you functional and present for years, not brilliant for six months and then permanently broken."

To truly embrace rest as strategic infrastructure, we must fundamentally redefine what rest actually is and what it does. **Rest is not simply the absence of work. It is an active, strategic, and vital process of repair and recovery.** While you are resting, your body and brain are engaged in intensive construction work:

Your nervous system shifts states. You move from the high-alert, energy-burning sympathetic nervous system state (the Takeover mode we discussed in Chapter 1) to the restorative, energy-conserving parasympathetic state. This is when your Resilience Budget from Chapter 2 actually gets replenished. Without this shift, you're operating in chronic deficit spending with no way to make deposits.

Your brain performs critical maintenance. During rest, particularly during sleep, your brain activates what's called the glymphatic system, which clears out metabolic waste products and toxins that accumulate during the day. This process is absolutely crucial for cognitive function, decision-making, and emotional regulation. When you skimp on rest, you're literally allowing toxic buildup in your brain.

Your body repairs and regulates. Rest is when your body repairs muscle tissue, reduces inflammation, regulates stress hormones like cortisol, and strengthens your immune system. This isn't passive time. It's when the actual construction and repair work happens.

Your Resilience Budget gets funded. Remember from Chapter 2 that you start each day with a finite budget of mental, emotional, and physical resources. Rest is the only way that budget gets replenished. Without adequate rest, you're making withdrawals from an account that never gets deposits. Eventually, you overdraw completely, and that's when you become a Ghost in the Chair, or worse, when your body forces a complete shutdown like mine did.

Without adequate rest, you are operating with a compromised instrument. Your decision-making becomes impaired. Your emotional regulation plummets. Your creativity evaporates. Your ability to solve complex problems diminishes. And critically, you lose access to **Awareness**, the first A of The 3 A's Framework™, because your depleted system is operating purely in survival mode.

Rest, therefore, is not the opposite of work. It is the essential foundation of sustainable high performance. To lead others effectively, you must first lead yourself to a place of recovery. This is what I call **Rest as Strategic Infrastructure**, the non-negotiable foundation that makes everything else possible.

The Energy Protection System: Your Professional Boundaries

One of the most common reasons we fail to rest, one of the biggest drains on our Resilience Budget, is because our boundaries are either weak or nonexistent. When I conduct what I call **The Depletion Audit** with a new client (we'll walk through this process later in the chapter), boundary violations are almost always the primary source of their energy leaks.

I see it constantly:
The manager who says "yes" to a new project when her plate is already overflowing, because she's terrified of being seen as "not a team player."
The employee who answers emails at 10:00 PM because the company culture implicitly rewards constant availability and punishes disconnection.
The consultant who allows clients to call him at all hours, sacrificing family dinner to prove his dedication and value.

These violations are rarely malicious. They're not usually imposed by villainous bosses twirling their mustaches. They're often born from our own deep-seated needs: to be helpful, to prove our worth, to avoid conflict, to maintain control, to be indispensable. However, the cumulative effect is a state of chronic energetic depletion, constant withdrawals from The Resilience Budget with no deposits, leading directly to becoming a Ghost in the Chair.

I teach my clients to think of boundaries as **Your Energy Protection System**, the intelligent filtering mechanism that determines what gets access to your limited resources. A healthy immune system doesn't seal you off from the world in a sterile bubble. It intelligently allows in what is nourishing and beneficial while keeping out what is harmful and draining.

Similarly, healthy boundaries don't isolate you from your work or your relationships. They protect your internal resources, your time, your focus, your emotional capacity, and your physical energy, so that you can engage with the world from a place of strength and presence, not depletion and resentment.

Here's the truth most people miss: boundaries aren't walls. They're filters. They don't keep everything out. They strategically manage what comes in, when it comes in, and how much energy you allocate to it.

The idea of setting big, dramatic boundaries can feel overwhelming and confrontational, so I encourage people to start with what I've developed and call **The Boundary Ladder**, a progressive system of increasingly protective boundaries that you can implement based on your current capacity.

Rung 1: Time Containers (The Foundation)

These are simple, specific boundaries around when you're available and when you're not. They require no explanation or justification.

> *Examples:* "I have a hard stop at 5:30 PM for a family commitment." (You don't need to explain that the "family commitment" is protecting your sanity.) "I'm available for meetings between 10 AM and 4 PM, Tuesday through Thursday." Email auto-responder that activates at 6:00 PM: "I've ended my workday. I'll respond within 24 hours of the next business day."

Rung 2: Capacity Declarations (The Reality Check)

These boundaries acknowledge your finite Resilience Budget and state your current capacity clearly.

Examples: "My core priorities right now are Project X and Y. I can certainly look at this new request, but I won't have the bandwidth to engage with it until the week of [specific date]. Will that timing work?" "I'm at capacity with my current caseload. If this is urgent, let's look at what we could deprioritize or reassign to create space."

Rung 3: The Collaborative No (The Strategic Declination)
This is my proprietary framework for declining requests while preserving relationships and demonstrating strategic thinking. It follows a specific three-part structure:

Part 1: The Acknowledgment. You validate the request and show you understand its importance. This demonstrates respect and that you're listening. Example: "Thank you for thinking of me for this project. I can see why this matters to the team's success."

Part 2: The Reality Statement. You state your limitation clearly and concisely, without excessive apology or justification. This is a statement of fact, not a plea for understanding. Example: "My current workload is at full capacity. Taking this on would compromise the quality I could deliver, both on this project and my existing commitments."

Part 3: The Alternative (When Appropriate). You offer a different path forward that doesn't require you to violate your boundaries. This turns a potential conflict into collaboration. Example: "While I can't lead this project, I could attend the kickoff meeting to share insights from similar work I've done. Or we could revisit this conversation in Q3 when my current project completes."

Rung 4: The Non-Negotiable (The Hard Boundary)

These are the boundaries that protect your most essential needs and values. They are stated clearly and held firmly, regardless of pushback.

Examples: "I don't check work communications on weekends. If there's a genuine emergency, here's how to reach me: [specific emergency protocol]." "I take my lunch break away from my desk every day. This is non-negotiable for my health and performance."

Why This Works: The Psychology of The Boundary Ladder

The Boundary Ladder works because it gives you options based on your current capacity and the situation's actual needs. Not every situation requires a Hard Boundary. Sometimes a simple Time Container is enough. Other times, you need to climb to higher rungs for better protection.

The key is that each rung gives you language and a framework, so you're not improvising in the moment when someone makes a demand and your depleted Resilience Budget makes you want to either cave immediately (to avoid conflict) or lash out defensively (because you're already overdrawn).

Mastering The Boundary Ladder is a game-changer because **it is the practical, daily application of self-respect.** It is the declaration that your well-being, your Resilience Budget, and your capacity to show up as something other than a Ghost in the Chair are not negotiable.

Completing the Stress Cycle: Movement as Physiological Reset

For many modern professionals, the workday is a physically stagnant experience. We sit in chairs, staring at screens, our bodies locked in a state of low-grade tension for hours on end. We hold our breath during a tense meeting. We clench our jaw while reading a difficult email. We hunch our shoulders as a deadline looms, our entire body contracting into a defensive posture. **We are trapping the body's stress response in our tissues with nowhere for it to go.**

Remember from Chapter 1 that The Takeover, that moment when your amygdala hijacks your system, is preparing your body for intense physical action. The stress response floods your body with cortisol and adrenaline to make you faster, stronger, and more alert so you can fight or flee from danger. This is brilliant evolutionary design when you're facing an actual physical threat.

The problem is, **you can't physically fight your overflowing inbox. You can't run away from a critical boss. You can't punch a passive-aggressive email.** So all that mobilized stress energy, the cortisol, the adrenaline, the muscular tension, the elevated heart rate, gets stuck in your body with no outlet. It's like revving your car's engine while keeping the brake pressed down. Eventually, something breaks.

This trapped stress contributes to chronic muscle pain, tension headaches, digestive issues, cardiovascular problems, and a dysregulated nervous system that stays stuck in high-alert mode. You're living in a body that's perpetually prepared for a physical emergency that never comes and never resolves.

Movement is the body's natural and most effective way to complete the stress response cycle. It metabolizes the stress hormones coursing through your system. It releases the physical tension trapped in your muscles. It signals to your nervous system that the threat has passed and you survived. This is why I refer to movement as **The Stress Cycle Completion Protocol.** It's not just about "exercise" or "fitness." It's about processing emotion and resetting your physiology so you can make deposits back into your Resilience Budget instead of staying stuck in chronic deficit.

For my clients with demanding desk jobs, I don't prescribe intense gym routines or complicated fitness plans. Most of them don't have time for that, and honestly, their depleted Resilience Budget can't support it anyway. Instead, we focus on what I call **Cycle Completion Routines**, small, strategic movement practices integrated throughout the day that complete stress cycles before they accumulate into chronic tension.

The Meeting Recovery Walk (5-10 minutes): Immediately after a stressful meeting, especially one that triggered The Takeover, take a brisk walk. It doesn't have to be long. Even five minutes around your building or up and down a stairwell will metabolize the stress hormones and complete the cycle your body started during the meeting. One of my clients, a director who has back-to-back meetings all day, now blocks 10 minutes after any "high-stakes" meeting on his calendar with a label that just says "Processing." His team knows what it means. He walks, his system resets, and he shows up to his next meeting actually present instead of carrying accumulated stress from the previous five meetings.

The Tension Release Sequence (2-3 minutes): Set a timer for every 90 minutes during your workday. When it goes off, stand up and do this quick sequence: Roll your shoulders backward 10 times, then forward 10 times. Gently tilt your head side to side, holding each stretch for 5 seconds. Do 10 slow neck rolls in each direction. Twist your spine gently left and right, 5 times each direction. Take 3 deep belly breaths. This releases the physical tension that accumulates from sitting and staring at screens. It takes less than three minutes and can prevent the chronic pain that sends so many of my clients to physical therapy.

The Transition Routine (5-15 minutes): This is one of the most powerful practices I teach. Instead of going directly from your workday into your home life, bringing all your accumulated stress with you, create a physical transition routine that completes your work stress cycle before you walk through your door. For some clients, this is a 10-minute drive where they listen to specific music and practice breathing. For others, it's changing clothes immediately when they get home and doing 15 minutes of stretching or yoga. For one of my clients who commutes by train, it's walking two extra stops before getting on, using that time to consciously release the day. The purpose of the Transition Routine is to metabolize your work stress before it infects your home life. Remember Sarah from Chapter 2, who would snap at her husband the moment she got home? She wasn't angry at him. She was carrying unmetabolized stress from performing all day, paying enormous Performance Tax, and she had no routine to complete the cycle. Her anger was trapped stress looking for an outlet.

In addition to these movement-based Cycle Completion Routines, I teach two fundamental nervous system regulation techniques that can be used anywhere, anytime, even in meetings. These are the tools that interrupt The Takeover before it fully activates and help you build **Awareness** of your internal state.

The Regulation Breath (Diaphragmatic Breathing)
When we're stressed, our breathing becomes shallow and rapid, confined

to our upper chest. This is part of The Takeover response. Your body is preparing for intense physical action. However, this shallow breathing also sends a signal to your brain that you are in danger, which reinforces the stress response. It becomes a self-perpetuating cycle. **Deep belly breathing is the fastest, most effective way to signal to your nervous system that you are safe.** It activates the vagus nerve, which is the primary pathway of the parasympathetic nervous system, the system responsible for rest, recovery, and making deposits back into your Resilience Budget.

> **How to practice The Regulation Breath:** Sit or stand comfortably. Place one hand on your chest and the other on your belly. Inhale slowly through your nose for a count of 4, focusing on expanding your belly like a balloon. The hand on your chest should remain relatively still. All the movement should be in your belly. Hold for a count of 2. Exhale slowly through your mouth for a count of 6, feeling your belly deflate completely. Repeat for 6-10 cycles.

> **Why the longer exhale matters:** The exhale activates your parasympathetic nervous system more powerfully than the inhale. By making your exhale longer than your inhale, you're actively shifting your system out of stress mode and into recovery mode. This is why a few minutes of intentional breathing can calm you down when nothing else seems to work.

The Body Check-In (Interoceptive Awareness Practice)

This is one of the most powerful tools for building **Awareness**, the first A of The 3 A's Framework™. Most people have completely lost touch with their internal bodily sensations. They can tell you everything about their external environment, their email count, their meeting schedule, their project deadlines, but nothing about what's actually happening inside their body until something breaks down catastrophically.

Interoception is your ability to sense your internal bodily state. The stronger your interoceptive awareness, the earlier you can catch stress signals and take **Action**, the second A, before you hit crisis mode. This practice rebuilds that connection.

> **How to practice The Body Check-In:** Close your eyes or soften your gaze. Take one deep Regulation Breath to ground yourself. Bring your attention to the top of your head and slowly scan down through your entire body: Face and jaw (Are you clenching?). Neck and shoulders (Are they hiked up toward your ears?). Arms and hands (Are your fists clenched? Fingers tense?). Chest and upper back (Is your breathing shallow or deep?). Stomach and lower back (Do you feel tightness? Nausea? Emptiness?). Hips and pelvis (Are you holding tension here?). Legs and feet (Are they grounded or restless?). Simply notice, without judgment. You're not trying to fix anything. You're just gathering data about your current state.
>
> **Where are you holding tension? Where do you feel numb? Where do you feel relaxed?** This practice takes 30-60 seconds and can be done anywhere. It reconnects your mind with your body, turns down the volume on anxious, racing thoughts, and grounds you in the present moment.

Here's why this matters for The 3 A's Framework™: You can't take effective **Action** (the second A) if you don't have **Awareness** (the first A) of what's actually happening in your system. The Body Check-In builds that Awareness muscle every single time you practice it.

The Biochemical Foundation: Nutrition as Stable Performance Fuel

Think of your body as a high-performance vehicle. Even with the best driver and the most carefully mapped route, it cannot run well on cheap, low-quality fuel. Yet that is precisely how many high-achievers treat their bodies. In the name of efficiency and productivity, they skip breakfast, grab a sugary snack for lunch, work through dinner, and rely on a constant drip of caffeine to power through the day, all while wondering why they feel irritable, foggy, anxious, and exhausted.

Here's what most people don't realize: **Nutrition isn't just about physical health or weight management. It is inextricably linked to your emotional regulation, your cognitive function, and your capacity to handle stress.** What you eat, or don't eat, directly impacts your mood, your focus, your decision-making, and your ability to access The 3 A's Framework™ when you need it most. The science is clear and undeniable.

When you eat processed carbohydrates and sugary foods, your blood sugar spikes rapidly. Your body responds by releasing insulin to bring it back down. However, if you've eaten nothing but simple carbs and sugar, your blood sugar doesn't just come down. It crashes hard. That crash triggers your body to release cortisol and adrenaline, the exact same stress hormones involved in The Takeover response we discussed in Chapter 1. Your body interprets the blood sugar crash as a potential survival threat, so it activates your stress response to mobilize emergency energy. The result?

You feel anxious, irritable, shaky, unable to concentrate, and emotionally dysregulated. And then you reach for more caffeine or more sugar to "fix" it, which starts the whole cycle over again. This is one of the most common, and most preventable, drains on your Resilience Budget.

Even mild dehydration, as little as 1-2% fluid loss, can impair cognitive function, reduce focus, increase feelings of fatigue, and trigger anxiety. Your brain is approximately 75% water. It needs proper hydration to function optimally. When you're dehydrated, your brain literally cannot perform at full capacity. Yet most of my clients come to me drinking maybe one or two glasses of water per day, while consuming four to six cups of coffee or tea, both of which are diuretics that actually increase fluid loss.

Your gut is often called your "second brain," and for good reason. It is home to trillions of bacteria that make up your microbiome, a complex ecosystem that produces hundreds of neurochemicals, including up to 95% of your body's serotonin, a key neurotransmitter for mood regulation, emotional stability, and stress resilience. A diet high in processed foods, sugar, and artificial ingredients disrupts this delicate ecosystem, directly impacting your mental health, emotional regulation, and stress response.

I am not a nutritionist, and I don't prescribe complex diets or meal plans. Instead, I focus on helping my clients make three simple, high-impact changes that create the biggest difference in their Resilience Budget and daily functioning:

Shift 1: Hydrate First, Caffeinate Second. Start your day with a large glass of water before you touch coffee. Keep a water bottle on your desk at all times. Often, the feeling of afternoon fatigue that we interpret as needing more coffee is actually just dehydration. Try drinking a full glass of water first. You'll be shocked how often the water alone solves the problem.

Shift 2: Stabilize Your Blood Sugar with Protein and Fiber. To prevent the dramatic blood sugar spikes and crashes that trigger stress responses, focus on including a source of protein and fiber in every meal and snack. Simple swaps: Instead of a pastry for breakfast -> Greek yogurt with berries and a handful of almonds. Instead of a bag of chips for a snack -> Apple slices with peanut butter or a cheese stick. Instead of just pasta for lunch -> Add grilled chicken or beans and a side of vegetables.

Shift 3: Eat With Intention, Not Efficiency. This is perhaps the most powerful shift and the one most people resist because it requires actually stopping work to eat. The act of stepping away from your desk for even 15 minutes to eat your lunch without distraction is a profound act of resilience-building. It allows your body to properly digest your food, gives your brain a much-needed cognitive break, creates a moment to practice Awareness, prevents mindless overeating, and makes an actual deposit into your Resilience Budget.

The Depletion Audit: A Case Study in Transformation

These foundational practices, Rest as Strategic Infrastructure, The Energy Protection System (boundaries), The Stress Cycle Completion Protocol (movement), and The Biochemical Foundation (nutrition), are the building blocks of a resilient life. To see how they come together in real life, let's look at the story of a client I'll call Ryan.

Ryan was the epitome of the hard-charging corporate attorney. He billed over 70 hours a week, slept maybe five hours a night, and was convinced that rest was a form of laziness. His entire identity and sense of self-worth were fused with his professional output. However, his body was telling a very different story. He was suffering from stress-induced ulcers. His blood pressure was dangerously high. His sleep cycle was completely shattered. He was living in chronic Resilience Budget deficit, paying massive Performance Tax every day, and rapidly approaching complete collapse. When he first sat down in my office, his fear was palpable. "If I slow down," he said, "I'll lose everything I've worked for. Everything will fall apart." Ryan was terrified that rest would destroy him. He couldn't see that the absence of rest was already destroying him.

Our work together started with one simple exercise, which I call **The Depletion Audit.** I asked Ryan to walk me through his last 24 hours in as much detail as possible, not what he accomplished, but how he actually spent his time and energy. What surprises people most when I conduct The Depletion Audit is not how much they're doing. It's the **complete absence of any intentional recovery.** Ryan's audit revealed a day that started with checking emails at 5:00 AM while still in bed and ended with him falling asleep with his laptop on his chest after midnight, with absolutely no meaningful breaks in between. When we mapped out his Resilience Budget for that day, it was devastatingly clear:

Started the day: Already at 70 points (poor sleep)

Morning: -30 points (no breakfast, high-stress client calls, no breaks)

Afternoon: -25 points (skipped lunch, blood sugar crash, difficult negotiation)

Evening: -20 points (worked through dinner, no transition routine, brought work stress home)

Ended the day: -5 points (deeply overdrawn)

He'd been operating in this kind of deficit for years. The ulcers and high blood pressure weren't mysterious medical problems. They were his body presenting the bill for years of chronic depletion. This is **Awareness**, the first A. Ryan couldn't change what he couldn't see.

We started with **Action**, the second A, through tiny, manageable changes. Our first intervention was to schedule two 10-minute blocks into Ryan's calendar. He was instructed to treat them as non-negotiable client appointments. During these blocks, he could do anything except work. At first, he resisted hard. I asked him to treat it as a 30-day experiment. Within one week, Ryan came back looking genuinely surprised. "It's strange," he admitted. "I got just as much work done, maybe even more. But the afternoon contracts I reviewed had fewer errors. I think... I think the breaks actually improved my focus instead of hurting it." This small win, this evidence that recovery wasn't the enemy of performance, gave us the momentum to climb to the next rung of The Boundary Ladder.

Over the next several months, we continued to build on this foundation through **Adaptation**, the third A. Ryan wasn't just implementing random changes; he was learning to read his Stress Signature, recognize his Resilience Budget status, and adjust his approach based on what was actually working. We introduced:

An Energy Protection System boundary: An email auto-response that activated at 9:00 PM. Not a single client complained. His productivity increased.

A Transition Routine: A 15-minute walk before he walked into his house. His wife noticed the difference immediately. "You're actually present now," she told him.

Cycle Completion Routines: A short walk at lunchtime, and he started keeping a water bottle and a bag of almonds at his desk.

Rest as Strategic Infrastructure: He committed to a hard stop at 11 PM for sleep preparation.

Six months after our first session, Ryan's ulcers had completely healed. His blood pressure had dropped to normal range. His sleep had normalized. His billable hours had actually *increased* slightly because his work quality and efficiency had improved so dramatically. But the most profound change was internal. "I don't feel like I'm barely surviving anymore," he told me. "I actually feel like I'm living. Rest isn't weakness. It's what makes everything else possible." Ryan had learned the fundamental truth that I hope every reader takes from this chapter: **Sustainable high performance requires a foundation of strategic recovery.**

The Daily Architecture of Resilience

Resilience is not built in a single, heroic moment of crisis management. It is not about "powering through" one more time. **Resilience is built in the small, consistent, and often unglamorous choices we make every single day.**

It is built in:

The decision to take an actual lunch break instead of eating at your desk

The practice of The Regulation Breath before responding to a triggering email

The Boundary Ladder framework that helps you say no without guilt

The Transition Routine that keeps work stress from infecting your home life

The choice to hydrate before you caffeinate

The commitment to Rest as Strategic Infrastructure instead of treating it as optional

These practices don't feel dramatic in the moment. But they are what keep you functional, present, and effective over years and decades, not just months. **This is the foundation upon which The 3 A's Framework™ operates.** Without these practices, you don't have The Resilience Budget to maintain **Awareness**, the energy to take consistent **Action**, or the capacity to **Adapt** when circumstances change. You're just surviving. And survival is not resilience.

Reflection Questions for Chapter 3

Self-Assessment Question: What is your current state? Honestly assess your relationship with rest. Do you see it as a strategic necessity or an indulgence you can't afford?

Pattern Recognition Question: Where do you see this in your life? Conduct a mini-**Depletion Audit** for yesterday. What were the biggest "energy leaks" from your **Resilience Budget**? What boundary violations or absent recovery practices do you notice?

Application Question: What will you do differently? Identify the biggest energy leak from your audit. Which rung of **The Boundary Ladder** or which **Cycle Completion Routine** could you practice this week to begin to plug that leak?

Accountability Question: How will you track progress? Choose one small, active recovery practice (like a 5-minute walk or practicing The Regulation Breath) and schedule it into your calendar for three days this week. How did showing up for that commitment feel?

Future-Focused Question: What's possible if you master this? What would change in your life if you truly believed that rest was strategic infrastructure, not optional maintenance? What new level of performance and well-being would become available to you?

Chapter 4
THE 3-A'S RESILIENCE FRAMEWORK™

It was in the quiet, contained hum of my therapist's office, a space that had become my sanctuary during the 18-month siege of my histamine system collapse, that The 3 A's Resilience Framework™ truly began to take shape. I was sitting across from a kind, perceptive woman, attempting to articulate the maddening frustration of my condition. I described the feeling of being at war with my own body, the sense of betrayal by my own biology, and the utter failure of traditional medical models to offer me a coherent path forward.

My reality was a confusing jumble of prescriptions that treated symptoms but ignored the source, a long list of foods to avoid, and a handful of generic stress management "tips" that felt like putting a tiny Band-Aid on a gaping wound. I had a collection of disconnected tools, but I had no system. I had an abundance of advice, but I had no framework for integration. **My life felt like a bucket full of water with a dozen holes in it, and everyone was just handing me smaller and smaller cups to try to fill it back up, completely ignoring the fundamental structural problem.**

Then, a client of my own, the brilliant, high-achieving executive I mentioned in the introduction, sat across from me in my own office. She uttered the words that would become the catalyst for this entire book, words that echoed my own silent, internal suffering: "I am itching, and I'm running out." In her, I saw a perfect, painful mirror of my own experience.

She, too, had begun a journey of diagnostic exams and allergy assessments, chasing symptoms while the real problem, chronic, unmanaged stress, remained unaddressed.

In that moment of profound connection, I realized the deep inadequacy of how we've been taught to think about, and therefore engage with, stress. **Traditional models often fail high-performers not because they're wrong, but because they're incomplete.** They address stress as if it's a single, monolithic event we can somehow outsmart or eliminate, or they offer a disconnected, à la carte menu of coping mechanisms without a clear, sequential system for applying them when you're actually in crisis.

Think about the models most of us know. We're told about the stress response, that ancient survival mechanism that activates when we perceive threat. We're told our bodies prepare to fight, flee, or freeze. This framework is essential for understanding what's happening during The Takeover (remember from Chapter 1, when your amygdala hijacks your rational brain). It describes the biology brilliantly.

But here's what it doesn't tell you: **what to do about it.**

It doesn't offer you a path back from the ledge of reactivity to the solid ground of your rational mind. It's a powerful diagnosis without a clear prescription. It can leave you feeling like a helpless victim of your own biology, a prisoner of an ancient survival mechanism that's woefully unsuited for the nuanced complexities of a 21st-century workplace.

The tragedy is that **by the time you even recognize you're in a state of high stress**, heart pounding, thoughts racing, jaw clenched, **The Takeover has already occurred.** The alarm has been pulled. Your body is flooded with stress hormones. Your rational, executive brain is effectively offline. Your Resilience Budget (from Chapter 2) is being drained at an alarming rate.

The question, then, isn't how to prevent The Takeover. In many cases, the trigger is too fast and the response too primal. The far more empowering and practical question is: **What do we do in the moments *after* the alarm has been pulled? How do we move from a state of chaotic reactivity to one of regulated, intentional response?**

It was in answering this question, for my client, for myself, and now for thousands of professionals I've worked with, that I developed The 3 A's Resilience Framework™. It is a **practical, repeatable, trauma-informed system for navigating stress, preventing burnout, and building genuine, sustainable resilience.** It is not a collection of tips to be tried at random. It is a sequential framework that guides you from the initial, overwhelming moment of a stress trigger back to a place of centered control and, eventually, to a place of wisdom and growth.

The three pillars of this framework, which must be practiced in order, are **Awareness, Action, and Adaptation.** Let's explore each one in the depth it deserves.

The First A: Awareness—You Can't Navigate What You Don't Notice

Awareness is the bedrock of resilience. It is the foundational, non-negotiable first step without which no meaningful change is possible. And yet, for most high-functioning professionals, it is our most underdeveloped skill.

We are a culture of doers, fixers, and performers. From a very young age, we're trained to focus our attention outward, on the next task, the next project, the next goal, the next problem to be solved. We've been conditioned, and often handsomely rewarded, for our ability to override our internal signals in the name of productivity and perseverance. We learn to silence our body's whispers of fatigue with another cup of coffee. We ignore the pangs of anxiety in our chest to get through a presentation. We numb the feeling of overwhelm by working even harder. **We treat our bodies like inconvenient appendages to our brilliant minds.**

This is how we become Ghosts in the Chair (Chapter 2), physically present but mentally and emotionally absent. This is how we end up operating in chronic Resilience Budget deficit without even realizing it. This is how we miss every warning sign until our bodies force a catastrophic shutdown.

I teach my clients that **true Awareness is not passive navel-gazing. It is an active, courageous practice of turning your attention inward.** It is the conscious and, crucially, non-judgmental observation of your own internal landscape. It's the moment a client like Jason (from Chapter 1) finally realizes, "My jaw is so tight right now it's giving me a headache," or when a client like Sarah (from Chapter 2) admits, "The moment my principal walks into my classroom, I feel a knot in my stomach and I start holding my breath."

For years, those physical sensations were just background noise, the static of a busy life. The practice of Awareness turns that noise into a clear, discernible signal you can actually use.

Awareness operates in two interconnected domains, and mastering both is essential for navigating stress effectively:

Domain 1: Somatic Awareness (Your Body's Intelligence)

This is the skill of learning to listen to and decode the rich tapestry of physical signals your body sends you every moment of every day. Your body is the first responder to stress, and its signals are often far more honest and immediate than the stories your mind tells you. Your mind can rationalize, justify, and deny ("I'm not tired, I'm just busy"), but your body cannot lie. A clenched jaw is a clenched jaw. A racing heart is a racing heart. Shallow breathing is shallow breathing. These signals are not your weaknesses. **They are your Stress Signature** (remember from Chapter 1). They're your body's sophisticated early warning system, your internal dashboard providing real-time data about your nervous system state.

Domain 2: Mental and Emotional Awareness (Your Internal Narrative)

This is the complementary practice of noticing your thoughts and feelings without getting swept away by them. It's about cultivating the ability to become an impartial observer of your own mind, to stand on the riverbank and watch the currents of your thoughts and emotions flow by, rather than being caught in the rapids. It's the moment you can say to yourself, with curious detachment: "There's that familiar story of 'I'm going to fail and everyone will see I'm an imposter' running through my head again," or "I'm noticing a strong feeling of anger. It's centered in my chest. It feels hot and expansive, and it wants me to lash out." This requires building what I call **Emotional Precision**, the ability to name your internal experience with accuracy and nuance. **This precision is power.** When you can name your emotion accurately, you can understand its message and respond to it effectively. When you can only say "I'm stressed," you have no useful information and no clear path forward.

The reason this dual Awareness, somatic and emotional, is so critical is that **it creates a crucial space, a sacred pause, between the stimulus (the stressor) and your response.** As psychiatrist Viktor Frankl famously wrote, it is in this space that our growth and our freedom lie.

To build this Awareness muscle, I use a process I call **The Stress Signal Map**, a systematic process for identifying your unique, predictable stress patterns.

> **Step 1: Identify Your Top 3 Stressors.** Be specific. Not "my job" but "presenting to senior leadership," "receiving critical feedback from my manager," "back-to-back meetings with no breaks."

> **Step 2: Map Your Stress Signature for Each Trigger.** For each stressor, meticulously document your physical, emotional, and mental response across three phases: **Before (The Anticipation Phase), During (The Active Stress Phase),** and **After (The Recovery/Aftermath Phase).**

> **Step 3: Identify Your Patterns.** Once you've mapped several stressors, look for patterns. Do you always get a headache? Does your stomach always clench? These patterns are your unique Stress Signature, your body's predictable way of telling you, "Hey, we're in stress mode here."

This practice is profoundly empowering. A key teaching I emphasize: **"Stress signals are data, not drama."** They are not a sign that you're weak, broken, or failing. They are a sign that your body is working exactly as designed. The question is: Are you listening?

Once you have this Awareness, you have a choice. You have that precious window before The Takeover is complete. And that's where the second A becomes critical.

The Second A: Action—The Power of the Regulated Response

Once you have the data from your Awareness, you can move to the second, and arguably most pivotal, pillar: **Action.** But this is where The 3 A's Resilience Framework™ makes its most critical distinction.

It is not about taking just *any* action. It is about the profound, life-altering difference between a reactive action and a regulated action.

Reactive action is what happens when your amygdala is in the driver's seat during The Takeover. It is impulsive, defensive, primal, and driven by fear. These reactive behaviors may provide a fleeting sense of release, but they almost always have devastating long-term consequences. They damage relationships. They erode professional credibility. And critically, **they drain your Resilience Budget at an accelerated rate.**

Regulated action, on the other hand, is intentional, strategic, and aligned with your values. It is the action you consciously choose to take once you've used your Awareness to create a pause and allow your prefrontal cortex, your rational, thinking, executive brain, to come back online. To do this in the real world, you need a practical, in-the-moment tool. This is where **The Regulation Protocol** comes in.

The Regulation Protocol: Your Emergency Response System
This is a simple, powerful intervention you can use anywhere, anytime. It works because it targets your physiology first. **You cannot think your**

way out of a stress response. You have to shift your body's state first, and then your mind will follow.

Step 1: Notice the Signal (Activate Awareness). You feel the heat rising, the jaw tightening. That's your cue. Name it silently: "This is my stress response. The Takeover is beginning."

Step 2: Introduce the Pause (Create Space). This is the conscious act of pressing the pause button on your automatic reaction. Take a deliberate sip of water. Ask a clarifying question. Excuse yourself for a moment. You are creating sacred space.

Step 3: Regulate Your Physiology (Reset Your System). In that pause, use techniques from Chapter 3. Breathe deeply using The Regulation Breath. Ground yourself physically by pressing your feet into the floor. Release tension by dropping your shoulders.

Step 4: Choose Your Response (Regulated Action). With your rational brain coming back online, you can now *choose* your action from a place of clarity rather than chaos.

This shift from reactivity to regulation is not just about feeling calmer. **It is a fundamental act of reclaiming your agency and your power.**

The Third A: Adaptation—From Surviving to Redesigning

Awareness gives you the data. Regulated Action gives you control in the heat of the moment. The third A, **Adaptation**, is what creates deep, lasting, transformative change. This is where you move from a life of constant short-term coping to one of long-term, sustainable resilience.

Coping is what you do to survive a stressful situation. It's decompressing at the end of a brutal day. It's the cathartic vent session with a colleague. But here's the problem: **coping is temporary.** It's anesthetic. It takes the edge off the pain, but it does absolutely nothing to heal the wound. **It's like bailing water out of a sinking boat instead of fixing the hole.**

Adaptation, on the other hand, asks a more powerful and courageous question: "**How can I redesign my life, my work, and my boundaries so that I need to cope like this less often?**" Adaptation is strategic, proactive, and long-term. **It's fixing the hole in the boat so you don't have to spend all your energy bailing water.**

Every moment of stress, once The Takeover has passed and you've regulated yourself, is a data point. It's an invitation to get curious rather than judgmental. You can engage in what I call **The Adaptation Inquiry**, a set of powerful questions designed to extract wisdom from your stress:

"What is this stress teaching me about my current capacity and limits?"

"Is there a boundary I failed to set that contributed to this situation?"

"Is there a resource I need that I haven't asked for?"

"Is there an outdated belief I'm holding that's making this harder than it needs to be?"

"What pattern am I noticing that I can interrupt at an earlier point next time?"

The answers to these questions become **your blueprint for Adaptation.**

The 3 A's as a Living System

The 3 A's Resilience Framework™ is not a linear, one-time process. **It's a dynamic, cyclical system that you use over and over again, getting more skilled with each iteration.**

The more you practice **Awareness**, the earlier you catch your Stress Signature.

The more you take **Regulated Action**, the more you build neural pathways for responding from your prefrontal cortex instead of your amygdala. The more you engage in **Adaptation**, the more you learn what actually works for your unique system, and the stronger your overall resilience becomes.

This is not about perfection. You will still have moments when The Takeover happens. You will still sometimes react instead of regulate. That's part of being human. The difference is that **now you have a system, a framework, for getting back on track.** You are no longer at the mercy of your stress. **You are learning to navigate it with skill, wisdom, and grace.**

Reflection Questions for Chapter 4

Self-Assessment Question: What is your current state? Think of a situation in the past week where you took a **reactive** action (a fight, flight, or freeze response). What was the trigger and what were the consequences?

Pattern Recognition Question: Take 10 minutes to create a **Stress Signal Map** for one common stressor (e.g., a weekly team meeting, a recurring deadline). What patterns do you notice in the Before, During, and After phases that you weren't conscious of before?

Application Question: What will you do differently? Identify one predictable stressor you know is coming this week. How can you proactively use **The Regulation Protocol** to prepare for and navigate that moment with **Regulated Action**?

Accountability Question: How will you track progress? Commit to practicing one full cycle of the **Regulation Protocol** (Notice, Pause, Regulate, Choose) once a day for the next three days when you feel your Stress Signature activate. Journal briefly about what you learned.

Future-Focused Question: What's possible if you master this? Identify one area of your life where you're currently just "coping." Using the **Adaptation Inquiry** questions, what is one concrete adaptation (a new boundary, routine, or structural change) you could make to reduce your need to cope?

Chapter 5
CULTIVATING AWARENESS

Awareness is a word we hear so often it has almost lost its meaning. We're told to be self-aware, to raise our awareness, to be more mindful of our surroundings. It has become a soft, almost generic term in the lexicon of personal development, often stripped of its true, formidable power. But in the context of building genuine resilience, in the context of The 3 A's Framework™, **awareness is not a passive or gentle concept. It is a radical, courageous, and sometimes profoundly uncomfortable act.** It is the practice of intentionally turning on the bright, unforgiving lights in a room you have been navigating in the dark for a very long time.

For high-achieving professionals, that darkness is often a place of strange, paradoxical comfort. We learn to function on a sophisticated form of autopilot, our days a tightly scheduled blur of meetings, emails, and deadlines. This state of unconscious competence is what allows us to be incredibly efficient. We can drive to work, mentally rehearse a presentation, participate in a conference call, and plan our evening schedule all at the same time, without giving much conscious, focused thought to any single one of those activities.

The problem is, this same autopilot efficiency makes us blind and numb to the accumulating, corrosive toll of stress. We become profoundly disconnected from the very signals our bodies and minds are sending us to alert us to danger. We're like pilots ignoring the flashing warning lights on the dashboard because we're too focused on reaching our destination ahead of schedule. We miss The Takeover happening until we're already in it. We don't notice our Resilience Budget draining until we're completely overdrawn. We don't see ourselves becoming Ghosts in the Chair until someone finally says, "You're not yourself anymore."

Cultivating Awareness is the process of intentionally and deliberately disengaging that autopilot. It is a commitment to move through your life with your eyes wide open, to notice the subtle, fleeting shifts in your internal landscape with the same focused, analytical attention you would give to a critical business report or a complex legal document. It is the foundational skill, the first A of The 3 A's Framework™, that makes everything else possible. Without this data, you are flying blind.

In this chapter, we will dissect the practice of Awareness, breaking it down into its core, actionable components: expanding your Emotional Precision, developing what I call Somatic Decoding (reading your body's stress signals), understanding the deceptive patterns of your own thoughts through what I call The Narrative Trap, and seeing how this deeply personal practice transforms not only your well-being but also your leadership presence.

This is not about navel-gazing or self-indulgence. This is about gathering the essential, mission-critical data you need to become the conscious, skilled architect of your life and your career.

Emotional Precision: Moving Beyond "Stressed"

I once had a client, a brilliant and highly respected engineer named Tom, who, when I asked him how he was feeling, would consistently respond with one of three words: "Good," "Tired," or "Busy." For him, these were the only available categories for his entire internal experience. The rich, complex, and often contradictory tapestry of human emotion was a foreign language he had never been taught. He was, like so many incredibly intelligent and successful professionals, operating with what I call Emotional Bluntness, the inability to distinguish between different internal states with any meaningful precision.

And because of this Emotional Bluntness, he was at a profound disadvantage. **He couldn't manage his emotions effectively because he couldn't even name them.** It's like trying to be a chef when the only ingredient label you have is "food." You can't create something intentional when you don't know what you're working with.

Emotional Precision is the ability to recognize, understand, and label your own emotions with accuracy and nuance. Without it, your internal world is a blunt, confusing, and often overwhelming landscape. Every negative or uncomfortable feeling gets lumped into the generic, unhelpful, and ultimately meaningless category of "stressed."

But here's the truth: **"stressed" is not an emotion. It's a state.** And within that state are a host of distinct, specific emotions, each with its own unique texture, message, and function. When you can name the emotion precisely, you can understand what it's telling you and respond strategically instead of reactively.

Think about the critical difference in the data you receive when you can get more specific:

> **Anxiety** is a future-oriented emotion, a fear of what might happen. Its core message is: "You perceive a potential threat coming. You need to prepare or gather more information."

Anger is a powerful, energizing response to a perceived injustice or boundary violation. Its core message is: "A line has been crossed. Something is not right here, and this situation needs to be addressed or changed."

Disappointment is the particular sadness that comes from an unmet expectation or a hope that has been dashed. Its message is: "Something you valued and hoped for did not happen, and that loss needs to be acknowledged and processed."

Overwhelm is the specific feeling that demands have catastrophically exceeded your capacity. Its message is a primal alarm from your system: "You are in severe Resilience Budget deficit. You need to reduce demands or increase support immediately."

Resentment is accumulated, unexpressed anger that has festered over time. Its message is: "You have been violating your own boundaries repeatedly, saying yes when you mean no, and the bill is coming due."

Shame is the deeply painful feeling that something is fundamentally wrong with you as a person (different from guilt, which is feeling bad about something you did). Its message is often distorted and harmful: "You are defective. You are not enough."

When my client Tom learned to differentiate using Emotional Precision, he had a career-altering breakthrough. He realized that the feeling he had been labeling as generic "stress" before a big presentation was not just stress. It was acute anxiety. This shift in language was a shift from a passive state of suffering to an active state of problem-solving.

He could now ask himself a more powerful question: "What specific threat am I anxious about?" He drilled down and realized his core fear was that the company's CFO, a notoriously detail-oriented executive, would question his team's data and he wouldn't have the answers, making him look incompetent in front of senior leadership.

With this precise information, he could take targeted, strategic action. He scheduled an extra two-hour prep session with his team to role-play the toughest possible questions the CFO might ask. He prepared backup data. He practiced his Regulation Protocol (from Chapter 4) so he could stay calm if questioned. By accurately naming the emotion, by practicing Emotional Precision, he unlocked the path to a clear, effective solution. He walked into the presentation not just less "stressed," but genuinely more prepared and confident. **His Awareness led directly to effective Action.**

I encourage my clients to use a tool I call **The Internal Weather Report**, a brief, structured check-in three times a day: morning, midday, and end of workday.

The Internal Weather Report (90 seconds, three times daily):

Physical: What am I feeling physically in my body right now? (e.g., tension in neck, jittery energy, heavy fatigue). This is your Stress Signature giving you real-time data.

Emotional: What am I feeling emotionally right now? Use a more specific word than "good," "bad," "fine," or "stressed." Ask: Am I feeling apprehensive, irritable, gratified, calm, resentful?

Mental: What narrative is running through my mind right now? Notice the dominant story or internal commentary. What am I telling myself about myself, my situation, or my future?

This simple, 90-second practice, done consistently, begins to build and strengthen the neural pathways for greater Awareness. It's like learning a new language. At first, it feels clumsy, but with practice, you become more fluent, and an entire world of greater understanding, self-compassion, and strategic action opens up to you. For workplace success, this skill is not soft. **It is mission-critical.**

Somatic Decoding: Reading Your Body's Stress Intelligence

As we've discussed throughout this book, **your body is your primary sensor for stress.** It often knows you are in trouble long before your conscious, thinking mind does. The goal of Somatic Decoding is to reintegrate the mind and body, to recognize that **your body is a constant and reliable source of valuable, real-time information about your nervous system state.**

In Chapter 3, I introduced The Body Check-In. Let's deepen that with The Somatic Inquiry. **The goal is simply to notice, with gentle, non-judgmental curiosity,** as if you were a scientist observing a phenomenon for the first time.

Step 1: Grounding (1 minute). Find a quiet place. Feel your feet on the floor, your body supported by the chair. Take one deep Regulation Breath.

Step 2: The Cranial Scan (30 seconds). Scan from the top of your head down to your face. Notice your forehead, your jaw, your tongue. Just observe.

Step 3: The Tension Reservoir (1 minute). Move your awareness to your neck and shoulders. Are they relaxed or hiked up in "shoulder armor"? Notice the specific quality of the tension.

Step 4: The Emotional Core (1 minute). Bring your awareness into your chest and your belly. **This area is your emotional barometer.** Notice your breathing. Notice any sensations in your stomach, like a tight knot of anxiety or a hollow feeling of emptiness.

Step 5: The Periphery (30 seconds). Let your awareness travel down your arms and legs. Are your hands clenched? Are your legs jittery?

Step 6: Integration (30 seconds). Take one more deep breath and ask yourself: "If my body could speak right now, what would it be telling me?"

One client, a lawyer named Elena, discovered through this practice that every single time she was working on a case for a particularly demanding partner, she would develop a sharp, stabbing pain between her shoulder blades. This physical signal became her invaluable early warning system. Once she made the connection, the pain became useful data. Armed with this Awareness, Elena could take Action. She would practice her Regulation Protocol before meetings with this partner and set clearer boundaries. **Her body was providing her with predictive data, a precious gift she had been ignoring for years.**

The Narrative Trap: Understanding Your Mind's Distortion Patterns

Just as your body has predictable stress patterns, so does your mind. Under the influence of stress, our brains tend to create specific kinds of negative, distorted stories. I call these **Narrative Traps. Narrative Traps are the stories your stressed brain tells you that feel completely true in the moment but are actually distorted interpretations of reality.**

The Catastrophe Story (Catastrophizing): Jumping to the worst possible conclusion.

The All-or-Nothing Story (Black-and-White Thinking): Seeing things in absolute terms. If it's not a perfect success, it's a total failure.

The Personalization Story: Believing everything others do is a direct, personal reaction to you.

The Mind-Reading Story: Assuming you know what other people are thinking, and it's always negative.

The Fortune-Telling Story: Predicting the future with absolute certainty, and always predicting disaster.

The Should Story (Shoulding on Yourself): The relentless internal tyrant that tells you how you "should" be, feel, or handle things.

The Evidence Filter Story (Confirmation Bias): Selectively paying attention only to information that confirms your existing negative belief.

The most effective method to escape these is a process I call **The Three-Step Reality Check.**

Step 1: Catch It (Awareness). The cue is often a sudden, unexplained, and disproportionate negative shift in your mood. In that moment, pause and ask yourself: **"What story did my mind just tell me?"** Naming it as "a story" creates distance.

Step 2: Check It (Challenge). Put the narrative on trial. Ask reality-testing questions: "Is this story 100% true?" "What evidence supports this story? What evidence contradicts it?" **"The goal is to get to a more accurate, evidence-based assessment of reality so you can respond strategically instead of reactively."**

Step 3: Reframe It (Choose a Better Story). Deliberately choose a more balanced, helpful, and realistic narrative. **You're not engaging in blind, Pollyannaish 'positive thinking.' You're aiming for a perspective that is more accurate and less emotionally hijacking.** For example, instead of "I'm going to get fired," try "I don't actually know what this meeting is about. My first step is to regulate my nervous system and go into the meeting prepared to listen."

The Awareness Audit: Revealing Your Invisible Scripts

The most surprising pattern that often emerges when my clients begin to cultivate Awareness is the simplest: **they realize how often they hold their breath.** This habit, sometimes called "email apnea," is a perfect metaphor for how we often deal with stress. We brace. We tense up. We stop the natural flow.

The **Awareness Audit** is a method to bring these invisible, self-sabotaging scripts to light through specific field experiments in your own workday.

Audit 1: The Breath-Holding Investigation (Duration: One workday). Set a recurring silent alarm for every hour. When it goes off, simply notice the state of your breath. Are you holding it? Is it shallow? **No judgment. Just data collection.**

Audit 2: The Boundary Betrayal Tracker (The "Yes" Audit) (Duration: One workday). Make a note every time you say "yes" to a request. At the end of the day, categorize each "yes": **Hell Yes (Enthusiastic and aligned), Neutral Yes (Sure, why not)**, or **Resentful Yes (Obligated and depleting)**. This reveals powerful data about the state of your Energy Protection System.

Audit 3: The Energy Economy Tracker (Duration: One full week). At the end of each workday, take two minutes to identify the single interaction that most **energized** you (a deposit) and the single interaction that most **drained** you (a withdrawal). This reveals your sources of renewal and your biggest energy leaks with stunning clarity.

This new, data-driven Awareness provides the undeniable, personal evidence they need to finally commit to making substantive change.

A Final Awareness Tool: The Mindful Transition

One of the places we lose awareness most often is in the space *between* tasks. We finish a tense call and immediately open an email, carrying the residue of the first interaction into the second. The **Mindful Transition** is a brief exercise to consciously reset between activities.

The Practice (30-60 seconds):

Close: When you complete a task (e.g., hang up the phone, send an email), physically close the materials. Close the laptop lid, put the notebook away.

Pause: Before opening the next thing, pause. Close your eyes for just ten seconds.

Breathe: Take one, single, intentional Regulation Breath. Inhale for 4, hold for 2, exhale for 6.

Open: Consciously open the materials for the next task.

This simple act prevents stress from bleeding from one part of your day into the next. It creates a firewall, allowing you to arrive at each new task with a cleaner slate.

Awareness as Leadership: Your Presence is Your Impact

Cultivating Awareness, Emotional Precision, Somatic Decoding, escaping Narrative Traps, and conducting Awareness Audits, is not a selfish act of self-improvement. It is, in fact, the most generous and impactful thing you can do for your team, your family, and your organization. Your internal state is not a private experience. It radiates outward from you like heat from a fire. **A leader's self-awareness, or lack thereof, has a profound and measurable ripple effect.**

Remember The Contagion Effect from Chapter 2? The opposite is also true: **A leader who practices Awareness creates a culture of psychological safety, presence, and regulated performance.**

Kevin was a director at a prestigious university, known for his academic brilliance but also for being "unapproachable" and "intimidating." His unmanaged stress showed up in curt emails and visible impatience in meetings. His self-perception was that he was efficient, and his team was too sensitive. The wake-up call came when HR flagged multiple staff complaints and two valued team members left. His defensive narrative was, "I'm not the problem, they are."

It wasn't until his supervisor sat him down and said, "Kevin... Your leadership effectiveness is the issue. Something has to change," that he agreed to work with me. Through our work, Kevin began to learn that **Awareness is not weakness, it's the foundation of effective leadership.** We started with the practices from this chapter. Using The Internal Weather Report, he began to notice the tell-tale tension in his shoulders before staff meetings and the impatient narratives running through his head. He learned to catch his Mind-Reading Stories ("They think I'm being unreasonable") and replace them with more accurate ones ("I don't actually know what they're thinking unless I ask").

The difference was immediate and palpable. Because he was calmer, he listened more. Because he wasn't internally agitated, he stopped the pen-tapping that signaled impatience. The ripple effect was profound. Morale improved. Collaboration increased. The only thing that changed was Kevin's internal state, his level of Awareness. He learned that **you lead from your nervous system state.**

When you, as a leader, practice Awareness, you give your team an incredible and rare gift: You model that it is safe to be human, to have emotions, to take a moment to regulate before responding. Your calm becomes contagious.

Awareness as a Lifelong Practice

Awareness is not a one-time event, a weekend workshop, or a certification you complete. **It is a lifelong practice,** a daily commitment to show up in your own life with curiosity, courage, and compassion.

It is essential because it is the first A of The 3 A's Framework™. Without Awareness, you cannot take effective regulated Action. Without Awareness, you cannot Adapt intelligently because you don't know what actually needs to change.

Awareness is the bedrock. It is the foundation of resilience, of effective leadership, of a sustainable, fulfilling life. It is the practice of turning on the lights, seeing yourself clearly, your Stress Signature, your Resilience Budget status, your Narrative Traps, your boundary violations, and saying, "I see this. I understand what's happening. And now I can choose a different response."

That is power. That is agency. That is the beginning of genuine transformation.

Reflection Questions for Chapter 5

Self-Assessment Question: What is your current state? The next time you feel a strong negative emotion, pause and use the **Emotional Precision Map** to name it with more precision than just "stressed." Are you anxious, resentful, overwhelmed, or something else?

Pattern Recognition Question: Where do you see this in your life? Practice **The Somatic Inquiry** (the 5-minute version) every day for one week. What is the most surprising physical sensation or pattern you notice? Where does stress seem to "live" most consistently in your body?

Application Question: What will you do differently? Choose one of the **Awareness Audits** (Breath-Holding, Boundary Betrayal, or Energy Economy) to conduct for a full day this week. Based on the data you collect, what is one specific Action you can take?

Accountability Question: How will you track progress? This week, try the **Three-Step Reality Check** on one **Narrative Trap** that you catch in real-time. Write down the distorted story and your more balanced, evidence-based reframe. How did this shift change your emotional state and your behavior?

Future-Focused Question: What's possible if you master this? If you are a leader, honestly assess how your internal state (your mood, your stress level, your presence) impacts the people you interact with. What would change for your team if you consistently practiced the awareness tools in this chapter?

Chapter 6

TAKING REGULATED ACTION

In the last chapter, we turned on the lights. We began the courageous, and sometimes unsettling, practice of Awareness. The first A of the 3 A's Framework. We learned to tune into the rich, nuanced, and often ignored language of our bodies through Somatic Decoding, our emotions through Emotional Precision, and our thoughts by escaping Narrative Traps. We learned to see our Stress Signature clearly, to track our Resilience Budget, and to identify when we're paying excessive Performance Tax.

This is a monumental, game-changing first step. **But Awareness, on its own, is not enough.** To know that you are standing at the edge of a cliff is crucial information, but it is the next step you take or consciously choose *not* to take that determines your fate. Knowledge without skillful action is simply a more detailed, and often more painful, form of suffering.

This is often the most frustrating and vulnerable stage for my clients. They come into a session with a look of dawning horror and say: "Okay, I get it. I'm aware now. I'm *exquisitely* aware of how my chest tightens into a knot when my boss sends a one-word email, how my mind instantly spirals into a catastrophic Narrative Trap of my own failure before a deadline, and how I hold my breath for what feels like hours a day. I can see my Resilience Budget draining in real-time. I have all the data. It's overwhelming. But now what? What in the world do I *do* with it?"

This is the critical bridge we must build and learn to cross the space between knowing and doing. And in that space lies the second pillar of the 3 A's Framework: **Action**. But as we've discussed throughout this book, it cannot be just *any* action. It must be a very specific kind of action, one that moves us from the chaotic, primal, and often destructive world of The Reactive Response to the centered, powerful, and strategic world of **The Regulated Response.**

Understanding the Fork in the Road: Reactive vs. Regulated

Every moment of stress presents you with a fork in the road. You can go left into The Reactive Response, or you can go right into The Regulated Response. Understanding the profound difference between these two paths is essential.

The Reactive Response: Your Default Programming

The Reactive Response is easy. It's our biological factory setting, our evolutionary autopilot. It requires no thought, no pause, and no courage. It is the path of least resistance, the well-worn, deeply grooved neural highway our brain instinctively travels down when it perceives threat, real or imagined.

Remember from Chapter 1 how The Takeover works: your amygdala detects a threat, bypasses your rational prefrontal cortex, and floods your system with stress hormones. Your body is prepared for intense physical action; fight, flee, or freeze. In the modern workplace, this manifests as The Workplace Survival Response we discussed in Chapter 4.

The Reactive Response looks like:

Snapping at a colleague who raises a concern in a meeting

Firing off an angry, defensive email at 11 PM

Avoiding a difficult conversation for weeks

Saying yes to everything out of fear, draining your Resilience Budget further

Making decisions from fear, anger, or overwhelm rather than strategy

Operating as a Ghost in the Chair, physically present but mentally hijacked

The cost of The Reactive Response:

Damaged relationships and eroded trust

Poor decisions you'll regret by morning

Further depletion of your already overdrawn Resilience Budget

Increased Performance Tax as you deal with the aftermath

Perpetuation of the stress cycle rather than resolution

The Regulated Response: Your Conscious Choice

The Regulated Response is a skill. It is an intentional, conscious choice that must be practiced with the same diligence you would apply to learning a new language or a musical instrument. It requires us to pause in the midst of a storm, when every instinct and every cell in our body is screaming at us to react, and choose a different path.

The Regulated Response is, in essence, the art of creating a sacred pause between a trigger and your response. This is where your Awareness becomes actionable power.

The Regulated Response looks like:

Taking three deep breaths before responding to a triggering email

Acknowledging the tension in your body and using it as data rather than reacting from it

Asking clarifying questions instead of making defensive statements

Taking a brief walk to metabolize stress hormones before a difficult conversation

Choosing your response based on your values and goals, not your momentary emotional state

Making deposits into your Resilience Budget instead of further withdrawals

The benefits of The Regulated Response:

Preserved relationships and increased trust

Strategic decisions aligned with your long-term goals

Maintained professional reputation and self-respect

Improved team culture and psychological safety

Breaking the stress cycle rather than perpetuating it

This chapter is your toolbox for building that sacred pause and choosing The Regulated Response. These are not just superficial techniques to make you "feel better." They are powerful, evidence-based tools for shifting your physiology and your psychology in real-time. They are designed to help you reclaim your executive brain when it has been taken hostage by your primal survival instincts, allowing you to act from a place of wisdom, not wounding.

The Physiological Reset: Calming Your Body First

Here is the single most important principle in this entire chapter, and one of the most important principles in this entire book:

You cannot think your way out of a physiological stress response.

Let me say it again: **You cannot think your way out of The Takeover.**

When your body is in full-blown fight-or-flight mode, flooded with cortisol and adrenaline, your prefrontal cortex—your rational, thinking, problem-solving brain is functionally offline. The blood flow has literally been rerouted to the more primitive parts of your brain dedicated to survival. Trying to reason with yourself in this state is like trying to have a calm, nuanced, logical conversation with someone whose house is on fire. It's simply not possible. Their system is not equipped to receive that information.

The first and most critical step in taking Regulated Action, therefore, is to calm your physiology. You must send a clear, undeniable, bottom-up signal from your body to your primal brain that you are, in fact, safe. You have to soothe the frantic animal before you can engage the wise human. Only then can your executive brain come back online.

I call this **The Physiological Reset.** The intentional intervention that shifts your nervous system from sympathetic activation (stress mode) to parasympathetic activation (rest-and-recovery mode). The two most powerful and immediate tools for achieving this are what I call **The Regulation Breath** and **The Grounding Anchor.**

Tool 1: The Regulation Breath Your Nervous System Remote Control

Your breath is the most powerful, portable, and accessible tool you have for regulating your nervous system. It is the literal, physical bridge between your conscious and unconscious mind. While you don't have to consciously think to breathe, you *can* consciously and deliberately change the rhythm, depth, and pace of your breath. And in doing so, you can directly and immediately influence your physiological state.

Your breath is the remote control for your internal world.

When you're stressed, when The Takeover is happening, your breathing automatically becomes shallow, rapid, and located high in your chest. This is called thoracic breathing, and it's a key part of the fight-or-flight response, designed to quickly oxygenate your muscles for intense physical action. The problem is, this style of breathing itself signals to your brain that you are in danger, which keeps the vicious cycle of stress hormones perpetuating. **You're breathing like you're in danger, so your brain believes you're in danger, so you keep breathing like you're in danger.**

To interrupt this cycle, you must intentionally shift to diaphragmatic breathing, what we've been calling belly breathing throughout this book. This type of deep, slow breathing stimulates the vagus nerve, a massive nerve that wanders from your brainstem down through your neck, chest, and abdomen. The vagus nerve is the primary activator of your parasympathetic nervous system—your body's sophisticated braking system, the "rest-and-digest" state that promotes calm, recovery, and clear thinking.

Here are two powerful Regulation Breath protocols you can use anywhere, anytime invisibly at your desk, in the restroom before a big meeting, in your car after a difficult phone call, or even discreetly during a meeting.

The Triangle Reset (For Focus and Immediate Calm)

This is my go-to protocol for its elegant simplicity and its calming, rhythmic nature. The equal counts of the inhale, hold, and exhale prevent the panic of feeling like you're not getting enough air, a common fear that keeps people from practicing breathwork.

When to use it:

Before a high-stakes meeting or presentation

After receiving a triggering email or message

When you notice your Stress Signature activating (chest tightness, shallow breathing, racing thoughts)

As part of your morning grounding routine

The Protocol:

Sit upright in your chair with your feet flat on the floor to create a stable base. You can either close your eyes or soften your gaze on a neutral point in front of you. Imagine a simple, equilateral triangle in your mind's eye.

Side 1 (Inhale): Inhale slowly, smoothly, and silently through your nose for a count of four as you mentally trace the first side of the triangle upwards. Focus on the sensation of the cool air entering your nostrils and your belly expanding like a balloon.

Side 2 (Hold): Gently hold your breath at the top of the inhale for a count of four as you trace the top side of the triangle. This pause is important, it prevents you from rushing and gives your body a moment of stillness. It should be a gentle hold, not a strained one. You're not holding your breath in panic; you're creating a moment of calm suspension.

Side 3 (Exhale): Exhale slowly, completely, and quietly through your mouth for a count of four as you trace the final side of the triangle downwards. Imagine you are gently blowing out a candle, not forcefully extinguishing it.

Repeat: Complete this cycle three to five times. The entire practice takes less than one minute and is incredibly effective at hitting the reset button on your nervous system, interrupting the frantic rhythm of The Takeover and bringing your focus back to the present moment.

Why it works: The equal timing creates a sense of rhythm and control. The extended exhale (same length as inhale) begins the shift toward parasympathetic activation. The mental focus on the triangle gives your conscious mind something neutral to do, interrupting catastrophic thought spirals.

The Deep De-Escalation Breath (For Intense Stress and Overwhelm)

This protocol, adapted from Dr. Andrew Weil's 4-7-8 technique, is what I call **The Deep De-Escalation Breath,** a powerful, natural tranquilizer for your nervous system. It is particularly useful when you feel highly agitated, emotionally overwhelmed, on the verge of tears, or are having trouble sleeping because your mind won't stop racing.

When to use it:

After a particularly difficult confrontation or conflict

When you're experiencing intense emotional overwhelm

Before bed when your mind is racing about work

When you feel on the verge of losing control emotionally

The Protocol:

Sit with your back straight. Place the tip of your tongue against the ridge of tissue just behind your upper front teeth and keep it there throughout the entire exercise. This helps to ground the energy and creates a consistent pathway for the breath.

Step 1: Exhale completely and forcefully through your mouth, making an audible *whoosh* sound. Empty your lungs entirely. You're clearing out all the stale, held stress energy.

Step 2: Close your mouth and inhale quietly and gently through your nose to a mental count of **four**. Fill your belly, not your chest.

Step 3: Hold your breath for a count of **seven**. This is the most important part of the practice, it allows the oxygen to deeply perfuse your bloodstream and signals to your brain that there is no emergency. If you were actually in danger, you wouldn't be able to hold your breath.

Step 4: Exhale completely through your mouth, making another audible *whoosh* sound to a count of **eight**. Let everything go.

Repeat: This is one complete breath cycle. Inhale again and repeat the cycle three more times for a total of four breaths.

Why it works: The extended exhale (8 counts) is profoundly calming to your nervous system. The hold (7 counts) creates a moment of complete stillness that interrupts panic. You will likely feel a noticeable sense of relaxation, possibly even slight lightheadedness, after just two or three rounds. This is your parasympathetic system activating exactly what you want.

Important note: If you feel dizzy or uncomfortable, return to normal breathing. You're learning to regulate, not force.

Tool 2: The Grounding Anchor, Returning to the Present

When your amygdala is hijacked, when The Takeover is in full effect, your mind is typically anywhere but the present moment. It is either frantically time-traveling into the future, catastrophizing about all the terrible things that *might* happen (the anxiety response), or it is trapped in the past, ruminating on a mistake or an injustice (the shame or anger response).

Grounding techniques are simple, powerful exercises that pull your attention out of the chaotic, fictional stories in your head and anchor it firmly in the physical reality of the here and now. They do this by focusing your attention on the undeniable, neutral, concrete information being provided by your five senses.

I call this practice **The Grounding Anchor** because it anchors you, like dropping an anchor on a boat in turbulent waters, to the solid, stable reality of the present moment.

Here are three types of Grounding Anchors you can use, depending on your situation and what's available to you:

Physical Grounding: The Body Anchor

This involves using your sense of touch to reconnect with your physical body and your immediate environment. It's particularly useful in meetings or situations where you need to be discreet.

The Practice:

While sitting in your chair, **press both of your feet firmly into the floor.** Notice the texture of the carpet or the coolness of the tile through the soles of your shoes. Feel the solid, unmoving, reliable ground beneath you. This is the earth. It is holding you. It is not going anywhere.

Press your back firmly into the back of your chair. Feel it supporting your weight. You are being held. You are stable.

Squeeze your hands into tight fists for five seconds, feeling the tension build in your forearms and noticing the sensation. Then **release them completely,** noticing the warmth, tingling, and relief as the muscles relax and blood flows back in.

Why it works: This simple act sends proprioceptive feedback to your brain, information about your body's position in space, that reminds your primal brain that you are physically safe, stable, and held. You're not falling. You're not in physical danger. You are grounded.

Environmental Grounding: The 5-4-3-2-1 Anchor

This is a wonderful and completely discreet technique for interrupting a powerful spiral of anxious thoughts or catastrophic Narrative Traps, especially in a public setting like a meeting where you can't leave or close your eyes.

The Practice:

Look around your current environment and silently name to yourself, with the focus of a detective looking for clues:

Five things you can SEE (Be as specific as possible)

"I see the grain of the wood on the conference table. I see a blue pen with a chewed cap. I see a picture of a beach on my colleague's desk. I see a tiny crack in the ceiling tile. I see the way the fluorescent light is reflecting off my watch face."

Four things you can FEEL

"I feel the texture of my pants against my legs. I feel the smoothness of the desk under my fingertips. I feel the subtle tension still remaining in my neck. I feel the cool air from the AC vent on my left arm."

Three things you can HEAR

"I hear the persistent hum of the computer fan. I hear a siren in the far distance outside. I hear the sound of my own quiet breathing."

Two things you can SMELL

"I can smell the faint scent of my coffee. I can smell the toner from the printer down the hall."

One thing you can TASTE

"I can taste the lingering mint from the gum I chewed earlier."

Why it works: This exercise forces your brain to focus on the concrete, sensory, real details of the present moment, making it biochemically impossible to simultaneously entertain catastrophic, abstract, future-oriented thoughts. Your brain cannot be in two places at once. By bringing it into the senses, you bring it out of the Narrative Trap.

Mental Grounding: The Cognitive Anchor

This involves using your cognitive brain for a simple, low-stakes, neutral task that requires just enough focus to interrupt rumination but not so much that it creates more stress.

The Practice (Choose One):

Silently name all the U.S. state capitals you can remember, in alphabetical order by state

Count backward from 100 by sevens (100, 93, 86, 79...) — surprisingly difficult and engaging

Pick a color (like green) and mentally scan the room to name all the objects you can see of that color

Recite the alphabet backward

Name one thing in the room for each letter of the alphabet

Why it works: This engages your prefrontal cortex in a simple, non-emotional task, effectively diverting energy and blood flow away from the emotionally hijacked and over-activated amygdala. It's like giving your anxious brain a neutral puzzle to solve, which interrupts the catastrophic thinking loop.

The Cognitive Reset: Escaping Narrative Traps in Real-Time

Once you have used The Regulation Breath and The Grounding Anchor to calm your body's frantic alarm system, you can then, and only then, begin to work with the deceptive and often damaging stories your mind is telling you. This is the crucial step of what I call **The Cognitive Reset,** actively escaping the Narrative Traps we identified in Chapter 5.

The Cognitive Reset is not about slapping a coat of happy, positive paint on a negative situation. It is not about lying to yourself or engaging in toxic positivity that dismisses real problems. **It is the sophisticated practice of consciously and deliberately challenging your initial, distorted, and often catastrophic interpretation of an event and finding a more balanced, realistic, and empowering perspective.**

It's about recognizing that **the first story your stressed brain tells you is usually a work of poorly-written fiction, and you, as the author of your experience, have the power to edit it.**

The Three Strategic Reframes: Your Narrative Escape Tools

The most powerful tool for escaping Narrative Traps is a well-posed question. A strategic question can slice through the fog of emotional reactivity and open up new possibilities. Here are the three most effective reframing questions I teach my clients, each designed to counter a specific type of Narrative Trap:

Strategic Reframe 1: The Depersonalization Question

When to use it: When you're caught in The Personalization Story Narrative Trap (everything is about you)

The Question: *"What does this actually have to do with me?"*

Why it works: This question is a powerful antidote to the ego-centric belief that everything is about us, a common cognitive distortion we discussed in Chapter 5.

Example in action:

The Trigger: Your boss walks past your desk without saying good morning.

The Narrative Trap (The Personalization Story): *"She's angry with me. I must have done something wrong. The project I submitted yesterday must have been terrible. She's avoiding me. I'm probably going to get fired."*

The Intervention: Pause. Take three Triangle Reset breaths. Then ask: **"What does this actually have to do with me?"**

The Reframe: *"Maybe she had a fight with her spouse this morning. Maybe she's preoccupied and stressed about a deadline. Maybe she was lost in thought about a budget crisis and literally didn't see me. Maybe she's dealing with a personal health issue. Maybe she's just having a bad day that has absolutely nothing to do with me."*

The shift: This question creates a critical separation between someone else's behavior and your internal reaction, stopping you from internalizing stress that isn't yours to carry. It reminds you that **you are not the center of everyone else's emotional universe.**

Strategic Reframe 2: The Perspective Expansion Question

When to use it: When you're caught in The All-or-Nothing Story or The Catastrophe Story (binary thinking, worst-case scenarios)

The Question: *"What's another way to look at this situation?"*

Why it works: This question is an invitation for your creative, strategic, problem-solving brain to come back into the conversation. It acknowledges that there are multiple possible interpretations of any situation, and the first one your stressed brain offers is rarely the most accurate or helpful.

Example in action:

The Trigger: You receive direct, critical feedback on a project you poured your heart into.

The Narrative Trap (The All-or-Nothing Story): *"I failed. This is a disaster. I'm terrible at this. All my work was worthless. I should just quit."*

The Intervention: Pause. Take three Deep De-Escalation Breaths. Use The 5-4-3-2-1 Anchor. Then ask: **"What's another way to look at this?"**

The Reframe (Generate Multiple Alternatives):

"This feedback, while painful to hear, is a gift that will make the final product stronger and my skills sharper."

"This is not a judgment of my fundamental worth as a person, it's a single data point about one aspect of my performance on one project."

"This is a fantastic opportunity for me to practice receiving feedback with grace and without defensiveness, which is a crucial leadership skill."

"My boss took the time to give detailed feedback because they believe I can improve. If they thought I was hopeless, they wouldn't bother."

"This is exactly the kind of growth challenge I said I wanted when I asked for more developmental opportunities."

The shift: You move from catastrophic, all-or-nothing thinking to nuanced, growth-oriented perspective. The situation hasn't changed, your interpretation of it has, which changes everything about how you respond.

Strategic Reframe 3: The Agency Reclamation Question

When to use it: When you're feeling powerless, overwhelmed, or out of control (The Overwhelm response)

The Question: *"What is the one thing I can control right now?"*

Why it works: Stress and anxiety often skyrocket when we feel powerless and out of control. This question deliberately shifts your focus from the vast, turbulent sea of things you *cannot* control to the small, solid island of what you *can*. It moves you from victimhood to agency, from helplessness to leadership.

Example in action:

The Trigger: You learn that a major project timeline has been moved up by two weeks by senior leadership, with no consultation.

The Narrative Trap (The Fortune-Telling Story + The Catastrophe Story): *"This is impossible. My team will be crushed. We're going to fail. This will destroy our morale. They're setting us up for failure. I'm going to look incompetent. This is going to be a disaster."*

The Intervention: Pause. Use The Body Anchor (feet on floor, back in chair). Take five Triangle Reset breaths. Then ask: **"What is the one thing I can control right now?"**

The Reframe (Identify Your Sphere of Control):

"I can't control the deadline, but I CAN control the clarity and compassion with which I communicate this news to my team."

"I CAN control how we re-prioritize our existing tasks and identify what can be postponed or eliminated."

"I CAN control the well-reasoned request I make to leadership for additional resources or a reduction in project scope to accommodate the compressed timeline."

"I CAN control my own response, staying calm and strategic instead of panicking, which will help my team stay calm."

"I CAN control the immediate next step: calling a team meeting to brainstorm solutions together."

The shift: You move from a position of victimhood ("This is being done TO me") to a position of leadership ("Here's what I can influence"). This doesn't solve the problem, but it activates your strategic mind and puts you back in the driver's seat of your response.

Putting It All Together: The Reset Protocol

Now, let's weave these powerful tools. The Regulation Breath, The Grounding Anchor, and The Cognitive Reset—into a simple, repeatable protocol that you can use in the midst of a stressful workday. I call it **The Reset Protocol,** your emergency response system for moments when you feel emotionally hijacked, overwhelmed, or triggered.

When to Use The Reset Protocol

Immediately after a difficult or triggering interaction (like a tense phone call, a critical email, or a confrontational meeting)

Just before a high-stakes meeting or a difficult conversation you're dreading

Anytime you notice your Stress Signature activating (chest tightness, jaw clenching, breath holding, catastrophic thinking)

When you feel The Takeover happening and you need to interrupt it before you do something you'll regret

When you've just made a withdrawal from your Resilience Budget and need to make a small deposit back

The Reset Protocol: Step-by-Step (3-5 Minutes)

Step 1: Recognize & Pause (The First 30 Seconds)

The moment you recognize your Stress Signature activating, your body tensing, your thoughts spiraling, your breath becoming shallow, **pause**. This is your Awareness (the first A) in action.

If you can, find a private space: your office, a restroom stall, your car, an empty conference room, even a stairwell. If you're in a meeting with others and cannot leave, you can still pause internally and simply say out loud: "That's a good point. Give me a moment to think about that."

Announce to yourself, silently or out loud: "I am using The Reset Protocol." This simple act of declaring your intention is a powerful step in reclaiming control. You're not being hijacked anymore, you're consciously intervening.

Step 2: Breathe (The Next 60-90 Seconds)

Practice one to two minutes of intentional, regulated breathing using either:

The Triangle Reset (3-5 cycles) if you need focus and calm

The Deep De-Escalation Breath (4 cycles) if you need intense de-escalation

Focus all of your attention on the physical sensation of your breath moving in and out of your body. This is **The Physiological Reset,** the anchor of the entire protocol. Your primary goal in this step is to soothe your nervous system and interrupt The Takeover response.

Step 3: Ground (The Next 30 Seconds)

Engage in a quick but focused Grounding Anchor. Choose the one that fits your situation:

The Body Anchor (feet on floor, back in chair, fists and release)

The 5-4-3-2-1 Anchor (if in a meeting or can't be obvious)

The Cognitive Anchor (count backward by 7s or another mental task)

This brings your attention firmly back into the safety and solidity of the present moment, away from the catastrophic future scenarios or painful past events your mind is spinning.

Step 4: Reframe (The Next 60 Seconds)

With a calmer body and a more present mind, engage in **The Cognitive Reset**. Choose the Strategic Reframe that fits your situation:

If you're personalizing: *"What does this actually have to do with me?"*

If you're catastrophizing or thinking in black-and-white: *"What's another way to look at this?"*

If you're feeling powerless: *"What is the one thing I can control right now?"*

Generate a more balanced, less catastrophic, and more resourceful interpretation. Write it down if you can, seeing it on paper makes it more concrete.

Step 5: Choose Your Response (The Final 30 Seconds)

Based on your more regulated and resourceful state, consciously choose your next best step. This is **The Regulated Response,** the culmination of the entire protocol.

Your choice might be:

To draft a calm, professional response to an email

To seek more information before acting ("I need to think about this and get back to you tomorrow")

To schedule a direct conversation rather than responding via email

To delegate the issue to someone else

To simply decide to table the issue until you've had more time to process

To set a boundary using The Boundary Ladder (from Chapter 3)

The key is that it is a conscious *choice*, not an automatic reaction. You are acting from your prefrontal cortex (your strategic, thinking brain), not your amygdala (your survival brain).

Why The Reset Protocol Works

This entire protocol takes less time than it takes to make a cup of coffee or scroll through social media for a few minutes. **Yet it can completely alter the trajectory of your day, your week, or even your career.** It prevents a reactive moment from spiraling into a day of turmoil, a damaged relationship, or a regrettable decision that takes weeks to repair.

The Reset Protocol works because:

It addresses physiology first (you can't think your way out of a hijack)

It creates the sacred pause between trigger and response

It gives you specific, concrete steps instead of vague advice to "calm down"

It integrates all three aspects of regulation: body, mind, and conscious choice

It's portable, you can use it anywhere

It builds the neural pathways for regulation with each use

From Reactive to Proactive: The Scheduled Restoration Break

While The Reset Protocol is a powerful reactive tool, something you use when you're already in stress mode, the ultimate goal of a resilient lifestyle is to build a life where you need emergency interventions less often. This requires a fundamental shift from a reactive stance to a proactive one, which is achieved through what I call **Scheduled Restoration Breaks.**

I tell the busiest professionals I work with that **proactive breaks are non-negotiable infrastructure, not optional luxury.** If you want to *stay* productive, creative, and effective, you *must* stay present and regulated. Breaks are not a threat to your productivity, **they are the essential fuel for it.**

The Productivity Paradox

The most common objection I hear is: "I don't have time for breaks."

My response is always the same: **"You don't have time NOT to take them."**

A brain that is overworked is a brain that is inefficient, error-prone, and uncreative. It makes costly mistakes. It misses important details. It can't access strategic thinking. It's operating as a Ghost in the Chair (from Chapter 2) physically present but cognitively depleted.

Research from the Draugiem Group found that the most productive employees were not those who worked the longest hours without breaks. They were those who worked in focused sprints followed by deliberate restoration periods. The specific rhythm they found most effective was 52 minutes of focused work followed by 17 minutes of complete mental disengagement.

While that specific timing may not be practical for everyone, you can't walk out of a meeting at the 52-minute mark, **the principle is sound and scientifically validated:** Your brain needs oscillation between engagement and recovery to maintain high performance.

How to Implement Scheduled Restoration Breaks

Schedule them like meetings. Put 5-10 minute restoration breaks into your calendar with the same seriousness and commitment you would schedule a meeting with your most important client. Label them something neutral like "Focus Block Transition" or "Strategic Thinking Time" if you're worried about perception.

Protect them fiercely. Treat these breaks as non-negotiable. When someone tries to schedule a meeting during one, you're not available. When you're tempted to skip it to "catch up on email," remind yourself: **"Skipping this break will make me less effective for the rest of the day. This is strategic, not selfish."**

Use them intentionally. These are not passive breaks where you scroll social media or check email. These are active restoration practices:

Walk outside (even 5 minutes changes your state)

Practice The Triangle Reset breathing

Do The Somatic Inquiry (from Chapter 5)

Stretch using movements from The Stress Cycle Completion Protocol (Chapter 3)

Eat a snack with protein mindfully (remember The Biochemical Foundation from Chapter 3)

Have a brief, non-work conversation with a colleague you like

Track the impact. Notice how your afternoon performance differs on days when you take your scheduled breaks versus days when you skip them. Most clients report that their decision-making quality, creativity, and patience are noticeably better on break-inclusive days.

Case Study: Tasha's Transformation Through Regulated Action

Tasha was a brilliant and passionate project manager in the high-pressure, fast-paced tech industry. She was incredibly effective at getting things done and moving projects forward. But when under pressure, which was most of the time, her default mode was pure, unadulterated reactivity. She was living in permanent Takeover mode, her Resilience Budget chronically overdrawn, paying massive Performance Tax every single day.

The Reactive Pattern

Her stress showed up as:

Snapping at colleagues in meetings when they raised potential problems, making people afraid to give her bad news

Sending late-night, anxiety-fueled, and often accusatory messages on Slack (messages she would regret by morning)

Micromanaging her team's every move to the point of their collective exhaustion

Making impulsive, fear-driven decisions that she'd have to walk back later

Operating as a stressed, reactive presence that everyone tried to avoid

The cost:

Team morale was in the basement

Turnover was rising, two valued team members had left citing her management style

Her own stress was escalating, she was having panic attacks in the bathroom

She felt a toxic cocktail of guilt, frustration, and helplessness

Her Narrative Trap: *"I have to control everything or things will fall apart. If I'm not constantly vigilant, my team will fail. The stress is just part of being a high-performer."*

She was stuck in a reactive loop and didn't know how to get out. When she came to me, she was on the verge of being put on a performance improvement plan, not for her technical skills, but for her impact on team culture.

Building Awareness First

Our work together started with the first A: **Awareness.** Tasha identified that her primary trigger was the feeling of losing control over a project's timeline. The moment a deadline was threatened or a problem emerged, The Takeover would activate.

Her Stress Signature:

Physical: Painful tightening in her chest, rapid and shallow breathing, jaw clenching, hands trembling

Emotional: Panic, rage, overwhelm

Mental Narrative Trap: The Catastrophe Story: *"This whole project is going to fail and it will be my fault. Everyone will see I'm incompetent. My career is over."*

This became her cue, her internal alarm bell signaling the need to intervene differently.

Implementing The Regulated Response

In meetings: Instead of snapping when a team member raised a problem, she learned to use **The Body Anchor**. The moment she felt the tightness in her chest activate, she would:

Press her feet firmly into the floor under the conference table

Press her back into her chair

Take one silent Triangle Reset breath cycle

Ask a clarifying question instead of reacting: *"Help me understand the specific concern. What information do you need from me?"*

This small, invisible intervention created just enough space for her to access **The Regulated Response** instead of The Reactive Response.

With digital communication: Her biggest breakthrough came with her commitment to **The Reset Protocol** for all potentially emotional communication. She made a strict rule for herself:

If an email, message, or situation triggered her Stress Signature, she would NOT respond immediately. Instead, she would:

Get up from her desk

Go to a small conference room or outside

Walk through the complete Reset Protocol

Only then would she draft her response

She used **The Cognitive Reset** religiously:

Catastrophic Narrative Trap: *"This whole project is going to fail and it will be my fault!"*

Strategic Reframe: *"This is a challenge, not a catastrophe. What is the next single logical step we need to take to address this? What can I control right now?"*

With her schedule: She implemented **Scheduled Restoration Breaks,** three 10-minute breaks per day, blocked on her calendar as "Strategic Thinking Time." She used these for:

Walking outside to complete stress cycles

Practicing The Triangle Reset

Doing quick Somatic Inquiries to check her Resilience Budget status

The Transformation

The changes were dramatic:

Within two weeks:

The late-night, anxiety-ridden communication tirades stopped completely

Her team noticed she was "actually listening" instead of just waiting to react

She stopped micromanaging and started asking questions

Within two months:

Team conflict dropped significantly

Collaboration and creative problem-solving improved

People stopped being afraid to bring her problems

Her panic attacks stopped

Within three months:

Her performance review noted "remarkable improvement in leadership presence and team culture"

Two team members who had been planning to leave decided to stay

Her own stress levels decreased dramatically

She was sleeping better and enjoying her work again

Tasha's reflection: "I didn't lower my standards. I didn't become less ambitious. I didn't work less hard. I just stopped operating in constant emergency mode. I learned that **regulated action is not weaker than reactive action, it's infinitely more powerful.** My team performs better, I feel better, and we get better results. I wish I'd learned this years ago."

The Key Lesson

What changed for Tasha? **Not her external circumstances.** The tech industry was still high-pressure. The deadlines were still aggressive. The projects were still complex.

What changed was her internal state and her response pattern. She learned to:

Recognize her Stress Signature (Awareness)

Use The Reset Protocol to interrupt The Takeover (Regulated Action)

Choose responses based on strategy, not survival (Leadership)

She learned that **you lead from your nervous system state.** When you're in constant Takeover mode, your team mirrors that chaos. When you're operating from regulation, your team mirrors that calm, focused presence.

The Practice of Regulated Action

Taking Regulated Action is a skill, and like any new skill, it requires diligent practice. **It will feel unnatural and even awkward at first.** Your brain will resist because The Reactive Response is faster and more familiar. You will stumble. You will have moments, even entire days, where your old, familiar reactivity wins.

That's not failure. That's learning.

Every time you successfully create that sacred pause, every time you use The Reset Protocol, every time you choose The Regulated Response over The Reactive Response, you are strengthening the neural pathways of resilience. You are literally rewiring your brain.

You are moving from being a victim of your circumstances to becoming the conscious, powerful author of your responses.

This is not about perfection. This is about progress. This is about building the skill, one regulated breath at a time, of showing up as the leader, professional, and person you want to be, even when stress is screaming at you to react.

Reflection Questions for Chapter 6

The Physiological Reset Experiment: The next time you feel your Stress Signature activating, chest tightening, breath shallow, thoughts racing, commit to a 60-second experiment. Practice three cycles of The Triangle Reset or one cycle of The Deep De-Escalation Breath. Then use one of The Grounding Anchors (Body, 5-4-3-2-1, or Cognitive). What do you notice shifts in your body and mind? Be as specific as possible. What changed physiologically?

The Cognitive Reset Practice: Identify a recurring, stressful situation at work (a weekly meeting, a regular report deadline, interactions with a specific person). What is your automatic Narrative Trap in that situation? (Catastrophe Story? Personalization? All-or-Nothing?) Practice escaping it by answering all three Strategic Reframe questions:

"What does this actually have to do with me?"

"What's another way to look at this?"

"What is the one thing I can control right now?"

The Reset Protocol Trial: Identify one predictable trigger in your work-week (a specific meeting, a particular type of email, a recurring deadline pressure). Proactively schedule The Reset Protocol in your calendar immediately before or after that trigger. Use the full 3-5 minute protocol. Afterward, journal: What was different about your experience? How did The Regulated Response differ from your usual Reactive Response? What impact did it have on the outcome?

The Scheduled Restoration Experiment: For one week, schedule three 10-minute Scheduled Restoration Breaks into each workday. Protect them like client meetings. Use them intentionally (walk, breathe, stretch, no email or social media). At the end of the week, assess: How did your afternoon performance differ on days with breaks versus days you skipped them? What was the impact on your Resilience Budget?

Chapter 7
PRACTICING ADAPTATION & RECOVERY

Imagine for a moment that you are the captain of a state-of-the-art ship on a long, arduous, high-stakes journey. In the last two chapters, we've equipped you with essential, sophisticated skills for this voyage.

Awareness—our first A is your advanced navigation system. It is the complex array of instruments that allows you to see the storms forming on the horizon, to understand the treacherous currents beneath the surface, and to accurately assess the internal conditions of your own vessel: your Resilience Budget levels, your Stress Signature activation, your Narrative Traps emerging, and the integrity of your Energy Protection System.

Regulated Action—our second A is your masterful seamanship. It is your ability to stand on the bridge in the midst of a turbulent squall, hands steady on the wheel, using The Reset Protocol to interrupt The Takeover, and skillfully navigating through the towering waves without panicking, without getting knocked off course, and without capsizing into reactive decisions you'll regret.

These skills are mission-critical. They are what allow you to survive the storm.

But survival is not the goal.

Anyone who has been through a truly difficult storm, a grueling project that drained your Resilience Budget to nothing, a corporate restructuring that left you operating as a Ghost in the Chair for months, a period of intense personal loss that bled into your work, knows that just making it through to the other side is not the end of the story.

The ship is battered. The sails are torn. The crew is physically and emotionally exhausted. The resources are critically depleted.

If you, as the captain, simply point the bow of your ship from the wreckage of one storm directly into the heart of the next without a period of intentional, strategic repair and replenishment, it is only a matter of time before your vessel suffers a catastrophic breakdown. The hull will breach, the mast will crack, and you will find yourself adrift and sinking.

This is the critical, and most often neglected, stage of the resilience journey: **Adaptation and Recovery**. This is the third and final A of the 3 A's Resilience Framework™. It is the conscious, deliberate practice of pulling your ship into a safe harbor after a storm, not to hide in fear, but to strategically repair, restock, refuel, and most importantly, *learn*.

It is about studying the ship's logs, analyzing the weather patterns, and integrating the hard-won lessons from the storm into the very structure of your ship, so you become stronger, wiser, and more seaworthy for the journey that lies ahead.

This is where we make the profound shift from in-the-moment stress management to the art of building a truly resilient and sustainable lifestyle. It's about shifting from a reactive posture of just surviving difficult experiences to a proactive one of actively and intentionally growing from them.

This chapter is your guide to that safe harbor. We will explore the tools for strategic adaptation, the frameworks for deep post-stress recovery, and the powerful routines that weave these practices into the very fabric of your daily, weekly, and monthly life.

Strategic Adaptation: Turning Stress Into Wisdom

In our culture, we tend to have a binary and profoundly unhelpful view of difficult work experiences. We either see them as something to be defeated, conquered, and quickly "put behind us" (the "move on" mentality), or we see them as a source of trauma from which we may never fully recover (the victim mentality).

The truth, as is so often the case, lies in a more nuanced, powerful, and ultimately more hopeful middle ground.

Difficult experiences, once we have safely navigated through their immediate chaos using Awareness and Regulated Action, are also our greatest and most potent teachers. **They contain a wealth of invaluable data and wisdom, but only if we have the courage, the humility, and the tools to extract it.**

This is what the third A-Adaptation is all about. It's about becoming what I call **The Intelligent Learner,** someone who systematically extracts wisdom from stress and uses it to rebuild their life more sustainably.

The Grounding Principle: What You Focus On Is What You Become

I teach my clients that genuine, lasting growth comes from structured reflection, not emotional rumination. To adapt and grow, you must ground yourself intentionally in the present moment and in the lessons available, not in the turbulent, emotionally charged waters of what just happened.

"What you focus on is what you ground yourself in."

If, after a difficult experience, you allow your mind to focus exclusively on:

The shame of your mistakes

The frustration of the outcome

The injustice of the situation

How you "should have" handled it differently

How unfair it was

You will ground yourself in a toxic, disempowering narrative of failure and victimhood. You'll feel the negative emotions intensify. Your Resilience Budget will remain depleted. You'll likely fall into multiple Narrative Traps (The Catastrophe Story, The All-or-Nothing Story, The Should Story).

If, however, you can consciously and intentionally shift your focus to:

The specific learning available

The strength you demonstrated even in the struggle

The clear opportunity for future growth

What you can control moving forward

How you can build from this experience

You will ground yourself in a narrative of resilience, competence, and agency. You'll feel empowered. You'll start making deposits back into your Resilience Budget. You'll be practicing true Adaptation.

This critical shift from reactive, emotional rumination to proactive, structured reflection is not a natural act, especially for a stressed and depleted mind. **It requires a formal, disciplined process.**

The Post-Storm Integration: Your Framework for Learning From Stress

The most powerful tool I have created for facilitating this shift is what I call **The Post-Storm Integration,** a structured inquiry to be used *after* a stressful event, a major project, a difficult week, or any experience that significantly drained your Resilience Budget.

This is not something you do in the immediate aftermath when you're still emotionally hijacked. You need to be regulated first. **Use The Reset Protocol (Chapter 6) to get yourself calm, then come to this framework with curiosity rather than judgment.**

The Post-Storm Integration has five essential questions that must be answered in order:

Question 1: What Actually Happened? (The Objective Record)

The first step is to state the event as objectively and dispassionately as possible, as if you were a neutral journalist reporting essential facts for a news story. **You're separating what actually happened from the story you're telling yourself about what happened.**

Example: *"The project deadline was moved up by two weeks by senior leadership without our input. My team had to work significant overtime, including two weekends. We delivered the project on the revised deadline. A post-mortem review revealed two significant errors in the final report that required a client-facing correction. Three team members expressed frustration about the compressed timeline. As a result, team morale is currently low."*

Why this matters: This step cleanly separates verifiable facts from emotional interpretation. It gets you out of Narrative Traps and into reality. You can't adapt from distorted information.

Common mistake: Mixing facts with interpretation. "The project deadline was cruelly moved up by leadership who don't care about us" is NOT objective. "The project deadline was moved up by two weeks" is objective.

Question 2: What Did I Feel? (The Emotional Landscape)

Here, you give yourself permission to identify, name, and validate the full spectrum of emotions you experienced, using the Emotional Precision skills from Chapter 5. **This is not wallowing, this is data collection about your emotional response pattern.**

Example: *"When I first heard the news about the deadline change, I felt a wave of pure panic and anxiety about failing. During those two weeks, my dominant feelings were pressure, irritability, and resentment toward leadership. When I discovered the errors, I felt deep professional shame and disappointment in myself. I also felt guilty about how my stress affected my team."*

Why this matters: Naming emotions without judgment validates your human experience and reduces their power over you. It also helps you identify your Stress Signature patterns. You're building Emotional Precision data.

Common mistake: Skipping this step as "too touchy-feely" or judging yourself for having emotions. Your emotions are data, not drama. They tell you what matters to you and what triggered your system.

Question 3: What Helped or Hindered Me? (The Performance Analysis)

This is a critical, honest, compassionate analysis of your own actions, decisions, and mindset during the event. **What did you do well? Where did your reactive patterns take over? Where did your Awareness serve you? Where did you fail to take Regulated Action?**

Example: *"What helped: I initially communicated the change to my team calmly and transparently, which built trust. I used The Reset Protocol twice when I felt myself spiraling. I maintained my morning walks three days that week, which helped my cognitive function."*

"What hindered: I fell into The All-or-Nothing Narrative Trap, I believed the project had to be perfect despite impossible circumstances, which led me to micromanage instead of delegate. I completely abandoned my other self-care practices, I skipped lunch, worked until 2 AM multiple nights, and stopped using Scheduled Restoration Breaks. My depleted Resilience Budget directly contributed to the cognitive errors I made. I didn't ask for help or push back on the timeline because I was afraid of looking weak."

Why this matters: This is where you identify your patterns, both your strengths and your vulnerabilities. You're gathering the specific data you need for Adaptation. You can't fix what you can't see.

Common mistake: Only focusing on what went wrong (falling into shame) or only focusing on what went well (missing the learning). You need both for complete understanding.

Question 4: What Do I Need Right Now? (The Immediate Recovery)

This question brings you powerfully into the present moment and focuses on your immediate, actionable needs for recovery. **It is an act of self-compassion and triage.** Your Resilience Budget is depleted, what deposits do you need to make immediately?

Example: *"Right now, I need to get a full eight hours of sleep tonight—that's non-negotiable. I need to have a transparent conversation with my manager about the errors without making excuses or catastrophizing. I need to call a team meeting with the sole purpose of publicly acknowledging their incredible hard work and creating space for them to decompress. I need to take tomorrow afternoon off to fully rest. I need to reinstate my daily walks starting today."*

Why this matters: This prevents you from immediately jumping into the next crisis while still depleted. It forces you to actually make deposits into your Resilience Budget instead of continuing to operate in deficit. It's the bridge between surviving the storm and learning from it.

Common mistake: Skipping recovery and immediately starting the next project. This guarantees you'll become a Ghost in the Chair and eventually burn out completely.

Question 5: What Can I Take Forward? (The Wisdom Integration)

This is the final and most important step. **It's where you turn the raw, painful experience into concrete, future-oriented strategy.** This is the very definition of wisdom. This is Adaptation in action.

Example: *"Moving forward, I will: (1) Build a 20% buffer into all project timelines I present to leadership to absorb unexpected changes. (2) Use pressure and anxiety as a cue to delegate MORE, not less the opposite of my current pattern. (3) Protect my sleep and daily Scheduled Restoration Breaks as* *non-negotiable elements of professional performance, not luxuries to sacrifice. (4) Practice The Boundary Ladder when presented with unrealistic demands instead of automatically saying yes. (5) Schedule a Post-Storm Integration after every major project to extract lessons instead of just moving on."*

Why this matters: This is where stress becomes wisdom. You're not just surviving, you're evolving. You're using the experience to upgrade your personal operating system. This is how you become more resilient over time instead of just more depleted.

Common mistake: Making the lessons too vague ("I'll try to take better care of myself") instead of specific and actionable ("I will block 10-minute Scheduled Restoration Breaks at 10 AM, 2 PM, and 4 PM in my calendar starting Monday").

The Power of The Post-Storm Integration

This structured reflection is the essence of strategic Adaptation. It transforms you from a passive experiencer of stress into an active, intentional learner. You're systematically upgrading your capacity to handle stress with every challenge you face.

The difference between professionals who burn out and those who build sustainable, thriving careers is often this: The ones who thrive do Post-Storm Integration religiously. They extract wisdom from every difficult experience. They don't just survive, they learn, adapt, and rebuild stronger.

The ones who burn out just keep pushing forward, never stopping to repair the ship, never learning from the storms, until one day the vessel simply can't take anymore and breaks apart completely.

The Boundary Rebuild: Reconstructing After Depletion

One of the most common and devastating consequences of chronic, unmanaged stress is what I call **Boundary Collapse,** the complete erosion of your Energy Protection System (from Chapter 3). When a client comes to me in a state of deep burnout or severe depletion, their boundaries aren't just weak, they're virtually nonexistent.

They are like a city that has just been hit by a catastrophic storm. Their professional and personal foundations are cracked. Their internal structures, their confidence, sense of purpose, motivation, are severely compromised. Their fundamental sense of safety in their own life has been shattered.

The process of rebuilding requires far more than just a two-week vacation or a spa day. It requires a slow, meticulous, deeply intentional process I call **The Boundary Rebuild,** the systematic reconstruction of your Energy Protection System.

Phase 1: The Boundary Archaeology (Understanding the Collapse)

We start by becoming archaeologists of their burnout, gently excavating through the layers of their past behavior to identify the patterns of boundary violation that led to the collapse.

We ask:

Where did they consistently say "yes" when every cell in their body was screaming "no"?

Where did they repeatedly compromise on their non-negotiables (sleep, exercise, family time) in the name of being a "team player"?

Where did they take on the emotional labor and anxieties of their colleagues or clients until they had no energy left for themselves?

Where did they allow their Resilience Budget to go into chronic deficit spending without ever making deposits?

Where did they ignore their Stress Signature until it escalated to crisis?

The pattern we usually find: A history of boundary violations so normalized that the person didn't even recognize they were violations. They thought they were "just doing their job" or "being helpful" when actually they were systematically dismantling their own wellbeing.

Phase 2: The Boundary Rebuild Protocol (Systematic Reconstruction)

Then, we begin the slow, intentional work of rebuilding. **This is not about building a massive, impenetrable wall that isolates them from the world.** It is about strategically rebuilding a healthy, flexible, resilient Energy Protection System using The Boundary Ladder framework from Chapter 3.

The Boundary Rebuild Protocol has three essential domains:

Domain 1: Reclaiming Time (The Calendar Reconstruction)

We look at their calendar, which is often a terrifying reflection of their boundaryless life, every minute packed, no white space, meetings scheduled during lunch, work bleeding into evenings and weekends.

The reconstruction:

Immediate actions:

Schedule "hard stops" at the end of each workday (using Time Containers from The Boundary Ladder)

Block lunch breaks as "meetings with CEO" so they're protected

Identify one evening per week that is designated as a sacred "work-free zone"

Create one full weekend day per month with no work contact

The resistance we encounter: "But my job requires flexibility." "My industry doesn't work that way." "I'll fall behind."

The reality: When they actually implement these boundaries, their productivity often *increases* because they're no longer operating in chronic Resilience Budget deficit. They have the cognitive capacity to focus and make good decisions.

Domain 2: Reclaiming Communication (The Digital Boundary Reset)

We craft new, clear, proactive communication protocols that protect their Resilience Budget from constant depletion.

The reconstruction:

Immediate actions:

> Create email signature that explicitly states working hours: "My working hours are 9:00 AM to 5:30 PM, Monday-Friday. I respond to emails during these times."

> Turn off ALL push notifications on phone and computer

> Establish three designated times per day for checking email instead of constant reactivity

> Create auto-responders that activate outside working hours

> Move Slack/Teams to "Do Not Disturb" mode outside of core hours

The resistance we encounter: "But what if there's an emergency?" "My boss expects instant responses." "Everyone else is always available."

The reality: True emergencies are rare. Most "urgent" communications can wait a few hours. When they set these boundaries clearly, most colleagues and supervisors respect them. And those who don't are revealing toxic workplace culture that should be addressed.

Domain 3: Reclaiming "No" (The Response Reconstruction)

For someone recovering from Boundary Collapse, especially if they have people-pleasing tendencies, saying "no" can feel terrifying—like an act of professional suicide.

The reconstruction:

We practice scripting and role-playing The Collaborative No (from The Boundary Ladder in Chapter 3). We start small with low-stakes situations and gradually build up their capacity.

Progressive practice:

Week 1: Say no to one optional, non-essential request. "No, I can't join that optional committee this semester, but thank you for thinking of me."

Week 2: Say no to one request that would compromise existing commitments. "No, I can't take on that extra project right now. My focus is on delivering excellent results on my current commitments."

Week 3: Say no to one request using The Collaborative No structure (acknowledge, state limit, offer alternative)

Week 4: Say no to something from authority figure

The transformation: Each successful "no" is a profound victory, a single brick laid in the foundation of their new, more bounded, self-respecting professional identity.

This Boundary Rebuild process is slow, often non-linear, and requires immense self-compassion. There will be setbacks. There will be moments of guilt and fear. But it is the essential, foundational work of moving from a state of chronic, soul-crushing depletion to one of sustainable—and even joyful—performance.

The Recovery Architecture: Building Sustainable Restoration

While strategic Adaptation (The Post-Storm Integration) is about extracting long-term lessons and making structural changes, and The Boundary Rebuild is about reconstructing your protective systems, **recovery is about the ongoing practices that help your nervous system downshift, repair, and return to equilibrium.**

After a stressful day, a difficult week, or even a single intense meeting, your nervous system can get "stuck" in the high-alert sympathetic state. You might feel wired but tired, physically exhausted but mentally unable to relax, your mind still racing and replaying events long after the workday is over.

I call this state The Recovery Gap—the space between when the stressor ends and when your nervous system actually completes the stress cycle and returns to baseline. Most professionals operate with a massive, chronic Recovery Gap. The stressor ends, but they never actually recover before the next stressor hits. This is how you end up operating in permanent Resilience Budget deficit.

Recovery practices are the tools you use to actively close The Recovery Gap—to intentionally guide your nervous system back into the restorative, parasympathetic state.

The Personal Recovery Toolkit: Your Emergency Restoration Practices

I encourage my clients to build what I call **The Personal Recovery Toolkit**—a curated collection of micro-recovery practices that feel doable, accessible, and even enjoyable. The key criteria:

Must take 10 minutes or less (so they can be realistically integrated into busy life)

> **Must be accessible** (no special equipment or locations required)

> **Must be evidence-based** (actually shifts physiology, not just distraction)

> **Must feel good to YOU** (what works for someone else may not work for you)

Here are the most effective nervous system recovery techniques I teach:

Recovery Tool 1: The Box Reset (Advanced Regulation Breath)

This is a variation on The Triangle Reset from Chapter 6, famously used by Navy SEALs and first responders to stay calm and focused under extreme pressure. Its perfect symmetry is incredibly regulating for the nervous system.

When to use: After high-stress meetings, before bed when your mind is racing, anytime you feel "wired but tired"

The Practice:

Inhale slowly through your nose: 4 counts

Hold your breath gently: 4 counts

Exhale smoothly through your mouth: 4 counts

Hold the breath out gently: 4 counts

This completes one "box"

Repeat for 1-2 minutes (4-8 boxes)

Why it works: The equal timing and the holds after both inhale and exhale create perfect balance in your autonomic nervous system. It's like hitting a reset button.

Recovery Tool 2: The Vagus Activation (Humming Practice)

This might sound strange, but humming is a fantastically effective and discreet tool. **The vibration created by humming physically stimulates the vagus nerve** in your throat and chest, sending a powerful, immediate calming signal throughout your entire body.

When to use: Between meetings, in your car, before a difficult conversation, anytime you need quick de-escalation

The Practice:

Take a normal, comfortable breath in through your nose

On the exhale, simply hum a low, gentle, continuous tone: "hmmmmmm"

Try to extend the hum for the full duration of your exhale

Notice the pleasant vibration in your chest and throat

Repeat 5-10 times

Why it works: The vagus nerve is the primary pathway of the parasympathetic (rest-and-digest) system. Direct physical stimulation activates it immediately. It's like pushing the "calm down" button directly.

Recovery Tool 3: The Tension Release Sequence (Progressive Muscle Relaxation)

This is particularly effective for releasing the deep, chronic physical tension that accumulates in your body when you're operating in constant stress mode—the shoulder armor, jaw clenching, and postural bracing we identified in The Somatic Inquiry (Chapter 5).

When to use: During lunch break, before bed, after particularly physically tense days

The Practice: Find a comfortable seated or lying position. Systematically work through the major muscle groups:

Hands: Clench into tight fists for 5 seconds. Notice the tension. Then release completely for 15 seconds. Notice the warmth and relaxation flooding in.

Arms: Tense your biceps and forearms. Hold 5 seconds. Release 15 seconds.

Shoulders: Pull shoulders up toward ears. Hold 5 seconds. Let them drop completely. Release 15 seconds.

Face: Scrunch all facial muscles together (forehead, eyes, jaw, mouth). Hold 5 seconds. Release completely. 15 seconds.

Chest and abdomen: Tense these core muscles. Hold 5 seconds. Release 15 seconds.

Legs and feet: Point toes, tense legs. Hold 5 seconds. Release 15 seconds.

Why it works: This practice powerfully illustrates the difference between tension and relaxation, helping you recognize where you're chronically holding stress. The contrast makes the relaxation deeper and more noticeable.

Recovery Tool 4: The Sensory Anchor (Intentional Sensory Engagement)

This involves intentionally engaging one of your five senses in a pleasurable, calming way to interrupt the stress cycle and signal safety to your nervous system.

When to use: End of workday transition, when you need to shift mental gears, when you feel emotionally flat or numb

The Practice (Highly Personal - Choose What Works for You):

Sound: Listen to a specific calming instrumental piece with headphones for 5 minutes

Taste: Mindfully sip warm herbal tea, noticing temperature, aroma, flavor

Smell: Use calming essential oils (lavender, bergamot, sandalwood)

Touch: Wrap yourself in a soft blanket, hold a smooth stone, pet an animal

Sight: Look at images of nature, watch clouds, observe flowing water

Why it works: Engaging your senses grounds you in the present moment and signals safety. Your nervous system can't be in stress mode and sensory appreciation mode simultaneously.

The Recovery Routines: Making Restoration Automatic

Recovery tools are individual techniques. Recovery Routines are how you build those tools into a consistent, reliable, automatic system.

Routines are powerful because they remove guesswork and moment-to-moment willpower from the equation. They are pre-committed, scheduled appointments you make with yourself for your own wellbeing. **When recovery becomes routine, it becomes reliable.**

I work with clients to design what I call **The Recovery Architecture**—a three-tiered system of recovery routines that build on each other and create sustainable restoration: Daily, Weekly, and Monthly.

Layer 1: Daily Recovery Routines (The Foundation)

These are the non-negotiable daily practices that prevent The Recovery Gap from widening and keep your Resilience Budget from going into chronic deficit.

The Hard Stop (End of Workday Boundary):

This is not just about logging off your computer. **It is a clear, intentional transition routine that signals to your brain and body that the work portion of your day is over and it is now safe to downshift.**

Your Hard Stop might include:

Changing out of work clothes into comfortable clothes

Taking a 10-minute walk around your neighborhood (completing any residual stress cycles)

Listening to a specific playlist or podcast on your commute that's completely unrelated to work

Doing five minutes of The Tension Release Sequence

Writing three things that went well today

Why it matters: Without a Hard Stop, work stress bleeds into your evening, preventing recovery and stealing time from your relationships. You never actually leave work—you just bring it home with you.

The Wind-Down Routine (Preparing for Restorative Sleep):

For at least 30-60 minutes before bed, you must disengage from screens (which emit blue light that disrupts melatonin production) and engage in calming, analog activities.

Your Wind-Down might include:

Reading a physical book (not on a device)

Taking a warm bath with Epsom salts

Light stretching or gentle yoga

Journaling or The Internal Weather Report (Chapter 5)

Practicing The Box Reset or Deep De-Escalation Breath

Why it matters: Sleep is the ultimate recovery tool. Without quality sleep, your Resilience Budget cannot be replenished. The Wind-Down Routine prepares your nervous system for deep, restorative sleep.

Layer 2: Weekly Recovery Routines (The Recalibration)

Once a week, it's essential to schedule deeper restoration that allows your system to fully reset.

The Digital Detox (Disconnection Practice):

A period of intentional disconnection from the relentless stream of information, demands, and digital stimulation.

Your Digital Detox might look like:

A full 24-hour "Sabbath" from all screens (Friday evening to Saturday evening)

A 4-hour block on Sunday morning with your phone in a drawer

One full day per week with no work email checking

An evening per week with no social media

Why it matters: Your overstimulated, dopamine-addicted brain needs regular rest. Constant digital engagement prevents deep recovery and keeps you in a state of low-grade stress activation.

The Weekly Integration (Structured Reflection):

A modified, 15-minute version of The Post-Storm Integration where you extract lessons from the week.

Your Weekly Integration questions:

What went well this week?

What was my biggest challenge?

What did I learn?

Where was my Resilience Budget most depleted?

Where was I most restored?

What is my single most important intention for next week?

Why it matters: Without reflection, you repeat the same patterns endlessly. The Weekly Integration ensures you're learning and adapting continuously, not just surviving week after week.

Layer 3: Monthly Recovery Routines (The Deep Restoration)

Once a month, conduct higher-level restoration that allows your system to fully repair and recalibrate.

The Resilience Audit (High-Level Review):

A check-in on the bigger picture of your life and your capacity.

Your Resilience Audit questions:

Looking at the last month, where do I feel most depleted?

Where do I feel most restored and energized?

Is my Resilience Budget consistently overdrawn?

Are my boundaries holding or collapsing?

What one structural change would make the biggest difference?

Using the 3 A's Framework, what do I need to adapt?

Why it matters: Monthly perspective allows you to see patterns you miss in the daily grind. You can proactively address chronic depletion before it becomes burnout.

The Reset Space (Deep Recovery Day):

A full day or weekend that is completely offline and unstructured, dedicated to deep rest and joyful, non-productive activities.

Your Reset Space might include:

A nature retreat or simple camping trip

A full day of reading, walking, and doing nothing

A weekend away with zero work contact

Time with loved ones doing activities you enjoy

Why it matters: Your nervous system needs periods of complete disengagement to repair at a deeper level than daily and weekly routines allow. This prevents the accumulation of chronic stress that leads to burnout.

Case Study: Javier's Journey From Burnout to Sustainable Success

Let's see how The Post-Storm Integration, The Boundary Rebuild, and The Recovery Architecture come together in a real transformation.

The Breaking Point

Javier was a senior analyst at a major government agency, a classic high-achiever who had built his entire successful career on the foundation of 60-hour workweeks. For years, this pace had worked, earning him promotions, respect, and a reputation as the go-to crisis manager.

But now, in his late forties, the bill for that unsustainable pace was coming due:

Physical: High blood pressure diagnosis, chronic insomnia, weight gain, persistent fatigue

Professional: Making uncharacteristic errors, missing details, operating as a Ghost in the Chair

Personal: Marriage strained from years of being physically present but emotionally absent

Emotional: Feeling trapped, resentful, and hopeless

His words in our first session: *"I've built a career I can't survive. And I feel like it's too late to change."*

His Resilience Budget had been chronically overdrawn for years. His Energy Protection System (boundaries) had completely collapsed. He was paying massive Performance Tax daily. He had no recovery practices whatsoever.

The Awareness Phase: Understanding the Collapse

Our work began with Awareness—the first A. We conducted The Post-Storm Integration on his typical workweek. The insights were shocking to him:

What actually happened: He was working 60-65 hours per week, checking email from 6 AM to 11 PM, eating lunch at his desk while working, taking zero breaks, sleeping 5 hours per night, and hadn't taken a true vacation in three years.

What he felt: Constant pressure, resentment toward his job, guilt about neglecting his marriage, shame about his health decline, fear about his future.

What hindered him most: His deeply ingrained, unconscious belief that his value as an employee and as a man was directly proportional to the number of hours he worked and how available he was. He'd fallen into The Should Story Narrative Trap: "I should be able to handle this. Real leaders don't need breaks. If I slow down, I'll become irrelevant."

What he needed: Sleep, boundaries, recovery time, and a completely different relationship with his work.

What he could take forward: The realization that his unsustainable pace wasn't a sign of dedication—it was a sign of dysfunction. He needed to rebuild everything.

The Action Phase: The Boundary Rebuild

We began The Boundary Rebuild Protocol slowly and incrementally.

Domain 1: Reclaiming Time

Week 1 commitment: Leave office at 6:00 PM three nights per week (Monday, Wednesday, Friday)

His resistance: "I'll fall behind. My boss will notice. My team needs me. This feels irresponsible."

The reality: The first week felt agonizing. He was flooded with guilt and anxiety. He was sure his career would suffer.

The surprise: His boss didn't notice. His colleagues didn't see him as less committed—they began to respect his discipline. By having a firm deadline, he became MORE focused and efficient during his work hours. His actual productivity increased.

Progressive expansion: Over three months, he extended this to five nights per week, then added protected lunch breaks, then one work-free weekend day per month.

Domain 2: Reclaiming Communication

New protocols:

No email checking after 7 PM or before 8 AM

Auto-responder activated outside work hours

Email signature stating his working hours

Moved work Slack to Do Not Disturb mode evenings and weekends

His resistance: "What if there's an emergency?"

The reality: In six months, there was exactly one true emergency outside his hours. For that, he created a protocol: "True emergencies can be handled by calling my cell phone directly. If it's not worth a phone call, it can wait."

Domain 3: Reclaiming "No"

Progressive practice:

Declined optional committee that would require evening meetings

Said no to taking on a junior analyst's project that wasn't his responsibility

Used The Collaborative No when asked to lead a task force: "I'm honored you thought of me. My current workload is at capacity. I could participate as an advisor rather than lead, or we could revisit this next quarter."

The transformation: Each "no" became easier. His guilt decreased. His sense of professional identity shifted from "the person who never says no" to "the person who maintains high standards by protecting his capacity."

The Adaptation Phase: The Recovery Architecture

We then meticulously designed Javier's Recovery Architecture:

Daily Layer:

Hard Stop at 6:00 PM: His sacred transition routine became listening to a history podcast on his drive home—something completely unrelated to work that signaled "work is over."

Wind-Down: 30 minutes before bed, no screens. He read physical books and practiced The Box Reset breath work.

Weekly Layer:

Weekly Integration: Friday afternoon, 15 minutes before end of day, he'd journal through the Weekly Integration questions. This gave him profound agency over his experience.

Digital Detox: Saturday morning, 8 AM to noon—phone in drawer, no work email, time in nature or with his wife.

Monthly Layer:

Resilience Audit: First Sunday of each month, 30-minute reflection on his Resilience Budget status and what needed to adapt.

Reset Space: One full unplugged weekend per month with his wife—hiking, visiting small towns, phones off Friday evening to Sunday afternoon.

His confession: "The Reset Space was the hardest routine to maintain but the most restorative for my marriage and my soul."

The Transformation

Six months into implementing The 3 A's Framework consistently:

Physical: Blood pressure normalized without medication. Sleep improved to 7-8 hours per night. Lost 15 pounds. Energy returned.

Professional: Promotion to a senior leadership role specifically citing his "balanced, strategic approach" and "sustainable leadership model." Fewer errors. Better decisions. More strategic thinking.

Personal: Marriage transformed. Wife said, "I have my husband back. You're actually present now."

Emotional: From trapped and hopeless to empowered and purposeful. "I'm not just surviving my career anymore—I'm actually enjoying it again."

His key insight: "Adaptation isn't retreat—it's intelligent redesign. I learned that true resilience isn't about doing more or pushing harder. It's about aligning your work with your fundamental human capacity to thrive. It's about knowing when to sail hard and when to pull into harbor to repair, refuel, and prepare for the journey ahead."

The Sustainable Success Model

Javier learned that the third A—Adaptation—is what makes the entire 3 A's Framework sustainable. Without Adaptation:

Awareness just makes you painfully conscious of problems you don't solve

Regulated Action prevents immediate disasters but doesn't prevent future ones

You're constantly in reactive mode, never learning, never improving

With Adaptation:

You extract wisdom from every stressful experience

You rebuild your systems stronger after each challenge

You prevent future crises instead of just managing current ones

You evolve into someone who can sustain high performance indefinitely

This is the difference between high-performers who burn out by 45 and those who thrive well into their 60s and beyond. It's not talent. It's not luck. It's whether they practice Adaptation or just keep pushing until they break.

Making Adaptation Your Operating System

Adaptation—the third A of the 3 A's Framework—is not a one-time event or a crisis intervention. **It's a way of life.** It's how you transform from someone who survives stress to someone who learns from it, grows through it, and builds an increasingly resilient, sustainable, fulfilling professional life.

The three essential elements of Adaptation:

The Post-Storm Integration - Extracting wisdom from difficult experiences

The Boundary Rebuild - Reconstructing your Energy Protection System when it collapses

The Recovery Architecture - Building sustainable daily, weekly, and monthly restoration routines

When you practice all three consistently, you create a virtuous cycle:

Stress happens (it always will)

You navigate it with Awareness and Regulated Action

You extract lessons through Post-Storm Integration

You rebuild stronger through Boundary Rebuild

You recover fully through your Recovery Architecture

You're ready for the next challenge, stronger than before

This is true resilience. Not the ability to endure endless stress without breaking. The wisdom to learn from stress, rebuild from it, and emerge more capable than you were before.

Reflection Questions for Chapter 7

The Post-Storm Integration Practice: Think about a recent challenging experience at work that significantly drained your Resilience Budget. Set aside 20-30 minutes with a journal and work through all five questions of The Post-Storm Integration: (1) What actually happened? (2) What did I feel? (3) What helped or hindered me? (4) What do I need right now? (5) What can I take forward? What is the single most important lesson you can apply this week?

The Boundary Rebuild Assessment: Where is the weakest or most porous boundary in your professional life right now? Is it time boundaries? Communication boundaries? Your ability to say no? Using The Boundary Rebuild Protocol, identify: (a) What pattern of boundary violation led to this weakness? (b) What one concrete step can you take this week to begin reconstruction? (c) What resistance or fear comes up when you think about setting this boundary?

The Recovery Toolkit Experiment: Of the recovery tools presented (The Box Reset, The Vagus Activation, The Tension Release Sequence, The Sensory Anchor), choose the one that feels most accessible and appealing. Commit to using it once per day for five days after a stressful moment or at end of day. Journal briefly about its effect. Did you notice a shift in your nervous system? Did it help close The Recovery Gap?

The Recovery Architecture Design: Look at your calendar for the coming week and month. Design your personal Recovery Architecture: (1) Daily: What will your Hard Stop and Wind-Down routines be? Schedule them. (2) Weekly: When will you do your Digital Detox and Weekly Integration? Block the time. (3) Monthly: When will you conduct your Resilience Audit and schedule your Reset Space? Put it in your calendar now. Treat these as non-negotiable, mission-critical appointments with your wellbeing. What resistance comes up? How can you address it?

Chapter 8
Building Your Personal Resilience Toolkit

For the past seven chapters, we have been on a journey of deep understanding. We have dissected the complex anatomy of stress through concepts like The Takeover and Stress Signature. We have counted its often invisible but devastatingly high costs through frameworks like The Performance Tax, The Resilience Budget, and The Ghost in the Chair. We have laid the essential foundations of a resilient lifestyle through Rest as Strategic Infrastructure, The Energy Protection System, and The Stress Cycle Completion Protocol.

We have explored the powerful, sequential framework of the 3 A's Resilience Framework™, Awareness, Regulated Action, and Adaptation, as our guiding philosophy. We have gathered the knowledge. We have analyzed the maps. We have studied the principles of navigation.

Now, it is time to build your ship.

This chapter marks the pivotal transition from theory to practice. It is the moment where all the concepts we've explored coalesce into a tangible, personalized, deeply actionable plan. A generic, one-size-fits-all approach to resilience is destined for the scrap heap of failed self-help initiatives because **you are not a generic human being.**

Your nervous system is a unique and intricate tapestry, shaped by your genetics, your personal history, and your cumulative life experiences. Your Stress Signature is yours alone. Your Resilience Budget operates according to your specific capacity. Your Narrative Traps follow your particular patterns. Your work environment has its own distinct culture, unwritten rules, and specific, predictable stressors.

The tools and strategies that work brilliantly for a trial lawyer who thrives on adversarial energy in a high-conflict courtroom may be entirely different from what works for a software engineer who needs long, uninterrupted blocks of quiet focus on a collaborative team. What closes The Recovery Gap for one person might not work at all for another.

Therefore, your resilience plan cannot be a pre-packaged, off-the-shelf solution. It must be what I call your Resilience Operating System™, a bespoke, personal blueprint customized specifically for you.

It must be built around your unique Stress Signature, your personal Narrative Traps, your specific Resilience Budget patterns, and the tools that feel most authentic, accessible, and regulating to your particular nervous system.

Please hear me on this: **This is not another self-improvement project to be added to your already overwhelming to-do list. This is not about achieving perfection.** Think of this instead as the essential and empowering work of building your personal navigation system for the complex, beautiful, and often unpredictable voyage of your life and career.

It is the work of creating a clear, reliable, compassionate guide that you can turn to in moments of calm to prepare and strategize, and in moments of storm to find your way back to the safety and clarity of your own inner harbor.

In this chapter, we will walk step-by-step through the process of building **Your Resilience Operating System™,** the living, breathing core of your personal resilience toolkit.

The Resilience Operating System™: Your Five-Layer Architecture

Your Resilience Operating System™ is not meant to be a static document carved in stone. It is a living, breathing guide, a dynamic tool that you will create and then continue to refine and evolve as you grow and as your life changes.

It consists of five essential layers that build upon each other:

Layer 1: Map Your Stress Signature (Identify your unique warning system) **Layer 2: Curate Your Response Toolkit** (Select your core intervention tools) **Layer 3: Design Your Implementation Architecture** (Build systems that make tools automatic) **Layer 4: Schedule Your System Updates** (Plan regular reviews and adaptations) **Layer 5: Establish Your Emergency Protocols** (Define your crisis response plan)

I strongly encourage you to get a dedicated notebook, a physical journal that you can connect with, or open a new digital document and actively work through these layers as you read. **This is an active, not a passive, process.** This is you taking authorship of your own resilience.

Let's begin the essential work of building your Resilience Operating System™, one crucial layer at a time.

Layer 1: Map Your Stress Signature

As we established in Chapters 1 and 5, you cannot navigate what you don't notice. **The first and most critical layer of your Resilience Operating System™ is mapping your unique Stress Signature with scientific precision.**

Remember from Chapter 1: Your Stress Signature is your body's and mind's predictable pattern of alarm bells, the early warning signs that your internal system is moving from a state of balance (homeostasis) into a state of stress and high alert. For some, the alarm is a loud, blaring, impossible-to-ignore siren. For others, it's a subtle, almost imperceptible hum they've long ago tuned out as background noise.

The goal of this layer is to document the unique frequency and signature of your own internal alarm system so you can catch it early, before The Takeover is complete, before your Resilience Budget is fully depleted, before you become a Ghost in the Chair.

The Stress Signature Mapping Exercise

Take a clean page in your notebook and create three columns. At the top of each column, write one of your three most common or most potent workplace stressors.

CRITICAL: Be incredibly specific here. Generic labels like "Work" or "Stress" are not helpful. Drill down with precision. Is it:

"Weekly team meetings with senior leadership where I'm expected to present"

"Receiving unsolicited critical feedback from my manager via email"

"Juggling multiple competing deadlines in the last week of the quarter"

"Difficult conversations with underperforming team members"

"Back-to-back video calls with no breaks for 4+ hours"

Precision is power. The more specific you are about the stressor, the more accurately you can identify your response pattern.

Now, under each specific stressor, meticulously list your predictable signals across three distinct domains:

Domain 1: Physical Signals (The Body's Alarm System)

What happens in your physical body? This is often where The Takeover first shows up, before you're even consciously aware you're stressed.

Examples:

Subtle shallowing of breath (remember The Breath-Holding Investigation from Chapter 5?)

Unconscious clenching of jaw or grinding teeth

Familiar knot of tension in neck or shoulders (The Tension Reservoir from Chapter 5)

Churning or acidic feeling in stomach (The Emotional Core from Chapter 5)

Onset of dull headache behind eyes

Sudden wave of fatigue or heaviness

Restless fidgeting, leg shaking, hand trembling

Feeling uncomfortably hot or suddenly cold

Chest tightness or pressure

Hands becoming cold and clammy

Be as detailed as you can. Your body is giving you incredibly valuable data if you learn to read it.

Domain 2: Emotional Signals (The Feeling Response)

What is the primary emotion or mood that arises? **Use the Emotional Precision skills from Chapter 5.** Push past the generic label of "stressed."

Examples:

Free-floating anxiety or dread about the future

Sharp spike of irritability or impatience with others

Prickly feeling of defensiveness

Surge of frustration or anger at the situation

Heavy sense of overwhelm or hopelessness

Detached feeling of emotional numbness (early sign of becoming a Ghost in the Chair)

Resentment at having to do this again

Shame about your performance or capabilities

Disappointment that things aren't going as planned

Domain 3: Mental Signals (The Narrative Trap Activation)

What is the automatic story your mind begins to tell you? What specific Narrative Traps (from Chapter 5) do you fall into?

Examples:

The Catastrophe Story: *"I'm going to fail. This will be a disaster."*

The All-or-Nothing Story: *"If this isn't perfect, it's worthless."*

The Personalization Story: *"They all think I'm incompetent."*

The Mind-Reading Story: *"Everyone can see that I'm an imposter."*

The Fortune-Telling Story: *"This is definitely going to go badly."*

The Should Story: *"I should be able to handle this. What's wrong with me?"*

Document the specific thoughts that loop through your head. These are your personal Narrative Traps in action.

Identifying Your Early Warning System

Once you have completed your three columns, take a different colored pen and look for patterns. **Circle the signals that appear most frequently across all three stressors.** These are your primary, high-frequency stress signals, the ones that show up regardless of the specific situation.

Then, and this is crucial, **identify your *earliest* warning sign.** What is the very first, most subtle cue that tells you your stress response is just beginning to activate, before The Takeover is complete?

Real client examples:

A CEO realized his earliest signal was repeatedly clearing his throat before difficult conversations

A graphic designer noticed her hands would suddenly feel cold just before feedback sessions

A teacher recognized she would start organizing her desk compulsively when avoiding a difficult parent phone call

An engineer discovered he would start checking email obsessively when he was anxious about a code review

This earliest signal is your golden ticket. It is your invitation to intervene early in the stress cycle, when you have maximum leverage, before The

Takeover hijacks your prefrontal cortex completely, before you've drained your Resilience Budget significantly, before you've said or done something you'll regret.

At the bottom of your page, write this sentence and fill in the blank:

"My earliest and most reliable Stress Signature is: _____."

Example completed statements:

> "My earliest and most reliable Stress Signature is: my breathing becomes shallow and I notice myself holding my breath."

> "My earliest and most reliable Stress Signature is: I feel a knot form in my stomach and my shoulders creep up toward my ears."

> "My earliest and most reliable Stress Signature is: my mind starts racing with catastrophic what-if scenarios and I can't focus on the present."

This is the cornerstone of your entire Awareness practice and the foundation of your Resilience Operating System™.

Layer 2: Curate Your Response Toolkit

Now that you know the specific signature of your alarms, you need to decide with clarity and intention what you will do when they go off.

This is where we build what I call **Your Rapid Response Toolkit,** your in-the-moment intervention tools.

The internet and the self-help world are full of an overwhelming number of stress management techniques. The goal here is **not** to create an exhaustive, encyclopedic list of every technique you've ever heard of. That would be completely useless in a moment of stress when your cognitive function is impaired by The Takeover.

The goal is to choose a small, curated, easily memorable selection of 3 to 5 Core Response Tools that you can practice, master, and deploy at a moment's notice with minimal cognitive load.

The Three Selection Criteria

Your Core Response Tools should be chosen based on three essential criteria:

Criterion 1: Personal Resonance They should resonate with your personality and your unique nervous system. If sitting still for meditation makes you more anxious and agitated, don't choose that as a primary tool. Perhaps a walking practice or The Stress Cycle Completion Protocol from Chapter 3 is a better fit.

Criterion 2: Environmental Accessibility They should be practical and accessible in your specific work environment. A tool that requires you to lie down on the floor or go outside for 30 minutes may not be practical if you work in a high-security facility or during back-to-back video conferences.

Criterion 3: Balanced Integration You should have a healthy mix of:

Physiological tools (body-based) to calm your nervous system and interrupt The Takeover

Cognitive tools (mind-based) to escape Narrative Traps and activate strategic thinking

You need tools for both the body and the mind. Remember from Chapter 6: You cannot think your way out of a physiological stress response. You must regulate the body first, then reframe the mind.

Your Tool Selection Menu

From the categorized list below, choose 3 to 5 tools that feel most accessible, practical, and appealing to you right now. Write them down in your notebook under the heading **"My Core Response Toolkit."**

Category A: Physiological Regulation Tools (For Interrupting The Takeover)

These tools shift your nervous system from sympathetic (stress) to parasympathetic (recovery) mode:

The Triangle Reset (Chapter 6)

The 4-4-4 breath for focus and immediate calm

Best for: Quick resets between meetings, before presentations

The Box Reset (Chapter 7)

The 4-4-4-4 breath for balance and deep regulation

Best for: Post-stressful events, evening wind-down

The Deep De-Escalation Breath (Chapter 6)

The 4-7-8 breath for intense de-escalation when highly agitated

Best for: After confrontations, before bed when mind is racing

The Body Anchor (Chapter 6)

Feet on floor, back in chair, physical grounding

Best for: Discreet use during meetings, immediate grounding

The 5-4-3-2-1 Anchor (Chapter 6)

Using five senses to anchor in present moment

Best for: Interrupting catastrophic thought spirals, anxiety attacks

The Tension Release Sequence (Chapter 7)

2-minute Progressive Muscle Relaxation focusing on hands and shoulders

Best for: Lunch breaks, releasing accumulated physical tension

The Stress Cycle Completion Walk (Chapter 3)

5-10 minute purposeful walk to metabolize stress hormones

Best for: After difficult meetings, midday restoration

The Vagus Activation (Chapter 7)

Humming practice to stimulate parasympathetic system

Best for: Between meetings, in car, quick de-escalation

Strategic Stretching (Chapter 3)

Simple neck rolls, shoulder shrugs, spinal twists at desk

Best for: Hourly micro-resets, releasing The Tension Reservoir

Category B: Cognitive Regulation Tools (For Escaping Narrative Traps)

These tools help you reframe catastrophic thinking and activate your prefrontal cortex:

Strategic Reframe #1: The Depersonalization Question (Chapter 6)

"What does this actually have to do with me?"

Best for: When caught in The Personalization Story

Strategic Reframe #2: The Perspective Expansion Question (Chapter 6)

"What's another way to look at this situation?"

Best for: When caught in The Catastrophe Story or All-or-Nothing Story

Strategic Reframe #3: The Agency Reclamation Question (Chapter 6)

"What is the one thing I can control right now?"

Best for: When feeling overwhelmed or powerless

The Three-Step Reality Check (Chapter 5)

Catch It, Check It, Reframe It protocol for challenging automatic negative thoughts

Best for: When you recognize a Narrative Trap activating

The Collaborative No (Chapter 3)

Your boundary script for declining requests without guilt

Best for: Protecting Resilience Budget from depletion

The Personal Resilience Mantra

A short, powerful, compassionate phrase you repeat to yourself

Examples: "This is temporary." "I can handle this, one step at a time." "This feeling is a wave; it will pass." "Just the next best step."

Best for: Moments of panic, maintaining calm during long stressors

Sample Balanced Toolkit

Here's what a well-curated, balanced Core Response Toolkit might look like:

My Core Response Toolkit:

The Triangle Reset (Physiological - 1 minute)

The 5-Minute Stress Cycle Completion Walk (Physiological - 5 minutes)

Strategic Reframe: "What can I control right now?" (Cognitive)

The Body Anchor (Physiological - 30 seconds, discreet)

My Mantra: "Just the next best step." (Cognitive)

Why this works: This toolkit has 3 physiological tools (different time commitments for different situations) and 2 cognitive tools (one reframe question, one mantra). It's memorable, covers multiple scenarios, and can be deployed in less than 5 minutes in most cases.

Your toolkit should fit on one index card. If you need a manual to remember it, it's too complicated for a stressed brain to access.

Layer 3: Design Your Implementation Architecture

This is where theory meets reality. **A beautifully curated toolkit that sits on a shelf is nothing more than a well-intentioned decoration.** Tools only work if they're used, and in the heat of a stressful moment when The Takeover is happening, when your Resilience Budget is depleted, when your cognitive function is impaired, our brains are not wired to remember new, complex routines.

Therefore, we must build Implementation Architecture, systems that make it as easy as possible to use our tools when we need them most. We must account for the fact that we are beautifully, predictably, fallibly human.

The Common Implementation Obstacles

The most common obstacles to using these tools are limiting narratives and self-abandonment patterns:

>*"I don't have time for this."* (False: these tools take 1-5 minutes; you spend more time scrolling social media)

>*"This won't work for me."* (False: these are evidence-based techniques used by Navy SEALs, surgeons, and high-performers globally)

>*"People will think I'm weird if I sit here breathing."* (False: most people are too focused on themselves to notice, and those who do notice will likely be curious or impressed)

"I should be able to handle stress without tools." (The Should Story Narrative Trap in action)

"I'll use them when I really need them." (False: you won't remember to use them unless they're habitual)

Implementation Architecture is a pre-commitment. It is a structure you build in a moment of calm, with your wise, rational, prefrontal cortex, to support your future self in a moment of stress when The Takeover is trying to hijack you.

The Five Implementation Strategies

For each of the Core Response Tools you selected in Layer 2, implement at least one of these strategies:

Strategy 1: Calendar Integration (Time-Based Triggers)

Schedule your practices as recurring, non-negotiable appointments.

Examples:

Block 10:30 AM daily: "Strategic Reset: Walk + Breathe"

Block 1:00 PM daily: "Resilience Break: Lunch away from desk"

Block 3:30 PM daily: "Energy Check: Triangle Reset"

Block End of Day: "Transition Routine: Review + Reframe"

Label them professionally so colleagues respect the blocks: "Strategic Thinking Time," "Focus Block," "Leadership Reflection," "Planning Session."

Why this works: It legitimizes the practice and protects that time from being booked over. Your future self doesn't have to remember or decide, it's already scheduled.

Strategy 2: Environmental Cues (Visual Triggers)

Place physical reminders in your environment that prompt your tools.

Examples:

Small sticky note on computer monitor edge: "BREATHE"
or "What can I control?"

Blue dot sticker on phone: Reminds you to practice Triangle
Reset before checking messages

Index card on dashboard: "Before driving home: 3 Triangle
Resets to complete stress cycle"

Object on desk: Smooth stone that reminds you to practice
grounding when you touch it

Make them small and discreet so they don't become clutter, but visible
enough to catch your attention.

Why this works: Visual cues bypass your need to remember. They interrupt autopilot and prompt conscious choice.

Strategy 3: Digital Automation (Technology-Based Triggers)

Use technology to create automatic prompts.

Examples:

Phone alarm (silent/vibrate): 10 AM, 2 PM, 4 PM - pause for
1-minute Triangle Reset regardless of what you're doing

Smart watch reminder: "Check your Stress Signature" three times daily

Calendar popup reminder: "Before this meeting: Body Anchor + 3 breaths"

Computer screensaver: "Your Resilience Budget needs deposits today"

Why this works: Technology creates accountability without requiring another person. It's consistent, unemotional, and you can't forget.

Strategy 4: Social Accountability (Relationship-Based Support)

Enlist support from trusted colleagues or friends.

Examples:

Find a "Resilience Buddy": Check in weekly via text: "Did you use your tools this week? What's one win?"

Walking partner: Schedule afternoon Stress Cycle Completion Walks together 2-3x per week

Team agreement: "Our team takes actual lunch breaks away from desks" - mutual permission and modeling

Accountability with manager: "I'm working on sustainable performance practices. Can we briefly check in monthly on what's working?"

Why this works: The simple knowledge that someone will ask creates motivation. Shared practices normalize what might otherwise feel awkward. You're more likely to follow through when someone else is counting on you.

Strategy 5: Implementation Intentions (If-Then Planning)

This is the most powerful and evidence-based technique. Create specific, detailed plans in the format: **"If [specific trigger], then I will [specific action]."**

Examples:

"**If** I feel my chest tightening before my weekly team meeting, **then** I will go to the restroom and practice The Triangle Reset for 3 cycles before entering the room."

"**If** I receive a critical email that triggers my Stress Signature, **then** I will not respond for 2 hours. I will first take a 5-minute walk and use The Reset Protocol from Chapter 6."

"**If** I notice myself falling into The Catastrophe Story, **then** I will immediately ask myself: 'What can I control right now?'"

"**If** it's Thursday at 3 PM (my weekly energy crash), **then** I will take a 10-minute walk outside, no exceptions."

"**If** someone makes a last-minute request that would drain my Resilience Budget, **then** I will use The Collaborative No: acknowledge + state my limit + offer alternative."

Write these down precisely. The more specific your plan, the more automatic the behavior becomes when the trigger occurs. You're pre-loading the decision so your stressed brain doesn't have to make it in the moment.

Why this works: Implementation Intentions create automatic behavior patterns. Research shows they increase follow-through by 2-3x compared to general goal-setting. You're essentially programming your brain: "When X happens, I automatically do Y."

Building Your Personal Implementation Architecture

Right now, in your notebook, create a simple table:

Core Tool

Implementation Strategy

Specific Plan

Triangle Reset

Calendar Integration

Daily 10:30 AM: "Strategic Reset" recurring appointment

Triangle Reset

Digital Automation

Phone alarm at 10 AM, 2 PM, 4 PM (silent vibrate)

Triangle Reset

Implementation Intention

"If I feel chest tightening before meetings, then I will practice 3 cycles in restroom first"

5-Min Walk

Calendar Integration

Daily 3:00 PM: "Strategic Thinking Walk"

5-Min Walk

Social Accountability

Tuesday/Thursday walking partner with Sarah

"What can I control?"

Environmental Cue

Sticky note on monitor: "W.C.I.C.?"

"What can I control?"

Implementation Intention

"If I feel overwhelmed by competing demands, then I will immediately ask: What can I control right now?"

Your goal: Every Core Response Tool should have at least 1-2 implementation strategies. The more, the better your odds of actually using them.

Layer 4: Schedule Your System Updates

Your stress patterns are not static. Your work demands will change, new projects will arise, life outside work will evolve. Your Resilience Budget capacity may shift with seasons or life events. New Narrative Traps may emerge. What worked brilliantly in Q1 may need adjustment by Q3.

Therefore, your Resilience Operating System™ cannot be a static document you create once and file away. It must be a living, breathing guide that you review, refine, and adapt regularly, this is the Adaptation piece of the 3 A's Framework in action.

I call this process **The System Update,** your dedicated, protected time to assess what's working, what's not, and what needs adjustment. It's your personal board meeting for your own wellbeing, and you are the CEO.

The Monthly System Update Protocol

Right now, pause and do this immediately before you continue reading:

Open your calendar and schedule a 30-minute, non-negotiable appointment with yourself for the **last Friday of every month**. Label it "System Update: Resilience Review" or something professional that you'll respect.

During this 30-minute appointment, work through these five essential questions in your notebook:

Question 1: What's Working? (Celebrate Your Wins)

It is absolutely crucial to start by acknowledging and celebrating what's working, no matter how small the wins.

Ask yourself:

Which of my Core Response Tools did I use most effectively this month?

Which boundaries held firm and made a real difference in protecting my Resilience Budget?

What recovery routines from Chapter 7 made me feel most restored?

Where did I successfully catch my Stress Signature early and intervene before The Takeover was complete?

What Implementation Architecture strategy worked best?

Example entries:

"The Triangle Reset before meetings has become automatic, used it 15+ times this month"

"My Tuesday/Thursday walking partner accountability is working perfectly"

"I successfully used The Collaborative No three times and didn't feel guilty"

"My evening Wind-Down Routine helped me sleep better, averaging 7 hours this month"

Why this matters: Your brain has a negativity bias and will naturally focus on what didn't work. Deliberately celebrating wins reinforces positive patterns and builds motivation to continue.

Question 2: What's Draining Me? (Honest Assessment)

Where were your biggest Resilience Budget drains this month? What patterns need attention?

Ask yourself:

What stressors were most potent or surprising?

Where did I consistently operate in Resilience Budget deficit?

Which boundaries were most challenging to hold, and why?

Where did I become a Ghost in the Chair this month?

What Narrative Traps did I fall into repeatedly?

Where did I pay the most Performance Tax?

Example entries:

"Back-to-back video calls with no breaks depleted me significantly, happened 8 times"

"I violated my 'no email after 7 PM' boundary multiple times when anxious about project"

"Fell into The Catastrophe Story every time senior leadership requested updates"

"Skipped lunch at desk 12 days this month despite my commitment"

Why this matters: This data tells you exactly where to focus your adaptation efforts. You can't fix what you can't see.

Question 3: What Needs Adjusting? (Strategic Pivot)

Based on what worked and what drained you, what one thing needs to change?

Ask yourself:

Does one of my Core Response Tools not feel as effective as I hoped?

Do I need to change the timing of my Scheduled Restoration Breaks to better suit my workflow?

Is my Implementation Architecture working, or do I need different strategies?

Do I need to add a new tool for a stressor I didn't anticipate?

Do I need to strengthen a boundary that keeps getting violated?

Example entries:

"The Box Reset isn't working well for me, I'll replace it with The Vagus Activation humming practice"

"My 3 PM walk keeps getting skipped, I need to move it to 11 AM before lunch rush"

"I need to add an Implementation Intention for the back-to-back video call pattern"

"I need to use The Boundary Ladder more consistently for last-minute requests"

Why this matters: This is Adaptation in action. You're using real data from your lived experience to refine your system.

Question 4: What's My Single Focus? (The Monthly Intention)

Choose ONE specific, achievable area to focus on for the coming month.

This should be:

Specific (not "manage stress better" but "practice Triangle Reset before every meeting")

Measurable (you can track whether you did it)

Achievable (realistic given your current capacity)

Time-bound (for this month only)

Example intentions:

"My focus for next month is: Get better at catching my Stress Signature early, I'll practice The Somatic Inquiry daily to build awareness"

"My focus: Use The Collaborative No every time someone requests something that would overdraw my Resilience Budget"

"My focus: Complete all Scheduled Restoration Breaks, no skipping, to prevent becoming a Ghost in the Chair"

"My focus: Practice The Three-Step Reality Check every time I notice The Catastrophe Story Narrative Trap"

Why this matters: One focused intention creates momentum. Trying to change everything at once leads to changing nothing. This is how sustainable transformation happens, one intentional month at a time.

Question 5: What Support Do I Need? (Resource Identification)

What would make your Resilience Operating System™ work better? What's missing?

Ask yourself:

Do I need more accountability? (Find a Resilience Buddy?)

Do I need more knowledge? (Re-read a specific chapter? Seek additional training?)

Do I need environmental changes? (Different workspace setup? Noise-canceling headphones?)

Do I need to have conversations? (With manager about workload? With team about boundaries?)

Do I need professional support? (Therapist? Coach? Medical consultation for sleep/health issues?)

Why this matters: Sometimes the issue isn't your system, it's that you need resources or support you don't currently have. Identifying this is strategic, not weakness.

This process of regular, structured System Updates ensures your Resilience Operating System™ remains relevant, effective, and alive. Growth comes from reflection and adaptation, not from perfection.

Layer 5: Establish Your Emergency Protocols

Even with the best, most consistent Resilience Operating System™, there will be times when your regular tools aren't enough. A major personal crisis, an unexpected organizational upheaval, a period of intense prolonged stress, a significant life transition, these can overwhelm your normal capacity to cope.

In these moments, your system can become so flooded that even The Reset Protocol feels inadequate. Your Resilience Budget may be so deeply overdrawn that you're operating in chronic deficit with no clear path back to equilibrium. You might be on the verge of, or already experiencing, Boundary Collapse (Chapter 7).

In these moments, you need pre-defined Emergency Protocols. This is your lifeline, the clear, simple plan you create in advance for what to do when your stress spikes beyond your normal system's capacity.

The Three-Tier Emergency Response System

In your notebook, create a new section titled **"Emergency Protocols: My Lifeline Plan."** Design a simple, tiered system from immediate action to significant intervention:

Tier 1: Immediate Circuit Breaker (0-10 minutes)

What is the one thing you can do immediately to create a moment of safety and interrupt crisis escalation?

This should be:

Immediately accessible (no scheduling required)

Simple enough to remember when panicking

Creates physical/environmental change

Examples:

"I will step outside and get fresh air and sunlight for 5 minutes, no matter what I'm doing"

"I will call [specific person] and use our code word 'Red Light' which means: I just need you to listen for 3 minutes, no advice"

"I will go to a private space (bathroom, car, empty conference room) and practice The Deep De-Escalation Breath for 2 full minutes"

"I will text my Resilience Buddy: 'Emergency check-in needed' and wait for their response before making any decisions"

Write yours now: "When I'm in crisis mode, my immediate Circuit Breaker is: _____ "

Tier 2: Professional Support Activation (Within 24-48 hours)

Who are the trained professionals you can call on for support? Have this information ready NOW so you don't have to search in crisis.

Document these with specific contact information:

Mental Health Support:

Therapist name: _____

Phone: _____

Emergency scheduling process: _____

Employee Assistance Program (EAP):

Company EAP phone: _____

Website: _____

Services available: _____

Crisis Hotline (if needed):

National: 988 (Suicide & Crisis Lifeline)

Text: Text "HELLO" to 741741 (Crisis Text Line)

Medical Support:

Primary care doctor: _____

When to call: _____

Manager/HR (for work-related crisis):

When I need to activate this: _____

How to request support: _____

Why have this documented: In crisis, your cognitive function is impaired. You don't want to be searching for phone numbers or trying to remember if your insurance covers therapy. Have everything written down and easily accessible.

Tier 3: Strategic Retreat (Within 1 week)

What is your plan for taking a strategic retreat when you recognize you're at breaking point or experiencing Boundary Collapse?

Pre-plan your retreat options:

Option A: Mental Health Day

Pre-conversation with manager (during calm): "I practice proactive mental health management. If I ever need to take a mental health day for wellbeing, I'll let you know as early as possible. I want to normalize this as preventive care."

How to request: "I need to take a mental health day tomorrow. I'll be back [date] and will catch up on urgent items."

Option B: Extended Weekend Reset

Schedule long weekend within 1-2 weeks of recognizing overwhelm

Plan: Completely unplug, go to nature/different environment, focus only on recovery

Pre-arrange coverage for urgent work matters

Option C: Professional Leave

Know your company's leave policies (FMLA, personal leave, medical leave)

Know your rights and options before you need them

Have therapist/doctor contact info ready for documentation if needed

Document your trigger for activating Tier 3: "I will activate my Strategic Retreat protocol when I notice these signs: _____ "

Examples of Tier 3 triggers:

"When I can't sleep for more than 3 consecutive nights despite using my tools"

"When I've operated as a Ghost in the Chair for 2+ weeks straight"

"When I experience panic attacks or can't stop crying"

"When I have thoughts of self-harm or feel completely hopeless"

"When my physical health is being significantly impacted (persistent illness, pain, etc.)"

Knowing you have this clear, pre-defined Emergency Protocol dramatically reduces the anxiety and panic that accompany crisis. You don't have to figure it out in the chaotic heat of the moment, you just have to follow the wise, calm, rational plan you created for yourself.

Case Study: Lena's Complete Resilience Operating System™

Let's see how all five layers come together in a real transformation story.

Lena's Starting Point

Lena was a mid-career finance professional and a classic "wellness information junkie." She had:

Read countless articles on stress management

Downloaded a dozen meditation apps

Had a bookshelf full of self-help books

Tried various techniques sporadically

But nothing stuck. Every new wellness tool felt like another temporary "band-aid," another thing she "should" be doing, which only added to her stress and sense of failure. She came to me wanting something comprehensive, sustainable, and most importantly, **personalized**.

Her words: *"I'm drowning in wellness advice but I have no system. Every Monday I start fresh with good intentions, and by Wednesday I've abandoned everything. I need something that actually works for MY life."*

Together, we built her complete Resilience Operating System™.

Layer 1: Lena's Stress Signature Map

Through detailed assessment, Lena discovered:

Her three main stressors:

Emails from senior leaders requesting urgent reports

End-of-quarter deadline pressure with multiple competing priorities

Giving presentations to executive team

Her Stress Signature patterns:

Physical:

Earliest signal: Subtle breath shallowing when opening emails from executives

Secondary: Sudden craving for sugary snacks around 3 PM (blood sugar crash from skipping lunch)

Tertiary: Tension headaches, shoulder armor activation

Emotional:

Anxiety (future-oriented fear about performance)

Overwhelm (too many demands, not enough capacity)

Resentment (at being constantly interrupted)

Mental (Narrative Traps):

The Catastrophe Story: "If this report isn't perfect, my credibility is ruined"

The Should Story: "I should be able to handle this without needing breaks"

The All-or-Nothing Story: "If I can't do it all excellently, I'm failing"

Her earliest warning system: "My earliest Stress Signature is: shallow breathing and the impulse to immediately respond to emails without pausing."

This awareness was revolutionary for her. She finally understood her patterns instead of just feeling generically "stressed."

Layer 2: Lena's Core Response Toolkit

Based on her Stress Signature and preferences, Lena curated this focused toolkit:

The Box Reset (Physiological - she liked its structural symmetry)

The Body Anchor (Physiological - discreet for meetings)

5-Minute Stress Cycle Completion Walk (Physiological - needed movement)

Strategic Reframe: "What can I control?" (Cognitive - for overwhelm)

Boundary Script (Cognitive - for protecting deep work time)

Her boundary script: "I'm in a deep focus block right now. Can we connect about this at [specific time later today]?"

Why this toolkit worked: It addressed her specific patterns (breath/body stress + overwhelm narrative), was simple enough to remember, and fit her work environment (corporate office, some flexibility).

Layer 3: Lena's Implementation Architecture

Calendar Integration:

Blocked 11:00 AM daily: "Strategic Reset Walk" (before lunch rush, harder to skip)

Blocked 2:30 PM daily: "Focus Block" (her afternoon energy dip time)

Blocked 5:30 PM daily: "Day Review + Reset" (transition home)

Environmental Cues:

Small sticky note on monitor: "Breathe before responding"

Phone background: "W.C.I.C.?" (What Can I Control?)

Digital Automation:

Phone alarm (silent vibrate) at 2:00 PM: "Stress Signature check + Box Reset"

Social Accountability:

Found colleague Sarah to be afternoon walking partner Tuesday/Thursday

Weekly Friday text with friend: "How'd your resilience week go? One win?"

Implementation Intentions:

> "**If** I feel my breath shallow when opening an executive email, **then** I will not respond immediately. I will practice one Box Reset cycle first."

> "**If** someone interrupts my Focus Block, **then** I will use my boundary script: 'I'm in deep focus right now. Can we connect at 3:30 PM?'"

"**If** it's Thursday at 3 PM (my predictable energy crash), **then** I will take my walk with Sarah, no exceptions, no matter how busy I feel."

The transformation in consistency: Within two weeks, Lena was using her tools 4-5 days per week instead of sporadically. **The Implementation Architecture made the difference**—she didn't have to rely on willpower or memory.

Layer 4: Lena's System Updates

Month 1 Review revealed:

What worked: Box Reset was becoming automatic; walking partner accountability was gold

What drained: Still struggling with afternoon walk consistency on non-Sarah days

What needs adjusting: Needs different strategy for solo walk days

Her adaptation: She asked her manager if she could schedule her afternoon walk as "Strategic Thinking Time" for working through problems. Manager said yes. Suddenly the walk felt "productive" not "indulgent", her limiting narrative shifted.

Month 3 Review revealed:

What worked: All tools being used consistently; Resilience Budget much more balanced

What needs adjusting: Formal evening journaling felt forced and wasn't happening

Her adaptation: Swapped written journaling for voice note reflections during her commute home. This felt more natural to her processing style. **This flexibility, guided by structured monthly review, kept her engaged with the system.**

Layer 5: Lena's Emergency Protocols

Tier 1 Circuit Breaker: "Call my sister and use code word 'Overload', she'll listen for 5 minutes no advice, then ask: What do you need right now?"

Tier 2 Professional Support:

Therapist: Dr. Martinez, (555) 123-4567, text for emergency session

Company EAP: (800) 555-EAP, available 24/7, up to 5 free sessions

Tier 3 Strategic Retreat: Pre-approved with manager during calm discussion: "I proactively manage my mental health. If I ever need a mental health day, I'll let you know morning-of. I've built enough buffer into my projects to accommodate this."

Trigger for Tier 3: "When I can't sleep for 3+ nights despite using all my tools, or when I notice I'm becoming a Ghost in the Chair for more than a week."

The Six-Month Transformation

What changed for Lena:

Resilience Budget:

From chronic deficit (operating at 30-40% capacity most weeks)

To sustainable balance (operating at 70-80% capacity with regular recovery)

Performance:

Fewer errors on financial reports

Better strategic thinking ("My brain actually works now")

More proactive problem-solving

Promotion to senior analyst

Relationships:

More present and patient with family

Better collaboration with colleagues

Less resentment, more genuine connection

Self-Perception:

From: "I'm failing at wellness and failing at work"

To: "I have a system that works for me. I'm building sustainable high performance."

Her key insight: *"I didn't need more information or more tools. I needed fewer tools that I actually used, and a system that made using them automatic. The Implementation Architecture was everything, it removed the decision fatigue and the guilt. And the monthly reviews meant I kept adapting instead of abandoning when something didn't work perfectly. This isn't a wellness hack. This is my operating system now."*

Your Resilience Operating System™ is Your Declaration of Self-Leadership

Building your Resilience Operating System™ is not about achieving perfection. It's not about never being stressed again. It's not about following someone else's prescription for wellness.

It is your declaration of self-leadership. It is the tangible expression of your commitment to not just survive the demands of your life, but to consciously, skillfully navigate them.

It is the essential, empowering work of building your own ship, plank by plank, layer by layer, so that you are not just prepared for the storms, but are made stronger, wiser, and more capable by them.

Your Resilience Operating System™ is:

Your personalized map of your unique Stress Signature

Your curated toolkit of proven interventions

Your infrastructure that makes resilience automatic, not aspirational

Your commitment to regular adaptation and growth

Your safety net for crisis moments

This is how sustainable, lasting transformation happens. Not through motivation or willpower. Not through generic advice. But through building a personalized system that works for your unique nervous system, your specific work context, and your real life constraints.

Now it's your turn to build yours.

Reflection Questions for Chapter 8

Commit to Building Your System: Set aside 60-90 minutes this week (schedule it now in your calendar as a non-negotiable appointment) to work through all five layers:

Layer 1: Map your Stress Signature

Layer 2: Curate your Core Response Toolkit (3-5 tools)

Layer 3: Design your Implementation Architecture

Layer 4: Schedule your first monthly System Update

Layer 5: Document your Emergency Protocols

Treat this as mission-critical strategic planning, because it is.

Identify Your Primary Obstacle: What is the biggest potential obstacle you foresee to implementing and maintaining your Resilience Operating System™? What limiting narrative or Narrative Trap might sabotage you? Write it down, then write down:

Evidence that contradicts this narrative

An Implementation Intention to override it when it appears

One person who can support you in overcoming this obstacle

Choose Your First Implementation Win: What is the single smallest, easiest step from your system that you can implement tomorrow? Not next week. Tomorrow. Choose something so small and achievable that you cannot fail. Then do it. Build momentum through small wins, not grand transformations.

Share Your Commitment: Tell one person about your Resilience Operating System™. Share your earliest Stress Signature signal and one tool you're committing to use. Making it visible makes it real. Accountability increases follow-through by 65%.

Chapter 9
Team & Culture Stress Dynamics

For the past eight chapters, our focus has been intensely and intentionally personal. We have been doing the essential, foundational work of building your own ship. We've inspected the hull for vulnerabilities through understanding your Stress Signature, upgraded the navigation systems of awareness using The Signal Map, learned the skillful seamanship of regulated action through The Reset Protocol, and designed the vital recovery routines of adaptation with The Recovery Architecture. This individual work is the absolute, non-negotiable starting point of the resilience journey. You cannot give what you do not have. You cannot create psychological safety for others if you are internally at war. And you cannot lead a team to a place of regulation, trust, and well-being if you do not know how to get there yourself.

But we do not work in a vacuum. Our ships do not sail on an empty ocean. We are part of a fleet, members of a team, and citizens of a complex, and often invisible, organizational culture. And in any fleet, in any ecosystem, the weather is contagious. The frantic, chaotic, and reactive energy of one ship can create a dangerous, destabilizing wake that jeopardizes the vessels around it. Conversely, the calm, steady, and purposeful presence of a well-captained ship can provide a safe harbor for others, a point of orientation and stability in the midst of a raging storm.

In this chapter, we zoom out. We shift our lens from the individual to the collective, from the internal world of one person to the intricate, interconnected dynamics of the group. We will explore the powerful, often unspoken, ways that stress operates not just *within* a person, but *between* people. We will dissect the anatomy of team and culture stress, examining how a leader's internal state becomes the team's external reality, how toxic stress can spread like an insidious contagion through an entire organization, and, most importantly, how to interrupt these destructive patterns and begin the intentional, courageous work of building a culture of shared, sustainable resilience.

This is the next frontier of leadership, and it is a profound departure from the old models. It is the critical shift from seeing stress as a personal problem, a sign of individual weakness for employees to manage on their own time, to understanding it as a systemic, cultural issue that leaders have a profound responsibility, and a powerful opportunity, to consciously and deliberately shape.

Living the 3-A Way: From Personal Practice to Professional Advantage

Before we dive into the complex dynamics of a team, it's crucial to understand how your personal, consistent practice of the 3 A's Resilience Framework™, Awareness, Regulated Action, and Adaptation, naturally and inevitably evolves into a powerful and discernible professional advantage. This is not just about feeling better; it is about performing better, connecting better, and leading better. When you consistently practice the 3 A's, you begin to operate from a fundamentally different place, a place of centered strength that others can feel.

Awareness in Daily Professional Life

This means you walk into a high-stakes negotiation not just with your talking points meticulously prepared, but with a clear, real-time, and non-judgmental understanding of your own Stress Signature. You notice the subtle, familiar tension creeping into your shoulders, that somatic data point we explored in Chapter 5, and use it as a cue to take a deep, grounding breath before you speak. You are aware of the precise moment your tone of voice begins to sharpen with impatience in a team meeting, catching yourself before The Takeover hijacks your professional presence. You can pause, soften, and choose a more collaborative and curious approach before it damages the fragile atmosphere of psychological safety. It's knowing, with profound clarity, the difference between responding from a place of strategic, long-term calm versus reacting from a place of short-term, ego-driven fear.

Regulated Action in Daily Professional Life

This is the visible, tangible manifestation of your inner awareness. It is the consistent, observable choice to deploy your Reset Protocol instead of a reactive response. It is the deliberate, almost imperceptible pause before you reply to a provocative or accusatory email, a pause in which you use The Triangle Reset or The Physiological Reset to regulate your own nervous system before you type a single word. It is the advanced skill of redirecting a conflict-ridden, circular conversation with a powerful, open-ended, and curious question instead of a critical, defensive, or blaming statement. It is the quiet courage to implement The Energy Protection System with a demanding client or a senior leader, not out of anger or resentment, but out of a deep professional commitment to delivering high-quality, sustainable work within a realistic and healthy framework.

Adaptation in Daily Professional Life

This is where resilience moves from a set of actions to your fundamental way of being. It means you have intentionally built The Recovery Architecture into your workday, structured breaks, realistic and protected deep-work blocks, and proactive team routines, that help you and your team recover from intense periods of Breaking Pressure (as opposed to healthy Growth Pressure) and stay steady for the long, marathon-like journey. Your boundaries become non-negotiable, not because you are rigid or unhelpful, but because you understand they are the very structure, the very container, that allows you to perform at your peak and to serve others from a full Resilience Budget.

When leaders and professionals practice the 3 A's daily, they gain a palpable and undeniable edge. They have better focus and make clearer decisions. They engage in healthier, more productive communication. They build a level of credibility and trustworthiness that can only be earned by someone who can handle intense, unpredictable pressure without cracking or causing collateral damage. This advantage builds trust, and trust, in any team, organization, or human relationship, is the ultimate and most precious currency of influence.

The Nervous System Broadcast™: A Leader's Unspoken, Powerful Impact

Every leader, whether they are a C-suite executive, a mid-level manager, or an informal team lead, has a crucial role they are likely entirely unaware they are playing: they are broadcasting their nervous system state to everyone around them. Your internal state, your level of regulation, your anxiety, your frustration, your calm, is not a private, contained experience. It radiates from you through what I call **The Nervous System Broadcast™**. It is constantly, silently, and powerfully setting the emotional and psychological temperature of the room.

Think of it this way: **your nervous system speaks before your mouth opens.** It communicates through micro-expressions, body language, vocal tone, pace of speech, and the energetic quality of your presence. Your team's mirror neurons, those specialized brain cells that help us unconsciously attune to others, are constantly reading and responding to your broadcast signal, often without anyone's conscious awareness.

If a leader runs "hot", chronically anxious, displaying a Fast-Burn Stress Signature (as we explored in Chapter 1), visibly irritable, emotionally reactive, and perpetually frantic, the whole team feels it. The ambient stress level in the room rises. What I call **The Reactive Cascade™** begins. People become more cautious, less likely to speak up with a new or dissenting idea, and more focused on simply surviving the meeting than on collaborating or innovating. A culture of fear, anxiety, and risk-aversion begins to take root, one meeting at a time, one dysregulated broadcast at a time.

Conversely, if a leader runs "steady", grounded, clear, present, responsive, and calm under pressure, the team's collective nervous system naturally co-regulates around them. Their regulated presence creates a powerful, invisible field of psychological safety, a palpable, unspoken sense that "we are safe here, we can handle this challenge, together." This is what I call **The Regulation Effect™,** when one person's nervous system stability creates a stabilizing influence on everyone around them.

Let me show you how this plays out with two very different leaders I coached in the same organization.

The Hot Broadcast (Maria)

Maria was a brilliant and deeply committed director in the organization's government affairs division. She was also a chronic workaholic who managed her own deep-seated anxiety, her Slow-Burn Stress we identified in Chapter 1, by sending a constant barrage of emails at all hours of the day and night. Even though she would often say things like, "You can just respond in the morning," her actions broadcasted a different, far more potent message through her Nervous System Broadcast: "I am anxious and working, so you should be anxious and working too."

Her team felt a constant, low-grade pressure to be "on call." They confessed to checking their phones before bed and first thing upon waking, their own nervous systems perpetually on high alert, waiting for the next urgent request. Maria's personal, unmanaged anxiety, her unregulated Stress Signature, had set the team's temperature to a state of chronic, low-grade urgency and impending exhaustion. Her Resilience Budget was depleted, and she was unconsciously depleting her entire team's budget as well. Unsurprisingly, her team suffered from some of the highest rates of burnout and turnover in the entire company. The Performance Tax (Chapter 2) was being paid by everyone.

The Steady Broadcast (David)

David was a manager in the same company's IT department. He was struggling with a team that he described as "constantly on edge and disengaged." Through our work, he began to practice the 3 A's, starting with a simple, personal adaptation from Chapter 7: he committed to practicing The Triangle Reset, a two-minute breathing protocol, in his office right before every weekly staff meeting. He didn't change the agenda, the attendees, or the topics of the meeting. The only variable that changed was his own internal state, his own Nervous System Broadcast.

He began to walk into the room from a place of calm, grounded regulation. Within three weeks, the change was remarkable. His team members reported in an anonymous pulse survey that they felt calmer and "more heard" in the meetings. One employee even commented, "I don't know what's different, but the meetings just feel less stressful now. I actually feel comfortable speaking up." David's personal regulation, his conscious use of The Regulation Effect, had single-handedly shifted the emotional temperature of the entire room.

The key truth here is one that every leader must grapple with, and it is profound: **Your nervous system leads before your words do.** Your team will always respond more to the non-verbal, energetic information you are broadcasting, your presence, your tone, your pace, your level of tension, than they will to the content of the slides you are presenting.

The Reactive Cascade™: Understanding Stress Transfer Systems

When a leader's unregulated stress consistently broadcasts a "hot" signal, it can create a dangerous phenomenon I call **The Reactive Cascade™**. This is the organizational equivalent of a biochemical chain reaction, one person's dysregulation triggers another's, which triggers another's, creating a downward spiral of collective stress that becomes embedded in the cultural DNA.

The Reactive Cascade operates through what behavioral scientists call "emotional contagion," but it's more nuanced and insidious than that simple phrase suggests. It's not just that people "catch" each other's emotions like catching a cold. It's that **unregulated stress creates systems-level changes in how teams communicate, make decisions, and relate to one another.**

The Four Stages of The Reactive Cascade™

Stage 1: The Initial Broadcast A leader's unregulated Stress Signature (anxiety, frustration, panic) broadcasts through The Nervous System Broadcast during interactions. The team's mirror neurons pick up the signal, even if nothing is explicitly said.

Stage 2: The Defensive Adaptation Team members unconsciously adapt their behavior to manage the leader's dysregulation. They become hypervigilant, overly cautious, or perform "emotional labor" trying to reg-ulate the leader's state instead of doing their actual work. This is The Performance Tax manifesting at the team level.

Stage 3: The Cultural Embedding These adaptive behaviors become "the way we do things here." Unspoken rules emerge: *"We don't talk about how stressed we are; it's a sign of weakness."* Or, *"If the boss is panicked and working until midnight, then we all must be panicked and working until midnight."* Or, *"Exhaustion is the price of admission to the inner circle."*

Stage 4: The Systemic Collapse The culture reaches a breaking point. What shows up is predictable and devastating:

> A rise in short tempers and impatience in meetings, with collaboration giving way to defensiveness

> A palpable silence in brainstorming sessions, as people become too afraid to offer new, innovative, or risky ideas

> A measurable increase in absenteeism, sick days, and employee disengagement

The formation of toxic cliques, persistent gossip, and destructive blame cycles, as people desperately try to manage their own anxiety by triangulating and creating an "us versus them" narrative

The Three Cascade Interrupters™

The good news is that The Reactive Cascade can be interrupted. The culture doesn't shift because stress magically disappears; stress is an inevitable part of ambitious work. The culture shifts when stress is acknowledged, normalized, and navigated collectively with skill and compassion. Here are three powerful interruptions that leaders can introduce:

Interrupter #1: Normalize the Signal

The single most powerful way to interrupt The Reactive Cascade is to courageously start talking about stress signals without shame or judgment. This doesn't mean holding long, unstructured, and potentially uncomfortable group therapy sessions. It means building in small, structured routines that make it safe and normal to talk about capacity, energy, and well-being using the language of The Stress Signal Map from Chapter 5.

A powerful and elegantly simple practice is the **One-Word Weather Report™**: Begin every team meeting with a one-word emotional check-in where each person names their current internal state. The leader must go first, modeling vulnerability and demonstrating The Regulation Effect: "My check-in today is 'stretched', feeling a bit thin after that deadline, but focused and optimistic about this conversation."

This simple act shatters the unspoken rule that everyone must pretend to be "fine" and normalizes the conversation about the human experience of work. It gives people permission to acknowledge their Stress Signature without apology.

Interrupter #2: Model the Recovery Architecture

In a culture dominated by The Reactive Cascade, rest is seen as a weakness, a sign that you are not committed enough. A leader can interrupt this destructive pattern by actively, visibly, and unapologetically modeling The Recovery Architecture we built in Chapter 7.

This means:

Taking a full lunch break away from your desk, maybe even going for a walk (practicing The Stress Cycle Completion Protocol)

Not sending emails at 10:00 PM or on a Sunday morning

Saying at the end of a long and grueling week: "Team, we did incredible work this week. I am signing off for the weekend to completely unplug and recharge with my family. I expect and encourage you all to do the same."

When a leader visibly maintains their Resilience Budget without guilt, it signals powerful permission for the entire team to do so. You are broadcasting through The Nervous System Broadcast that recovery is not optional, it's professional.

Interrupter #3: Create Collective Reset Routines

When a team is caught in The Reactive Cascade, their collective nervous system is stuck in the "on" position, perpetually braced for the next crisis. A leader can introduce structured pauses, or **Collective Reset Routines™**, to help the team's nervous system downshift together.

This could be as simple as:

Declaring a two-minute silent pause for individual reflection in the middle of a contentious, decision-making meeting when you sense The Takeover beginning to hijack the room

Starting every meeting with a 60-second guided breathing exercise using The Triangle Reset

Implementing a "No-Tech Transition", the first five minutes of a meeting are screen-free, allowing people to fully arrive and co-regulate before diving into content

These structured pauses interrupt the frantic, reactive momentum of The Reactive Cascade and allow the team's collective rational brain to come back online.

The Six Micro-Routines™: Building Team Resilience Layer by Layer

Building a resilient, high-performing culture can feel like a daunting, overwhelming, and abstract task. The biggest mistake organizations make is trying to overhaul their culture overnight with some massive, top-down, and often impersonal initiative. Sustainable change happens not through flooding the system with new rules and expectations, but through the gentle, consistent practice of layering. It happens through the consistent implementation of small, repeatable, and high-impact behaviors I call **The Six Micro-Routines™**.

Here are six quick, repeatable practices that teams can adopt to begin the slow but powerful process of building a culture of shared resilience. The key to successful implementation is that the leader must **model the practice first**, demonstrating The Regulation Effect, then explicitly invite, but not force, participation.

Micro-Routine #1: The One-Word Weather Report™

As mentioned above, this is a simple, powerful way to start meetings. Each person shares one word that describes their current internal state using language from their Stress Signature (e.g., "focused," "scattered," "energized," "depleted," "optimistic," "stretched"). It builds awareness, empathy, and human connection in under two minutes while normalizing the conversation about capacity.

Micro-Routine #2: The Regulation Opener™

For meetings that are known to be difficult, long, or contentious, the leader can start by saying, "Before we dive into this complex topic, let's all take just 60 seconds to fully arrive and get present. I invite you to join me in The Triangle Reset, three slow, deep breaths." This is not about forcing anyone to meditate; it is about using The Regulation Effect to co-regulate the nervous systems in the room and set the stage for a more productive and less reactive conversation.

Micro-Routine #3: The Boundary Demonstration™

The leader must model respectful, professional boundary-setting using principles from The Energy Protection System (Chapter 3). When the team sees their leader say in response to a new request, "That's a great idea and I see the value in it, but our team does not have the bandwidth to take that on this quarter without depleting our Resilience Budget and compromising our existing commitments. Let's discuss the strategic trade-offs," it makes it safe and acceptable for them to do the same. This is The Nervous System Broadcast in action, communicating that boundaries are not selfish, they're strategic.

Micro-Routine #4: The Energy Audit™

At the end of the weekly team meeting on Friday, the leader can pose two simple but powerful questions drawn from The Depletion Audit in Chapter 3: "As we head into the weekend, I want everyone to take a moment to identify one thing from this week that felt like an energy leak, a process that was frustrating, a communication that was unclear, a meeting that drained you, and one thing that energized you and felt like a win. We'll start our Monday meeting by brainstorming one small way we can plug one of those leaks."

This routine does three things simultaneously: it normalizes talking about energy management, it generates actionable improvements, and it activates The Recovery Architecture at the team level.

Micro-Routine #5: CLEAR™ Communication Rounds

The CLEAR™ Communication model (Connect, Listen, Express, Ask, Reinforce) is a powerful proprietary tool for navigating difficult conversations and feedback sessions. In a team debrief after a project, for example, the leader can structure the conversation using these five steps, ensuring that everyone feels heard and that feedback is delivered constructively and respectfully. This creates psychological safety and interrupts The Reactive Cascade before it can start.

Micro-Routine #6: The Recognition Close-Out™

End every meeting with one quick round of specific appreciation. The leader can ask, "What is one thing you appreciate about our work together today?" or "Who is one person on the team you'd like to acknowledge for their specific contribution this week?"

This simple practice intentionally and powerfully shifts the team's focus to the positive, counteracting the brain's natural negativity bias and strengthening relational bonds. It also models the kind of culture you're trying to create, one where people feel seen, valued, and psychologically safe.

These are small but incredibly powerful cultural shifts. They are low-effort, high-return practices that, over time, can fundamentally rewire a team's culture from one of chronic Reactive Cascade patterns to one of resilience, trust, and psychological safety.

The Implementation Ladder™: Culture Integration Without Overwhelm

Integrating these valuable practices into a team's existing, and often deeply entrenched, workflow requires a thoughtful, strategic, and patient approach. Here is my five-step **Implementation Ladder™** that I recommend to leaders to ensure the change is sustainable and doesn't ironically create more overwhelm for a team that is already at capacity:

Step 1: Anchor in Leadership

The first step is always, without exception, to train your leaders. If the managers, directors, and team leads do not personally understand, practice, and embody these behaviors, any broader initiative is doomed to fail. It will be perceived as hypocritical and "just another corporate initiative." The change must be authentic and embodied at the leadership level first. Leaders must learn to manage their own Stress Signature and master The Nervous System Broadcast before they can guide others.

Step 2: Choose One Routine

Start small. Be realistic. Don't try to implement all Six Micro-Routines at once. In consultation with your team, choose the one that feels most accessible and relevant to your team's most pressing pain points. For many teams, The One-Word Weather Report is a great, low-risk place to start because it requires minimal time and creates immediate psychological safety.

Step 3: Measure the Impact

After consistently implementing that one practice for a month (30-60 days), gather both qualitative and quantitative feedback. This can be done through a simple, anonymous pulse survey or an informal team conversation. Ask: "What has been the impact of this new practice? What's working? What could be better? How has this affected our Reactive Cascade patterns?"

Step 4: Layer the Next Step

Only after the first practice feels natural, has become a habit, and has demonstrated clear value should you consider adding a second one. This slow, deliberate layering approach prevents the team from feeling overwhelmed by "just another corporate initiative" and builds buy-in through experienced success. You're teaching the team that sustainable change is built routine by routine, not through dramatic overnight transformation.

Step 5: Sustain Through System Integration

To ensure the practices stick for the long term, they must be formally embedded into your team's existing structures and routines. Add The One-Word Weather Report as a permanent standing item on your weekly meeting agenda. Integrate the CLEAR™ Communication model into your official performance review process and documents. Build these practices into your onboarding process for new team members so it becomes part of "the way we do things here", part of the cultural DNA.

This approach of steady, incremental progress using The Implementation Ladder is what creates long-term, sustainable, and authentic culture shifts. Small, consistent wins create the momentum and the crucial buy-in for bigger, more ambitious changes down the road.

Elise's Story: Transforming an Entire Organizational Culture

Let's end with the story of Elise, a client whose journey exemplifies how a single, committed leader's dedication to managing The Nervous System Broadcast can transform the culture of an entire organization.

Elise was the passionate and deeply committed executive director of a mid-sized nonprofit focused on community health. She loved her mission-driven work with every fiber of her being, but she admitted to me in our first session, her voice heavy with a mix of shame and despair, that her staff were like "walking zombies." Turnover was alarmingly high, morale was devastatingly low, and all-staff meetings felt heavy with unspoken tension, cynicism, and resentment. Elise herself was deeply burned out, experiencing what we now recognize as the Depletion/Disconnection/Collapse sequence from Chapter 2, but she felt a profound sense of responsibility to change the toxic culture she had unintentionally helped create through years of broadcasting unregulated stress.

Phase 1: Mastering The Nervous System Broadcast

Our work began with her as the broadcaster. I taught her the CLEAR™ communication model and the personal, daily practice of The 3-Minute Reset (a combination of The Triangle Reset and The Grounding Anchor from Chapter 6). She began practicing The Six Micro-Routines in her own leadership behavior. She started pausing before responding in tense budget meetings, using The Reset Protocol. She began naming her own Stress Signature to normalize it for her team ("I'm feeling some anxiety around this budget shortfall, so I want us to talk about it openly and honestly instead of everyone trying to manage my stress for me"). She started inviting reflection from her team instead of demanding immediate answers, demonstrating The Regulation Effect in real-time.

The shift in her own leadership team was almost immediate. Her direct reports told her in their one-on-ones that they felt "seen and safe" for the first time in years. Their Resilience Budgets were beginning to refill. This initial success gave Elise the courage and the credibility to roll out team-wide practices.

Phase 2: Introducing The Six Micro-Routines™

We started with one, simple practice: The One-Word Weather Report at the start of their weekly all-staff meeting. At first, it was awkward, people weren't used to being asked about their internal state at work. The Reactive Cascade had taught them to hide their Stress Signatures. But Elise persevered, modeling vulnerability first every single time.

Then, after a month, we layered in a second practice: two minutes of shared, guided breathing using The Regulation Opener in the middle of long, draining meetings. People could opt out quietly, but most participated because they could feel the collective nervous system shift.

Then, we introduced a third, more advanced practice: "Cascade Reframes," where leaders were trained to proactively pose questions like, "What can we do differently as a team to prevent this kind of last-minute stress from spiraling into a Reactive Cascade next time?" This moved the culture from blame to collective problem-solving.

Phase 3: The Measurable Transformation

Within six months, the results were stunning and measurable. A follow-up anonymous employee engagement survey showed that scores had risen by an unprecedented 40%. The turnover rate, which had been a major financial and emotional drain on the organization, had decreased by half. And in the survey's qualitative comments, staff described the workplace with words that had been unimaginable just a year earlier: "lighter," "more collaborative," "supportive," and "more human."

Elise's own regulated, intentional, and courageous presence, her mastery of The Nervous System Broadcast, had inspired her managers to follow suit, creating a cascade of positive change throughout the organization. She had moved her organization from a culture of The Reactive Cascade to a culture of shared, sustainable, and high-performing resilience.

Her story is a powerful testament to a simple but profound truth: **When leaders regulate themselves, they create The Regulation Effect for the room. And when you consistently create The Regulation Effect, you ultimately transform the culture.** The work of building a resilient organization always begins with the deep, personal, and courageous inner work of the leader.

Reflection Questions for Chapter 9

Your Professional Advantage: How would consistently practicing the 3 A's Resilience Framework give you a professional advantage in your specific role? What is one small, regulated action using your Reset Protocol that you could take this week to build trust with your team or a key stakeholder?

The Nervous System Broadcast: Think about your last team meeting or one-on-one. What do you think you were broadcasting through your nervous system state? Was it a "hot" broadcast (anxious, rushed, tense) or a "steady" broadcast (calm, present, grounded)? What could you do before your next meeting to shift your broadcast toward The Regulation Effect?

The Reactive Cascade: What are the unspoken rules about stress in your team or organization? Can you identify which stage of The Reactive Cascade your team might be in? What is one of The Six Micro-Routines that you could realistically introduce to your team this week to begin interrupting the pattern?

Your Leadership Anchor: As a leader (formal or informal), what is your personal commitment to this work? What is the first, smallest, most manageable step on The Implementation Ladder you will take this week to begin anchoring these practices in your own leadership style? How will you model The Regulation Effect for your team?

Chapter 10
COPING WITH MAJOR EVENTS & BURNOUT

Life, and work, are not linear. The journey of any meaningful career is not a steady, predictable, upward climb, but a series of peaks, plateaus, deep valleys, and unexpected, ground-shaking tremors that can challenge our very sense of who we are. The resilience toolkit we have been so carefully and intentionally building throughout this book, The 3 A's Resilience Framework™, The Reset Protocol, The Recovery Architecture, The Energy Protection System, is designed for navigating the daily squalls and turbulent currents of our professional lives. But what happens when the 100-year storm hits? What happens when a major disruption, an organizational restructuring that eliminates your role, a sudden and shocking layoff, a personal health crisis that reorders your priorities, or the final, crushing weight of burnout, completely upends your world and shatters your sense of stability?

These major events don't just test our resilience; they demand a different and more profound level of stress navigation altogether. When the very floor drops out from under us, our most primal survival instincts kick in with a force that can be terrifying and all-consuming. The carefully constructed, well-captained ship we have built can feel like a tiny lifeboat in the midst of a tsunami. In these moments, survival becomes the immediate, and only, priority.

But survival, while essential, is not enough. The ultimate goal, even in the midst of a gut-wrenching crisis, is not just to make it through, not just to endure. It is to stabilize, to recover, and eventually, to find a way to grow stronger, wiser, and more compassionate from the experience.

This chapter is your guide for those deeply challenging moments. It is a crisis-response manual for your inner world. We will explore how to recognize the critical threshold where normal stress escalates into full-blown crisis. We will dissect the most common major disruptions with both clinical precision and deep empathy. And we will learn how to apply what I call **The Emergency Navigation System™**, a modified, compassionate version of our 3 A's framework designed specifically for when your Resilience Budget is completely depleted and your capacity is severely diminished. This is not about avoiding the inevitable pain of difficult events; it is about learning to move through them with your humanity, your dignity, and your fundamental sense of agency intact.

The Crisis Threshold™: When Stress Crosses the Line

Stress is a normal, and often even healthy, part of an ambitious and engaged life, what we've called Growth Pressure in Chapter 1. A crisis is not. It is absolutely essential to learn to differentiate between manageable Breaking Pressure and what I call **The Crisis Threshold™**, the point at which the demands placed upon you so catastrophically exceed your internal and external resources that your ability to function in daily life becomes significantly impaired.

Think of it this way: Normal stress is the ship's engine working hard to move you forward against strong currents. Breaking Pressure is when that engine is running at maximum capacity and starting to overheat. **The Crisis Threshold is when the engine catches fire, smoke fills the cabin, and the entire vessel loses power.** Your internal alarm bell is no longer just ringing, it is screaming, the sound is deafening, and the entire system is flashing red.

I remind my clients of a crucial, and often life-saving, truth: **If you wait until you're past The Crisis Threshold to act, the cost of recovery, in terms of your health, your relationships, and your career, is exponentially higher.** Recognizing the early warning signs that you are approaching this threshold is therefore a profound act of self-leadership and radical self-preservation.

The Four Warning Signals of The Crisis Threshold™

I've developed a framework called **The Four Warning Signals™** to help leaders recognize when they're approaching The Crisis Threshold. These are not generic stress symptoms, these are the specific indicators that your system is moving from overwhelmed to emergency. Think of them as the escalating alert levels in your internal navigation system.

Warning Signal #1: The Physiology Override™

Your body is in a constant state of "fight or flight," but it's moved beyond the acute Stress Signature responses we explored in Chapter 5. This is what I call **The Physiology Override,** when your nervous system has completely overridden your conscious control. It manifests as:

Chronic, debilitating insomnia where you either can't fall asleep or you wake at 3 AM with your heart pounding and racing thoughts you cannot quiet

Unexplained panic attacks that seem to come from nowhere, even in situations that previously felt safe

A constantly racing heart, even at rest, that no amount of deep breathing can calm

Chronic digestive issues that have become a constant companion

The persistent, deeply uncomfortable feeling of being perpetually jittery and on edge, unable to truly relax even in a safe and quiet environment

Physical symptoms that begin affecting your ability to perform basic tasks

This is your nervous system screaming that The Takeover has become permanent, that your Stress Cycle (Chapter 3) is never completing, and that your body is no longer able to downregulate on its own.

Warning Signal #2: The Foundation Collapse™

You have stopped engaging in what I call **The Four Pillars of Self-Care** from Chapter 3, rest, nourishment, movement, and connection. This is **The Foundation Collapse**, and it's a huge red flag. Your Recovery Architecture has completely crumbled:

Rest: You're not sleeping, or you're sleeping all the time as a form of escape. There is no restorative rest happening.

Nourishment: You're skipping meals because you have no appetite, or you're using food, often sugar, caffeine, or alcohol, to numb your painful feelings rather than fuel your body.

Movement: Your Stress Cycle Completion Protocol has disappeared. You've stopped any physical activity that used to help you regulate.

Connection: Most tellingly, you have withdrawn from your loved ones. You avoid calls from friends, you feel disconnected from your partner, and you have stopped engaging in the hobbies and activities that once brought you joy and renewal.

When all four pillars collapse simultaneously, you've crossed The Crisis Threshold. Your Resilience Budget isn't just depleted, the account is closed.

Warning Signal #3: The Double Siege™

At work, you feel completely and utterly overwhelmed, unable to focus on even simple tasks. What I call **The Performance Tax** from Chapter 2 has become so high that you can't pay it anymore, your performance, which may have been a primary source of your identity and self-esteem, is visibly crumbling, which only adds to your sense of panic and shame.

But here's what makes this a crisis rather than just a difficult period: your home life, which should be your sanctuary and your primary source of recovery, no longer feels like a safe harbor. This is what I call **The Double Siege,** when both your professional life and your personal life feel like war zones simultaneously.

Your home may feel like another source of pressure and demands, or you may feel so numb and disconnected that you are unable to engage with your family in a meaningful, loving way. The Ghost in the Chair from Chapter 2 has followed you home. There is no safe place to recover, which means The Crisis Threshold has been crossed.

Warning Signal #4: The Urgent Whisper™

This is perhaps the most important and most honest signal of all. It is the quiet, wise voice beneath the frantic, chaotic noise of your anxious thoughts that speaks with increasing urgency: *"I can't keep this up. Something is about to break."*

I call this **The Urgent Whisper** because it often starts quietly, easily dismissed or rationalized away. But as you approach The Crisis Threshold, it gets louder and more insistent. It's your deepest wisdom speaking directly to you, begging you to pay attention before you reach the breaking point.

When you see these Four Warning Signals in yourself, or in a colleague you care about, it is a clear and urgent message that the situation has moved past

Breaking Pressure and is approaching or has crossed The Crisis Threshold. Immediate, compassionate, and decisive intervention is required.

The Three Crisis Profiles™: Understanding Major Disruptions

In my years of clinical practice, I see three major crisis profiles that consistently have the power to throw even the most resilient and well-resourced professionals across The Crisis Threshold. Understanding the unique psychological and emotional dynamics of each can help us respond more effectively and compassionately, both to ourselves and to others. I call these **The Three Crisis Profiles™**.

Crisis Profile #1: The System Shock™ (Organizational Change)

This is one of the most common and profoundly destabilizing events in modern professional life, what I call **The System Shock**. The announcement of a layoff, a merger, or a major departmental restructuring sends a powerful shockwave of fear and uncertainty through an entire organization. Leaders often tragically underestimate the psychological and emotional ripple effect of these decisions, focusing with tunnel vision on logistical and financial aspects while failing to manage the human emotion that is unleashed.

The Typical Reaction

For those who lose their jobs: The experience is often one of profound grief, shock, and a sudden, violent crisis of identity. The loss is not just financial; it is a loss of routine, of community, and of a core part of who they are. Their professional Stress Signature suddenly has no outlet, nowhere to go. They may experience all Four Warning Signals of The Crisis Threshold simultaneously.

For the "survivors": The reaction is often a toxic and confusing cocktail of relief, guilt, and intense anxiety. The unspoken question hangs in the air of every meeting: *"Am I next?"* The Nervous System Broadcast from Chapter 9 becomes dominated by collective fear. In the absence of clear, consistent, and transparent communication from leadership, a vacuum is created, and that vacuum is almost always filled with fear, rumor, rampant speculation, and the most catastrophic of narratives. The Reactive Cascade accelerates into overdrive.

Silence from leadership in these moments is not neutral; it is profoundly and actively damaging. It signals that the organization doesn't care about the human impact, which destroys trust and psychological safety.

The Regulated Response

For leaders navigating The System Shock: Clear, consistent, and deeply compassionate communication using the CLEAR™ framework from Chapter 9 is non-negotiable. This is a time to over-communicate, to be relentlessly visible, to walk the floors, and to answer the tough questions with as much honesty and transparency as possible. The leader's Nervous System Broadcast must project The Regulation Effect, not additional panic.

For employees (both leaving and staying): The work is to allow and acknowledge the grief without shame, to actively seek mutual support from colleagues who are sharing the experience, and to focus with fierce intentionality on what they can control through their personal Reset Protocol. This is also the time to activate The Emergency Navigation System, which we'll explore shortly.

Crisis Profile #2: The Personal Earthquake™ (Loss or Health Crisis)

We do not leave our full, complex, and often messy humanity at the door when we badge into the office or log onto a Zoom call. A major life event that happens outside of the office, the death of a beloved parent or spouse, a difficult and frightening medical diagnosis for yourself or a child, a painful divorce, will inevitably and profoundly impact your capacity to function at work. I call this **The Personal Earthquake** because it shakes the very foundation of your life, and the tremors are felt in every area, including your professional performance.

The Typical Reaction

Many high-performers, conditioned by a culture that prizes stoicism and views vulnerability as weakness, try to "power through" The Personal Earthquake. They may see their work as a welcome distraction, a way to maintain a semblance of normalcy and control in a life that feels out of control. They may not disclose what they are truly going through to their colleagues or their manager for fear of being seen as weak, less committed, or professionally vulnerable.

The result is often what I call **The Silent Struggles,** heroic but unsustainable effort to maintain a facade of competence while their internal resources are being rapidly and completely depleted. Their Resilience Budget has been wiped out by the personal crisis, but they're still trying to pay The Performance Tax at work. This can eventually lead to a full-blown collapse that crosses The Crisis Threshold.

Grief, especially, lives in the body. It manifests as a heavy, leaden fatigue, a persistent brain fog that makes complex thought difficult, and a profound lack of motivation and purpose. The Physiology Override takes hold, but the person may not recognize it as a crisis signal because they're so focused on "holding it together."

The Regulated Response

The first step is an act of courageous honesty, first and foremost with yourself, and then, if it feels psychologically safe, with your manager or a trusted colleague. Acknowledging that your capacity is temporarily and legitimately reduced is not a sign of weakness; it is a sign of profound self-awareness and strength.

The work is to give yourself permission to rest without shame, to seek professional support from a therapist or a grief counselor, and to proactively build in micro-breaks throughout your workday using your Reset Protocol to process the powerful waves of emotion as they arise. This is also when activating The Emergency Navigation System becomes essential for survival and eventual recovery.

Crisis Profile #3: The High-Performer's Collapse™ (Burnout)

Burnout, as we've discussed through frameworks like The Performance Tax and the Depletion/Disconnection/Collapse sequence in Chapter 2, is not just a period of intense stress, it is an acute state of crisis. It is particularly insidious and dangerous for high-functioning professionals because they are often the last to recognize it in themselves. I call this **The High-Performer's Collapse** because it specifically targets those who have built their identity and self-worth on being exceptionally capable.

They have a lifetime of experience and a well-developed skill for overriding their body's Four Warning Signals. They have a deep and often unconscious belief that their worth is tied to their productivity. They can masterfully mask their growing cynicism with a veneer of professionalism and compensate for their declining effectiveness by simply working longer and harder hours. Their Stress Signature gets ignored until it becomes The Physiology Override.

But eventually, inevitably, the facade crumbles, and they crash through The Crisis Threshold.

The Typical Reaction

The High-Performer's Collapse often culminates in a sudden and dramatic breakdown. This can be:

Physical: A serious stress-related illness like shingles or an autoimmune flare-up, a panic attack that lands you in the emergency room thinking you're having a heart attack, or chronic pain that becomes debilitating

Emotional: A sudden, terrifying inability to get out of bed in the morning, a dramatic and completely out-of-character outburst at work that damages relationships and reputations, or The Double Siege where nothing feels safe anymore

In the weeks and months leading up to the collapse, the professional often doubles down on the very behaviors that are causing the burnout, believing with a kind of frantic desperation that if they just work harder, push through this one last project, they can finally get to a place of rest. This is The False Alarm Economy from Chapter 1 gone haywire, they've completely lost the ability to distinguish between real threats and manageable stress.

The Regulated Response

The first and most critical step is to accept, with radical and uncompromising honesty, that The High-Performer's Collapse is not a badge of honor; it is an alarm bell of the highest and most urgent order. It is a clear and undeniable signal from your body and your spirit that your current way of working and living is no longer sustainable and is, in fact, causing you harm.

The work of recovery requires a complete and unapologetic stop, a strategic and intentional retreat to allow your depleted nervous system and exhausted body to begin the long, slow process of healing. This is not something you can fix by just trying harder; it must be addressed through The Emergency Navigation System and a fundamental, courageous re-design of your relationship with work, with success, and with yourself.

The Emergency Navigation System™: The 3 A's in Crisis

When you are in the midst of a genuine crisis, your capacity is severely diminished. You do not have the same cognitive, emotional, or physical resources that you do when you are in a state of balance. Therefore, our approach to applying the 3 A's Resilience Framework must be modified. It must become simpler, more compassionate, more gentle, and more focused on immediate stabilization rather than long-term growth.

This is what I call **The Emergency Navigation System™,** a crisis-adapt-ed version of the 3 A's designed specifically for when you've crossed The Crisis Threshold and survival, not optimization, is the goal.

Emergency Step 1: Awareness as Acknowledgment™

In a crisis, the practice of awareness is not about detailed Stress Signal Mapping or sophisticated analysis of your patterns. It is about one simple, courageous, and often incredibly difficult act: **acknowledging the unde-niable truth of what is happening.** I call this **Awareness as Acknowl-edgment™**.

It is the practice of looking at your reality without denial, minimization, or toxic positivity. It is the simple, honest act of saying to yourself:

"I have been laid off, and I am terrified."

"I am completely burned out, and I desperately need help."

"I am grieving, and I cannot function the way I usually do."

"I have crossed The Crisis Threshold, and I need emergency support."

Once you have acknowledged the raw reality of the situation, the ongoing practice of awareness becomes about gently and compassionately noticing your Four Warning Signals without judgment or the expectation that you should "fix" them immediately. You are not trying to change them, make them go away, or analyze them deeply. You are simply acknowledging their presence with the kindness of a good friend:

"I notice that my heart is racing right now."

"I notice a feeling of deep, heavy sadness sitting in my chest."

"I notice that I'm struggling to think clearly."

"I notice that I'm having trouble sleeping."

This non-judgmental noticing can be incredibly grounding. It stops you from layering a secondary crisis of self-criticism ("I shouldn't be feeling this way! I should be stronger than this!") on top of the primary, and already overwhelming, crisis. It allows you to observe The Physiology Override without adding shame to the experience.

Emergency Step 2: Action as Next Best Step™

Regulated action in a crisis is not about creating a complex, long-term strategic plan or implementing your full Reset Protocol. Your brain is not capable of that right now, you're past The Crisis Threshold. The goal is to bring your focus from the overwhelming, catastrophic, and imagined future back to the immediate, manageable, and concrete present.

The guiding principle of action in a crisis is what I call **Action as Next Best Step™**: Focus with fierce, laser-like intention on the single smallest, most compassionate, and most stabilizing action you can take right now, in this moment. Not the entire staircase, just the next step.

What is the one thing you can do in the next five minutes that would bring even a micro-dose of regulation or relief?

Breathing actions:

Taking three slow, deep, intentional breaths using The Triangle Reset

Humming for 30 seconds to activate your vagus nerve

Grounding actions:

Feeling your feet on the floor and naming one thing you can see, hear, and touch (The Grounding Anchor from Chapter 6)

Holding an ice cube in your hand to interrupt a panic spiral

Boundary actions:

Turning off your phone and your email for one hour

Canceling one non-essential commitment to create breathing room

Connection actions:

Sending a text to one trusted friend that simply says, "I'm having a hard time. Can we talk later?"

Calling your therapist or a crisis hotline

Nourishment actions:

Drinking one full glass of water

Eating one piece of fruit or a simple, nourishing meal

These small, regulated actions are profoundly powerful because they restore a micro-dose of agency and control in a situation that feels completely and terrifyingly out of control. They are the small rudders that can begin to turn a massive, drifting, and storm-tossed ship. Each Next Best Step is proof that even in crisis, you still have some capacity to care for yourself.

Emergency Step 3: Adaptation as Safety Anchors™

Adaptation in a crisis is not about long-term growth, optimization, or building elaborate Recovery Architecture. It is about short-term stabilization. The primary goal is to create simple, predictable, and comforting routines that can serve as anchors in a turbulent and unpredictable sea. When your external world is in chaos, creating a sense of order and predictability in your immediate, personal world is essential for calming your dysregulated nervous system.

I call these **Safety Anchors™,** the non-negotiable, simple routines that provide psychological and physiological stability when everything else feels unmoored.

If you've experienced The System Shock (layoff or restructuring): The sudden and complete loss of your daily work structure can be profoundly disorienting. The adaptive response is to create a new, simple daily structure for yourself that is focused on recovery and stabilization, not just productivity:

Morning Anchor: A 20-minute walk outside first thing in the morning to get sunlight on your face and help regulate your circadian rhythm

Connection Anchor: A daily scheduled phone call with a friend or family member who is a known source of support

Evening Anchor: A clear and intentional transition routine like reading a physical book, listening to calming music, or taking a warm bath

If you've experienced The Personal Earthquake (grief or health crisis): Your Safety Anchors need to create pockets of peace in the midst of emotional turbulence:

Morning Anchor: Five minutes of gentle stretching or seated breathing before you check your phone

Midday Anchor: A brief walk or sitting outside, allowing yourself to feel whatever emotions arise without judgment

Evening Anchor: A simple gratitude practice, naming one small thing that felt manageable today

If you've experienced The High-Performer's Collapse (burnout): Your Safety Anchors must directly counter the behaviors that led to collapse:

Morning Anchor: Absolutely no work-related activity for the first hour after waking, only rest, nourishment, and gentle movement

Boundary Anchor: A hard stop time for work each day with a transition routine (change clothes, take a shower, light a candle)

Weekly Anchor: One completely work-free day where you practice doing absolutely nothing productive

These Safety Anchors are not about being productive in the traditional sense; they are about providing your over-activated, depleted nervous system with a sense of safety, predictability, and rhythm, which is the very foundation of healing after crossing The Crisis Threshold.

Catherine's Journey: Navigating The System Shock with The Emergency Navigation System™

Let me show you how The Emergency Navigation System works in practice through the story of Catherine, a high-level executive client who experienced The System Shock during an unexpected and brutal corporate merger.

The Crisis: Crossing The Crisis Threshold

Catherine lost her C-suite position in a single, impersonal phone call. Her entire professional identity was inextricably tied to her role. For 20 years, she had been "Vice President at a Fortune 500 company." In the space of that phone call, that identity was gone, and she immediately exhibited all Four Warning Signals:

Physiology Override: Within days, she was experiencing panic attacks, insomnia, and constant heart palpitations **Foundation Collapse:** She stopped eating regular meals, stopped exercising, and withdrew from friends **Double Siege:** Work felt impossible (she had no work), and home felt overwhelming (she was too ashamed to tell her family the depth of her distress) **Urgent Whisper:** She told me in our first session, "I feel like I'm losing my mind. I can't keep living like this."

Catherine had clearly crossed The Crisis Threshold. This was not manageable stress, this was a full emergency.

Phase 1: Awareness as Acknowledgment™

Her immediate instinct, as a classic high-achiever exhibiting The High-Performer's Collapse patterns, was to deny the severity of the crisis and to overwork. She felt a frantic, desperate need to "prove her value" to the world and to herself. She was spending 14 hours a day frantically networking, endlessly polishing her résumé, and applying for dozens of jobs. Her nervous system was broadcasting pure panic. She wasn't sleeping. She was skipping meals. Her instinct was to sprint, but this was a marathon for which she had not trained.

Our first work together was the courageous act of Awareness as Acknowledgment:

Me: "Catherine, I need you to hear this. What you're experiencing is not just stress. You've crossed The Crisis Threshold. This is an emergency. Your body is in Physiology Override. Your Foundation has collapsed. You're experiencing The Double Siege. Before we can talk about job searching, we need to stabilize you. Can you acknowledge that?"

Catherine: (Long pause, then tears) "I didn't just lose a job. I lost my tribe. I lost my routine. I lost my sense of purpose. I lost who I am. And I'm terrified."

That moment of radical honesty, naming the loss for what it was, acknowledging The Crisis Threshold had been crossed, was the first step toward healing. She stopped judging herself for her "weakness" and started treating her situation with the seriousness it deserved.

Phase 2: Action as Next Best Step™

We immediately shifted from her frantic 14-hour days of reactive activity to a much simpler question: *What is the next best step for your nervous system right now?*

Instead of trying to implement complex strategies, we focused on tiny, stabilizing actions:

Her first Next Best Step: Three deep breaths using The Triangle Reset before checking her email each morning, to interrupt the immediate panic spiral

Her second Next Best Step: One 10-minute walk outside each day, not for exercise, but for Stress Cycle Completion and nervous system regulation

Her third Next Best Step: Texting one trusted friend each day with a simple check-in: "Having a hard day. Just needed you to know."

We structured her day into manageable chunks. Her new "job" became:

Four hours of focused, strategic job-searching in the morning (her Next Best Step for her career)

The rest of the day dedicated to other stabilizing Next Best Steps: a walk, a healthy lunch eaten mindfully, coffee with a friend for genuine connection (not just networking)

Each small action was a deposit back into her completely depleted Resilience Budget. Each one proved she still had agency, even in the midst of the crisis.

Phase 3: Adaptation as Safety Anchors™

We completely and intentionally redesigned her daily routines using Safety Anchors. Her life had been defined by her role at the company, now we needed to create new anchors that existed independently of her job:

Morning Safety Anchor: 30 minutes of non-work activity, reading, journaling, or gentle yoga, before she looked at job listings **Midday Safety Anchor:** A walk in a nearby nature preserve, rain or shine, to complete The Stress Cycle **Evening Safety Anchor:** Absolutely no job-searching after 6 PM. Instead, she reconnected with an old hobby (painting) that she had abandoned years ago

But here's what made the biggest difference: We worked on consciously and deliberately mapping her identity beyond her job title. She started volunteering at a local animal shelter. She joined a book club. She slowly, intentionally, and sometimes painfully began to build a new, more expansive, and more resilient sense of self that was not dependent on an external title or the logo on her business card.

The Transformation: Rebuilding Differently

Within six months, Catherine secured a new and exciting leadership role. But she entered this new role as a fundamentally different person. She did so with:

A set of **non-negotiable Safety Anchors** already in place

Clear boundaries about working hours that she communicated from day one

A **Resilience Budget** she was committed to maintaining, not depleting

A **broader identity** that included but was not defined by her work

As she told me in our final session, her voice clear and strong: **"The crisis didn't just take something from me. It forced me to rebuild differently, to build a life and a career that is stronger, wiser, and more authentically my own. I would never wish The System Shock on anyone, but I'm grateful for what I learned from navigating it."**

The Three-Tier Support Architecture™: You Cannot Do This Alone

In a crisis, our most primal instinct can often be to withdraw, to retreat into isolation, to hide our perceived failure or vulnerability from the world. This is the single most dangerous thing you can do when you've crossed The Crisis Threshold. You cannot and should not try to navigate a major crisis alone. Intentionally seeking, building, and activating a robust support network is a critical and non-negotiable part of the recovery process.

I've developed **The Three-Tier Support Architecture™** to help clients identify and leverage the specific types of support they need during and after a crisis.

Tier 1: Professional Support (The Expert Layer)

This is the time to call in the experts, people who are trained to help you navigate The Crisis Threshold. This tier is non-negotiable for anyone who has crossed into crisis territory:

Therapists and Counselors: A licensed mental health professional can provide a safe, confidential, and objective space to process the complex emotions of a crisis and can offer evidence-based tools and strategies. If you're experiencing The Physiology Override or The Foundation Collapse, this is essential.

Coaches: For career-related crises like The System Shock, a skilled executive or career coach can help you navigate the practical aspects of transition while also supporting your emotional resilience.

Medical Professionals: If your crisis includes physical symptoms, consult with your physician. The Physiology Override may require medical intervention, not just emotional support.

The key: Do not wait until you are completely drowning to call for this level of support. Seeking professional help early, when you first notice The Four Warning Signals, dramatically reduces recovery time.

Tier 2: Peer Support (The Shared Experience Layer)

Connecting with others who have been through a similar experience can be incredibly validating, destigmatizing, and powerful. This tier provides the "you're not alone" reassurance that counters the isolation of crisis:

Professional Networks: If you've experienced The System Shock (layoff), find or create a networking group of other professionals in transition. Many cities have formal groups; online communities also exist.

Support Groups: For The Personal Earthquake (grief, illness, divorce), support groups provide a space to share experiences with others who truly understand what you're going through.

Trusted Colleagues: If you're experiencing The High-Performer's Collapse (burnout), seek out a trusted colleague who has been through it and come out the other side. Their story becomes proof that recovery is possible.

The key: Knowing you are not alone, that others have crossed The Crisis Threshold and survived, is a powerful antidote to the shame and isolation that so often accompany crisis.

Tier 3: Personal Support (The Safe Harbor Layer)

Identify the 2-3 people in your personal life who are your true "safe harbors", people who can hold space for you without judgment, who won't try to "fix" you, and who can simply witness your humanity in a moment of vulnerability:

The Characteristics of a Good Safe Harbor:

They listen without immediately jumping to advice or solutions

They don't minimize your experience with toxic positivity ("Everything happens for a reason!")

They don't make your crisis about them ("That reminds me of when I...")

They can tolerate strong emotions without getting uncomfortable

They check in consistently without being intrusive

The key: Be explicit with your Safe Harbor people about what you need. You might say: "I don't need advice right now, I just need to vent for ten minutes and have you tell me I'm not crazy. Can you do that?"

Building Your Architecture Before Crisis Hits

The ideal time to build The Three-Tier Support Architecture is before you cross The Crisis Threshold, when you're still operating from your normal Resilience Budget. Identify your people now:

Who is my Tier 1 person? (Do I have a therapist or coach I can call?)

Who is my Tier 2 community? (What groups or networks exist that could support me?)

Who are my Tier 3 Safe Harbors? (Name 2-3 specific people)

Having this architecture in place means that when crisis hits, you don't have to figure out where to turn, you already know. You can immediately activate your support system instead of wasting precious energy in The Crisis Threshold trying to build it from scratch.

The Truth About Crisis and Growth

Major disruptions are an inevitable and often painful part of a long and meaningful career. They are the powerful storms that test the integrity of our ships and reveal our vulnerabilities. But here is the truth that I want you to hold onto:

Crisis does not build character; it reveals it. And more importantly, crisis recovery builds resilience.

By learning to recognize The Crisis Threshold early through The Four Warning Signals, by applying The Emergency Navigation System (Awareness as Acknowledgment, Action as Next Best Step, Adaptation as Safety Anchors), and by courageously activating The Three-Tier Support Architecture, we can learn to not just survive these storms, but to emerge from them as more resilient, more self-aware, and ultimately, more compassionate and effective leaders and human beings.

You will face crisis in your career. That is not a matter of if, but when. What you do have control over is how prepared you are to navigate it, how quickly you recognize you've crossed The Crisis Threshold, and how willing you are to reach out for support instead of suffering in isolation.

The storms will come. But with The Emergency Navigation System, you don't have to drown.

Reflection Questions for Chapter 10

The Crisis Threshold Assessment: Looking at The Four Warning Signals (Physiology Override, Foundation Collapse, Double Siege, and Urgent Whisper), have you ever experienced a time in your career where you crossed The Crisis Threshold? What were the specific signals your body and mind were sending you that you may have missed or ignored at the time? Are you experiencing any of these signals right now?

Your Crisis Profile: Which of The Three Crisis Profiles (System Shock, Personal Earthquake, or High-Performer's Collapse) resonates most with your past or current experience? What did you learn from navigating that crisis, or if you're in it now, what support do you need?

The Emergency Navigation System: Think of a past or current major disruption in your life. How could you apply The Emergency Navigation System to that situation?

Awareness as Acknowledgment: What is the one core truth you need to admit to yourself about this situation, without judgment or shame?

Action as Next Best Step: What is the single, smallest, most stabilizing step you can take today, not tomorrow, but today?

Adaptation as Safety Anchors: What is one simple Safety Anchor you could create for yourself to provide a sense of predictability and stability?

Your Support Architecture: Take a moment to map out your current Three-Tier Support Architecture:

Tier 1 (Professional): Who is your therapist, coach, or trusted medical professional? If you don't have one, who could you research this week?

Tier 2 (Peer): What groups, communities, or colleagues could support you through shared experience?

Tier 3 (Personal): Who are your 2-3 Safe Harbor people, the ones who can hold space for you without judgment?

Are there any gaps in your architecture? Who is one person you could reach out to this week to strengthen your support network before the next storm hits?

Chapter 11

Your Personalized Stress Navigation Plan

We have arrived at the final and most crucial stage of our journey together. For the past ten chapters, we have embarked on a deep exploration, a guided expedition into the often-turbulent waters of stress and the powerful, steadying landscape of resilience.

We have dissected the anatomy of **The Takeover,** understanding stress not as an external enemy, but as an internal signaling system broadcasting through your **Stress Signature**. We have painstakingly counted its hidden costs through the lens of **The Performance Tax**, **The Ghost in the Chair**, and the three-stage descent of **Depletion, Disconnection, and Collapse**. We have laid **The Four Pillars** as the foundational architecture of resilient living. We have navigated **The 3 A's Framework™,** Awareness, Action, Adaptation, learning to move from unconscious reactivity to conscious, intentional response. We have understood how **The Nervous System Broadcast** creates contagion in our teams through **The Collective Climate**. We have learned to recognize **The Crisis Threshold** and activate **The Emergency Navigation System™** when life demands it.

You now possess the knowledge. You have the frameworks. You hold the tools.

This final chapter is about integration. It is the pivotal moment where knowledge is forged into deliberate practice, and where practice, over time, is transmuted into embodied, unconscious wisdom.

This chapter is your implementation guide. It is designed to help you synthesize everything you have learned into a single, cohesive, and deeply personalized document: **Your Resilience Blueprint™**. Please do not see this as a final exam or yet another self-improvement project to add to your already overwhelming to-do list. See this, instead, as the essential and empowering work of creating your personal operating manual, the architectural blueprint for the resilient, well-captained ship you have so carefully and intentionally designed throughout this book.

Many books on this topic leave you with a fleeting, temporary sense of inspiration but no clear, structured, and sustainable path to implementation. My goal for you is profoundly different. I want to leave you not just inspired, but fully and confidently equipped. This chapter will provide you with **The Integration Architecture™,** the specific questions, the detailed exercises, and the robust structures to create a blueprint that is not just elegant in theory, but powerfully effective in the messy, beautiful, and unpredictable reality of your daily life.

We will cover the practical steps of implementation, the art of deep customization for your unique life, the science of building unshakable accountability, and the wisdom of troubleshooting the inevitable obstacles you will face on this rewarding, lifelong path.

The Integration Architecture™: Putting It All into Practice

Building **Your Resilience Blueprint™** is an act of profound self-leadership. It is a powerful declaration to yourself and to the world that you are ready to move from being a passive reactor to your circumstances to becoming the conscious, deliberate author of your responses.

I strongly encourage you to set aside **The Integration Week™,** seven days where you commit to working through this process with focus and intention. You don't need seven consecutive hours; you need seven intentional touchpoints with yourself. Each day, carve out just 15-20 minutes of protected, sacred, and uninterrupted time. Turn off your phone and put it in another room. Close your email and all other tabs on your computer. Treat this with the same seriousness, focus, and deep respect you would a critical strategic planning session for your career, because that is precisely what it is.

Day 1: The Foundation Inquiry™, Anchoring in Your Deepest "Why"

Before you dive into the specific details, tactics, and tools of your blueprint, it's crucial to anchor yourself in your "why." This is **The Foundation Inquiry™**, the cornerstone of everything that follows.

Why are you truly doing this work? What is the single most important, most meaningful, and most deeply felt shift you want to make in your relationship with stress? Remember back to Chapter 2, what is the **Performance Tax** you're no longer willing to pay? What would it look like to reclaim your **Resilience Budget** and invest it in what truly matters?

What would success look like, sound like, and, most importantly, *feel* like for you in three months? This is not about a vague, generic, and ultimately uninspiring goal like "be less stressed." You must get specific, tangible, and visceral. You must connect this work to what you value most.

Examples of Foundation Statements:

> *"Success would be ending my workday feeling tired in my body but fulfilled in my spirit, closing the chapter on Depletion and reclaiming my energy for what matters most outside of work."*

"Success would be getting through my weekly leadership meetings without The Takeover, without my jaw aching from tension, my stomach in knots, and my mind replaying every interaction for hours afterward."

"Success would be being fully present with my family in the evenings, having completed The Stress Cycle rather than bringing The Ghost in the Chair to my dinner table."

"Success would be waking up on Monday morning below The Crisis Threshold, feeling calm preparedness instead of that familiar, heavy knot of dread."

Take a moment right now. In your dedicated notebook, write down **Your Foundation Statement** at the very top of the page. Frame it as a positive, affirmative, and emotionally resonant declaration. This will be your North Star, the guiding principle, the lighthouse in the distance, that will keep you focused, motivated, and compassionate with yourself when the challenging work of building new habits feels difficult.

Days 2-4: The Three-Dimensional Assessment™, Creating Your Blueprint Core

Now, we will use **The Three-Dimensional Assessment™** to create the core content of your blueprint. This is where you synthesize the deep awareness you have cultivated throughout this book and translate it from insight into actionable data. Each dimension takes approximately 20 minutes.

Dimension 1: The Stressor Map™

Let's get honest and specific. List your top 3-5 recurring workplace stressors. Remember, ruthless specificity is your greatest ally here. Generic labels like "My Boss" are not helpful. Drill down.

Think back to Chapter 1: What triggers your unique **Stress Signature**? What situations consistently activate **The Takeover**? Is it **Flash Fire Stress** (sudden, acute) or **Slow Burn Stress** (chronic, accumulating)?

Effective Stressor Mapping:

Vague: "My Boss"
Specific: "The feeling of being unprepared when my boss asks for unexpected data in meetings"

Vague: "Too much work"
Specific: "The pressure to respond immediately to emails that arrive after 6 PM when I'm already depleted"

Vague: "Difficult conversations"
Specific: "The emotional weight of delivering critical feedback to an underperforming but well-liked team member while managing my own narrative trap of 'If I'm direct, I'm mean'"

For each stressor, also note:

Frequency: How often does this occur? (Daily, Weekly, Monthly)

Intensity: On a scale of 1-10, how much does this drain your **Resilience Budget**?

Pattern: Is this **Growth Pressure** (challenging but manageable) or **Breaking Pressure** (consistently overwhelming)?

Dimension 2: The Pattern Recognition Audit™

This is a critical diagnostic tool that brings together everything you've learned about your automatic responses. For each of the stressors you just mapped, I want you to audit your typical pattern using **The 3 A's Framework™** as the lens.

Create a chart for each stressor with these three sections:

AWARENESS: My Stress Signature

What are your go-to physical, emotional, and mental signals for this specific stressor? Review Chapter 5's **Somatic Decoding** work. Be as detailed as possible.

Example:

> *Physical Signals:* Heat rising in my face, shallow breathing, tight chest, jaw clenching

> *Emotional Signals:* Defensiveness, shame, fear of exposure

> *Mental Signals:* The Narrative Trap: "This is an attack on my competence"

ACTION: My Reactive Pattern

What is your typical, automatic reactive behavior when this stressor appears and **The Takeover** begins? Be honest, no judgment here.

Examples:

"I avoid the conversation for as long as possible, which only increases my anxiety"

"I get defensive and interrupt, trying to explain myself before fully listening"

"I work longer hours to try to compensate, depleting my Resilience Budget further"

"I become silent, withdrawn, and passive-aggressive, broadcasting my stress through The Nervous System Broadcast"

ADAPTATION: My Current Coping Pattern

What are your current, often unconscious, coping mechanisms? How do you manage the painful aftermath of this stress? Distinguish between:

Healthy Adaptation: Practices that genuinely restore you (Chapter 3's Four Pillars)

Compensatory Behaviors: Quick fixes that don't complete The Stress Cycle

Maladaptive Patterns: Behaviors that create additional problems

Example:

Compensatory: "I vent to my partner for 30 minutes, which exhausts them and me"

Maladaptive: "I scroll on my phone to numb out rather than completing The Stress Cycle"

Healthy (but inconsistent): "Sometimes I take a walk, and it genuinely helps, but I rarely prioritize it"

This **Pattern Recognition Audit™** provides you with a clear, honest, and non-judgmental picture of your current reality. You're essentially documenting your existing **Resilience Operating System™** before you upgrade it.

Dimension 3: The Tool Selection Matrix™

Based on your unique **Stress Signature** and your specific work environment, it is now time to formally and intentionally select your toolkit. Remember the wisdom from Chapter 6: the goal is not to have the most tools; it is to master a few essential and reliable ones.

The **Tool Selection Matrix™** has four categories:

1. Core Physiological Tools (Choose 2-3)

Which body-based tools from Chapter 6 feel most accessible, practical, and effective for *your* specific signals? Consider:

The Regulation Breath™ (Box Breathing for baseline regulation)

The Triangle Reset™ (for high-intensity moments)

The Grounding Anchor™ (when dissociation or overwhelm appears)

Movement Micro-Doses (5-minute walks, desk stretches)

Selection Criteria: Which tools address your specific somatic signals? If you experience chest tightness and shallow breathing, prioritize breathwork. If you experience restless energy and agitation, prioritize movement.

2. Core Cognitive Tools (Choose 2-3)

Which mind-based tools will best counteract your specific, habitual **Narrative Traps** from Chapter 5?

The Cognitive Reset™ (for catastrophizing and worst-case thinking)

The Three Strategic Reframes™ (What can I control? What's the evidence? What would I tell a friend?)

The Reality Check Protocol™ (for separating story from fact)

Empowering Mantras (context-specific phrases you'll actually use)

Selection Criteria: Match the tool to your most common narrative trap. If you struggle with "This is permanent," focus on temporal reframing. If you struggle with "This is personal," focus on depersonalization questions.

3. Boundary Protocols (Choose 1-2)

From Chapter 3's **Energy Protection System**, which boundaries are most urgent for your situation?

Time Boundaries (work hours, meeting limits, email protocols)

Emotional Boundaries (what you will/won't take responsibility for)

Relational Boundaries (how you'll engage with specific difficult people)

Physical Boundaries (workspace protection, interruption management)

Selection Criteria: Where is the biggest leak in your **Resilience Budget**? Start there.

4. Recovery Routines (Choose 2-4)

From Chapter 7's **Recovery Architecture**, select routines at multiple time scales:

Daily Transition Routine (completing The Stress Cycle between work and home)

Weekly Restoration Practice (deeper recovery to prevent accumulation)

Monthly Integration Review (checking your Blueprint's effectiveness)

Quarterly Reset Space (if you're at risk of hitting The Crisis Threshold)

Selection Criteria: What does your current lifestyle realistically support? Start with what you can actually sustain, then build from there.

This detailed **Three-Dimensional Assessment™** provides the rich, personalized raw data for your blueprint. You now have a clear map of your stressors, an honest audit of your patterns, and a thoughtfully curated toolkit designed specifically for you.

Day 5: The Context Calibration™, Tailoring to Your Professional Reality

Your Resilience Blueprint™ must be tailored to the unique demands, constraints, and cultural nuances of your profession and your life. A plan that works for a government employee navigating a slow-moving, risk-averse bureaucracy will look very different from a plan for a university professor juggling the chaotic demands of teaching and research, which will look different still from a plan for a corporate executive in a fast-paced, "always-on" environment.

The Context Calibration™ process asks you to honestly assess:

1. Your Professional Environment's Stress Drivers

What are the systemic, structural stressors built into your industry or organization? (Reference Chapter 9's **Collective Climate**)

Government/Public Sector: Bureaucratic constraints, limited resources, slow change, high accountability

Academia: Conflicting demands (teaching/research/service), isolation, publish-or-perish pressure

Corporate: Profit pressure, "always-on" culture, rapid change, constant performance evaluation

Healthcare: Life-or-death stakes, emotional labor, under-resourcing, moral injury

Nonprofit: Mission-driven exhaustion, limited resources, vicarious trauma, funding instability

2. Your Cultural Constraints

What are the unwritten rules in your workplace about resilience, boundaries, and self-care? Will implementing your Blueprint require you to actively push back against toxic norms, or will you find cultural support?

3. Your Season of Life

What personal demands are you managing right now? (Caregiving responsibilities, health challenges, relationship transitions, financial stress) Your Blueprint must account for your actual available capacity, not an idealized version.

Let's explore how **The Context Calibration™** shapes three different blueprints:

Blueprint Example 1: Javier (Government Agency Director)

Primary Stressors (from Stressor Map™): The glacial pace of change, bureaucratic red tape, feeling powerless, rigid hierarchies, high-stakes work with limited resources.

Context-Calibrated Toolkit:

Core Cognitive Tool: The reframing question, "What is within my sphere of influence right now?" becomes an essential daily practice. This directly addresses his **False Alarm Economy,** his nervous system treating systemic problems as personal emergencies.

Primary Boundary Strategy: Less about pushing back against the entire system (which leads to **Breaking Pressure**) and more on building strong personal time boundaries (leaving at a set time, taking a full lunch away from desk) and emotional boundaries to avoid taking on the systemic frustration of the entire agency as a personal burden.

Non-Negotiable Recovery Routine: A daily "transition routine" after work (listening to a specific podcast on the commute) is absolutely critical to complete **The Stress Cycle** and create psychological separation from the draining work environment. Without this, he brings **The Ghost in the Chair** home every night.

Blueprint Example 2: Dr. Evans (University Professor)

Primary Stressors: Conflicting demands of the "three-legged stool" (teaching, research, service); invisible emotional labor of mentoring students; relentless publication pressure; fragmented, unpredictable schedule.

Context-Calibrated Toolkit:

Core Physiological Tool: Micro-resets between classes or meetings are non-negotiable. A 2-minute **Triangle Reset™** in her office can regulate her nervous system before transitioning from a large, energetic lecture to an intense one-on-one student meeting. This prevents accumulation toward **The Crisis Threshold**.

Primary Boundary Strategy: Ruthlessly protecting time for deep, focused work. This means scheduling "unavailable" deep-work blocks in her public calendar and learning to say a graceful but firm "no" to non-essential committee requests. Her **Resilience Budget** must prioritize core academic work over service obligations that don't align with her career goals.

Non-Negotiable Recovery Routine: Weekly connection with academic peers *outside* her institution, a powerful antidote to professional isolation and departmental politics. This addresses **The Collective Climate** issue: when your immediate environment is toxic, you need to find healthy climates elsewhere.

Blueprint Example 3: Catherine (Corporate Executive)

Primary Stressors: Relentless profit and deadline pressure, "always-on" culture that celebrates exhaustion, back-to-back virtual meetings causing screen fatigue, weight of high-stakes decision-making.

Context-Calibrated Toolkit:

Core Physiological Tool: The Reset Protocol™ (the complete 3-5 minute sequence) becomes critical to use proactively *before* high-stakes presentations, difficult feedback conversations, or major decision-making meetings. This ensures she's leading from clarity, not anxiety, preventing **The Takeover** from hijacking crucial moments.

Primary Boundary Strategy: Clear, top-down communication boundaries. This includes establishing explicit email and Slack protocols with her team ("I will not respond after 7 PM, and I do not expect you to either") and, most importantly, *visibly modeling* these sustainable work habits. As a leader, her **Nervous System Broadcast** sets **The Collective Climate,** her boundaries give permission for others to set theirs.

Non-Negotiable Recovery Routine: Monthly, completely unplugged "Reset Space" (a full weekend day with no screens, no plans, no agenda) is essential. Her over-stimulated nervous system needs this depth of recovery to prevent the accumulation that leads to **Collapse**. This also creates the quiet mental space necessary for the strategic, innovative thinking her role demands.

The key is to look honestly and compassionately at the specific demands of your life and choose the tools and strategies that are most relevant, realistic, and practical for *you*. **The Context Calibration™** ensures your Blueprint isn't generic advice, it's a precision instrument designed for your unique reality.

Day 6: The Commitment Architecture™, Staying True to Your Blueprint

A Blueprint without a robust accountability system is just a wish. It is a set of good intentions that will almost certainly crumble under the immense pressure of old, deeply ingrained habits, unexpected crises, and the powerful gravitational pull of your current life.

The Commitment Architecture™ is your system for maintaining consistency. Remember, on this journey, consistency is far more important than intensity.

What works best is highly personal. Choose a system that feels supportive and motivating to you, not punitive or shaming. Here are **The Four Pillars of Commitment Architecture™:**

Pillar 1: The Daily Anchor™

This is the simplest and often most powerful system. At the very end of each workday, as the last thing you do before you shut down your computer, take 60 seconds to ask yourself:

> **"On a scale of 1-10, how well did I honor my Resilience Blueprint today?"**

Followed by a gentle, curious inquiry:

> **"What is one small thing I can do tomorrow to move that number up by just one point?"**

This is not about achieving a perfect 10; it is about cultivating a daily practice of gentle, non-judgmental course correction. You're checking in with your **Resilience Budget,** where did you invest it well today, and where might you invest it differently tomorrow?

Pillar 2: The Accountability Alliance™

This can be a colleague, a friend, a partner, or a coach. The key to making this work is to be incredibly specific and clear about what you are asking for.

Effective Accountability Request:

"Can we agree to text each other every Friday afternoon with our biggest resilience win and our biggest challenge of the week? I don't need you to solve my challenges or fix me, I just need you to witness them and remind me of my Foundation Statement when I lose sight of it."

The best **Accountability Alliances™** are reciprocal. You're not asking someone to be your compliance officer; you're creating mutual support for two people navigating similar challenges.

Pillar 3: The Visual Progress System™

For some people, a visual system provides a powerful and satisfying reinforcement. This could be:

A simple habit tracker app on your phone

An old-fashioned calendar on your wall where you mark days you practiced your core routines

A journal where you record your **Daily Anchor™** score each evening

Photos or screenshots that document your progress over time

This provides a tangible, visual record of your commitment, which can be incredibly motivating on difficult days. When **The Takeover** whispers, "You're failing at this," you have objective data showing otherwise.

Pillar 4: The Habit Tethering™

This is a brilliant technique from behavioral science. The idea is to "tether" your new desired habit to an existing, automatic one. This makes implementation dramatically easier because you're not relying purely on willpower or memory.

Examples of Effective Habit Tethering™:

> "*After* I pour my first cup of coffee in the morning (existing habit), I will practice **The Regulation Breath™** for two minutes (new habit)."

> "*After* I shut down my computer for the day (existing habit), I will immediately put on my walking shoes and take my 5-minute Stress Cycle completion walk (new habit)."

> "*After* I send the last email before a big meeting (existing habit), I will close my eyes and do **The Triangle Reset™** (new habit)."

The key is: **After [existing reliable habit], I will [new Blueprint practice].**

Choose at least two of these four pillars for **Your Commitment Architecture™**. The goal is to find a system that feels supportive, not punitive. This is not about creating another stick to beat yourself up with; it's about gently, compassionately, and consistently guiding yourself back to your deepest intentions.

Day 7: The Obstacle Navigation Plan™, Preparing for Resistance

As you begin to implement your Blueprint, you will inevitably encounter obstacles. This is not a sign that your Blueprint is failing or that you are failing. It is a normal, predictable, and even essential part of any meaningful change process.

The key is to anticipate these obstacles and have **The Obstacle Navigation Plan™,** a clear, pre-defined strategy for how you will respond when they arise. Here are the four most common obstacles and how we navigate them:

Obstacle #1: The "No Time" Trap

This is the most common, most seductive, and most powerful obstacle. Your **False Alarm Economy** will insist that everything is urgent and there's no time for resilience practices.

The Reframe:

Resilience practices are not something you do *instead* of your work; they are the very thing that allows you to do your work sustainably and at a higher level. They are a high-leverage investment in your **Resilience Budget**, not a time-wasting expense. A 5-minute reset that allows you to have a more focused, creative, and productive hour is a massive return on investment.

The Strategy:

Start ridiculously small. If 10 minutes feels like too much, start with one minute. Practice one single cycle of **The Regulation Breath™**. The initial goal is not to achieve a perfect duration; it is simply to build the neural pathway of pausing and turning inward. Once the habit is established, you can gradually expand it.

Obstacle #2: The Guilt Script

Many of us, especially those in helping professions, in leadership roles, or with deeply ingrained people-pleasing tendencies, feel profound guilt when prioritizing our own well-being. Your inner critic may say, "This is selfish. Other people need me."

The Reframe:

You cannot pour from an empty cup. This is not a cliché; it is a fundamental law of human energetics. Taking time to replenish your own resources is not a selfish act; it is the most generous and responsible thing you can do for the people you lead, serve, and love. Every time you practice **The Reset Protocol™**, you're ensuring you don't bring **The Takeover** into your next interaction.

The Strategy:

Intentionally and explicitly link your resilience practice to your sense of service. Before you take your lunch break away from your desk, tell yourself: *"I am taking this break so I can complete The Stress Cycle and be a more patient, present, and effective leader for my team this afternoon. This IS my work."*

Obstacle #3: The Perfectionism Collapse

This is the insidious all-or-nothing mindset. You miss one day of your practice, and your inner critic concludes, "See? I've already failed. I might as well give up entirely." This is a classic **Narrative Trap** from Chapter 5.

The Reframe:

The goal is not, and never will be, perfection. The goal is progress and, most importantly, *repair*. Every single moment, every single breath, is a new opportunity to begin again. Missing one practice doesn't erase all the practices that came before it. Your **Resilience Budget** doesn't zero out overnight.

The Strategy:

Have a specific, pre-planned "course correction protocol." For example:

> *"If I miss my morning practice, I will commit to a 2-minute* **Triangle Reset™** *at lunchtime. There will be no shame, no blame, no story about failure, just a gentle, compassionate return to my Foundation Statement and my next best action."*

Write this protocol directly into your Blueprint so it's already decided before the moment arrives.

Obstacle #4: The Environment Pushback

You start setting new, healthy boundaries, and your team, your boss, or your clients, who are accustomed to your old, boundaryless patterns, push back with confusion, frustration, or even anger. Remember from Chapter 9: you've been broadcasting a certain pattern through **The Nervous System Broadcast**, and now you're changing the signal.

The Reframe:

This pushback is a normal and predictable part of any system change. It is not a sign that your boundary is wrong; it is a sign that the boundary is *working* and the system is being forced to adjust. Systems resist change by design, that's homeostasis. Your job is not to eliminate the pushback; it's to hold your boundary with compassionate firmness despite the pushback.

The Strategy:

Communicate your new boundaries with calm, confident, and non-defensive language. Whenever possible, link your boundary to a shared goal or mutual benefit:

> *"I am now turning off my Slack notifications after 6 P.M. I'm doing this to ensure I'm fully rested and can bring my most focused, strategic, and creative thinking to our work tomorrow morning. I'm protecting my capacity to serve this team well for the long term."*

Notice: No apology, no justification, no defensiveness. Just clear, values-aligned communication.

The Obstacle Navigation Plan™ means you're not caught off-guard. You've already scripted your response to these predictable challenges, which means you can implement it even when your cognitive resources are depleted.

The Progress Indicators™: Knowing Your Blueprint Is Working

How do you know if your Blueprint is actually working? **The Progress Indicators™** are both qualitative and quantitative, and it's important to track both.

Indicator Category 1: The Internal Shift (Qualitative)

These are the powerful shifts in your lived, subjective experience. You can track these in your monthly review:

Awareness Indicators:

Do you notice **The Takeover** earlier in the sequence than you used to?

Can you identify your **Stress Signature** signals with greater precision?

Are you catching **Narrative Traps** before they fully activate?

Action Indicators:

Are you using your tools proactively instead of only reactively?

Do you feel more agency and less helplessness in stressful situations?

Are you completing **The Stress Cycle** more consistently?

Adaptation Indicators:

Do you recover faster from difficult days or weeks?

Are you protecting your **Resilience Budget** more effectively?

Do you feel less frequently at **The Crisis Threshold**?

Relational Indicators:

Do you feel more present and less reactive with your family in the evenings?

Are you bringing **The Ghost in the Chair** home less often?

Has your **Nervous System Broadcast** shifted in a way that improves **The Collective Climate** around you?

Indicator Category 2: The External Data (Quantitative)

You can also track objective, verifiable metrics:

Physical Health Markers:

Sleep quality (you can use a sleep tracking app to monitor deep sleep and resting heart rate)

Resting heart rate trends (decreasing over time signals improved nervous system regulation)

Blood pressure readings (if you were in concerning ranges)

Frequency of stress-related symptoms (headaches, digestive issues, muscle tension)

Performance Markers:

Number of sick days taken

Quality of work output (creativity, strategic thinking, error rates)

Meeting effectiveness (shorter, more focused, better outcomes)

End-of-day energy levels (rated 1-10 each evening)

Behavioral Markers:

Frequency of using your core tools (tracked in your **Visual Progress System™**)

Consistency of your **Daily Anchor™** practice

Number of times you successfully held a boundary

How quickly you implemented your **Obstacle Navigation Plan™** when challenges arose

The beauty of **The Progress Indicators™** is that they give you concrete evidence of change, which becomes especially important when your inner critic tries to dismiss your progress.

The Evolution Protocol™: Growing With Your Blueprint

Finally, and perhaps most importantly, you must remember that your Blueprint must evolve as you evolve. The tools and routines that serve you in one season of your life may need to be adjusted or even completely replaced in the next.

The Evolution Protocol™ consists of:

Monthly Review (15-20 minutes)

Set a recurring monthly appointment with yourself. Review:

What's Working: Which tools are you actually using? Which feel effective? Double down on these.

What's Not Working: Which tools are you consistently avoiding? Why? Are they genuinely not helpful, or are you hitting an obstacle that needs navigation?

What's Changed: Has your life circumstance shifted? New stressors appeared? Old stressors resolved? Does your **Context Calibration™** need updating?

Progress Check: Review your **Progress Indicators™**. What evidence do you see of positive change? Where are you still struggling?

Blueprint Update: Based on the above, what one or two adjustments will you make for the coming month?

Quarterly Deep Dive (1-2 hours)

Every three months, do a more thorough review:

Re-take The Three-Dimensional Assessment™: Has your **Stressor Map™** changed? Are new patterns showing up in your **Pattern Recognition Audit™**?

Evaluate Your Commitment Architecture™: Is your accountability system still serving you, or does it need refreshing?

Check Your Foundation Statement: Does it still resonate, or has your "why" evolved?

Celebrate Progress: Intentionally acknowledge how far you've come. Review your early journal entries. Notice the changes.

What works today may need to shift tomorrow, and that's not a sign of failure. It is the very definition of conscious, intentional adaptation. This is the third A of **The 3 A's Framework™** in action at the meta-level: you're adapting not just your daily responses, but your entire resilience system.

Lena's Blueprint Evolution: One Year Later

Let's revisit Lena, our client from Chapter 8, a year after she first built her Blueprint. Her company went through a major, incredibly stressful acquisition. The old Lena would have immediately abandoned all her self-care practices, worked 18-hour days fueled by caffeine and anxiety, and ended up at **The Crisis Threshold** within weeks, spiraling through **Depletion, Disconnection, and Collapse**.

But the new Lena had **The Resilience Blueprint™**.

She recognized **The Takeover** beginning, her **Stress Signature** was unmistakable: racing heart, catastrophic thoughts, the urge to work all night. But this time, she had tools. She immediately activated her **emergency protocols** from Chapter 10's **Emergency Navigation System™**, scheduling an extra session with her therapist to process the uncertainty.

She leaned heavily on her **Core Tools,** using **The Triangle Reset™** as a lifeline before every tense transition meeting. She practiced **The Regulation Breath™** in her car before entering the building each morning, intentionally shifting her **Nervous System Broadcast** so she wasn't amplifying the collective panic.

But most importantly, in her **monthly Evolution Protocol™ review**, she consciously and strategically adapted her Blueprint for the new reality. She knew that her leisurely 15-minute walks were no longer realistic in the short term. So she adapted. She swapped them for a non-negotiable

5-minute reset in her office every 90 minutes—just enough to complete **The Stress Cycle** and prevent accumulation.

She also realized that her need for support had increased exponentially, so she proactively reached out to two trusted colleagues who were also navigating the acquisition and created a weekly check-in call, a powerful **Accountability Alliance™** that became her lifeline.

Lena successfully navigated one of the most stressful periods of her career, not by being perfect or by avoiding the stress, but by using her Blueprint as a dynamic, flexible, and compassionate guide. Her Blueprint didn't prevent the storm, but it was the anchor that kept her from being swept out to sea. She protected her **Resilience Budget** fiercely, prevented **The Performance Tax** from bankrupting her, and emerged on the other side still intact, tired, yes, but not broken.

This is my ultimate vision for you.

Your Call to Action: From Knowledge to Embodied Wisdom

You now have everything you need. You have **The 3 A's Framework™**. You have **The Resilience Operating System™**. You have tools for regulation, protocols for crisis, strategies for team dynamics, and now, **The Resilience Blueprint™,** your personalized implementation guide.

The question is no longer *what* to do. The question is: *will you do it?*

Will you honor your **Foundation Statement**? Will you protect your **Resilience Budget** as fiercely as you protect your calendar? Will you practice **The Daily Anchor™** even on days when you feel "too busy"? Will you implement your **Obstacle Navigation Plan™** when resistance arises?

This is not just about managing stress better. This is about fundamentally changing your relationship with stress. It's about moving from unconscious reactivity to conscious response. It's about preventing **The Takeover** from hijacking your life. It's about ensuring that you don't just succeed in your career, but truly thrive as a whole, healthy, and resilient human being.

The journey doesn't end here. It begins here.

Start with **The Integration Week™**. Build your Blueprint. Choose your tools. Implement your **Commitment Architecture™**. And then, day by day, practice by practice, begin the beautiful, challenging, transformative work of becoming the person who no longer needs this book, because the wisdom has become embodied, automatic, and unconscious.

You have the knowledge. You have the frameworks. You hold the tools.

Now, build your Blueprint. And let it guide you home to yourself.

Reflection Questions for Chapter 11

Your Foundation Inquiry™: If you haven't already, set aside time this week to formally create **Your Resilience Blueprint™** using **The Integration Architecture™** in this chapter. What is your Foundation Statement, the single most important shift you want to make in your relationship with stress?

Your Assessment: Which dimension of **The Three-Dimensional Assessment™** will be most revealing for you: **The Stressor Map™**, **The Pattern Recognition Audit™**, or **The Tool Selection Matrix™**? Why?

Your Commitment Architecture™: Which of the four pillars feels most supportive and realistic for you right now: **The Daily Anchor™**, **The Accountability Alliance™**, **The Visual Progress System™**, or **Habit Tethering™**? Can you commit to implementing at least two?

Your Obstacles: What is the single biggest obstacle you anticipate encountering? Review **The Obstacle Navigation Plan™** and write down your specific strategy for navigating it *before* it arrives.

Your First Step: What is the single most important commitment you are willing to make to yourself, right now, as you close this book and begin the next chapter of your resilience journey? Write it down. Share it with someone you trust. Take the first small step today.

You are not alone in this work. And you are absolutely capable of it.

Welcome to the rest of your resilient life.

Conclusion

Your Transformation

We have reached the end of our journey together on these pages, but in the most meaningful and tangible sense, we have arrived at the true beginning of yours. If you have walked through this book not just as a passive reader absorbing information, but as an active participant, underlining passages that resonated deep within you, pausing to wrestle honestly with the questions, and courageously beginning to sketch out the architectural blueprint of your own resilience, then you have done more than simply read a book. You have engaged in a profound act of self-reclamation. You have stood at the helm of your own ship, taken an honest, unflinching inventory of your well-worn navigation systems, your automatic reactive tendencies, and your deeply ingrained patterns, and you have begun the courageous work of learning to steer with intention, wisdom, and agency.

I want you to take a moment, right now, before you turn this final page, to truly acknowledge the significance of that work. In a world that relentlessly, and with ever-increasing intensity, demands more *from* us, more productivity, more availability, more data, more speed, more performance, more optimization of every waking hour, you have made a conscious and counter-cultural choice to demand more *for* yourself: more presence, more well-being, more agency, and more of your own precious and irreplaceable humanity. That is not a small thing. In the context of our modern work culture, where burnout is worn like a badge of honor and exhaustion is mistaken for commitment, this is a revolutionary act. It is, in fact, the beginning of everything.

My deepest and most sincere hope is that you close this book feeling not just informed or temporarily inspired, but fundamentally and irrevocably transformed. The goal was never to simply give you a collection of interesting ideas to ponder or another list of stress-management techniques to add to your already overflowing mental inbox. The goal was to facilitate a fundamental, tectonic shift in your relationship with stress, with your work, with your leadership, and ultimately, with the very core of yourself.

The Core Transformation: From Unconscious Reactivity to Conscious Agency

The central transformation this book is designed to ignite is the profound and life-altering shift from a life of unconscious, exhausting, and often destructive reactivity to one of conscious, intentional, and empowering agency. It is the deliberate movement from being a passive victim of your circumstances, feeling tossed about by the unpredictable waves of deadlines, demands, and difficult people, to becoming the active, skilled, and confident author of your responses.

Before this journey, your experience of stress may have felt like being caught in a relentless, unpredictable, and deeply personal storm. A triggering email would arrive in your inbox, and before you had a chance to think, the gale-force winds of anxiety would be howling through your nervous system, the towering waves of anger or frustration would be crashing over the deck, and you would be thrown about, clinging to the wreckage, just trying to survive until the storm passed. You were, in essence, a passenger on your own ship, your destination and your state of being determined entirely by the whims of the external weather. A life lived in reactivity is a life of chronic, low-grade exhaustion, a feeling of being perpetually on the defensive, of never quite catching your breath, of being one crisis away from collapse.

The 3-A Approach™ is your path to reclaiming the helm, to becoming the captain of your own vessel.

Awareness is the act of turning on your sophisticated, internal navigation systems. It is the moment you learn to read the subtle but powerful weather patterns of your own nervous system with the skill of a seasoned navigator. It is the ability to notice the almost imperceptible drop in barometric pressure, the slight clenching in your jaw, the shallowing of your breath, the familiar knot in your stomach, the edge in your internal dialogue, that signals an approaching storm. You are no longer surprised or ambushed by the storm; you see it forming on the horizon, and you have precious time to prepare. The grainy, black-and-white film of your unconscious reactions begins to turn into vivid, high-definition color. You move from being a victim of your emotional weather to becoming a skilled meteorologist of your inner world.

Regulated Action is the practice of skillful, courageous seamanship in the midst of turbulent waters. It is the ability to stand on the bridge during that storm, to feel the powerful, primal pull of the reactive currents that want to drag you onto the jagged rocks of regret, and yet consciously choose to steer your ship with a steady, regulated, and intentional hand. It is the sacred creation of that pause, that breath-filled space, between the lightning flash of the trigger and the thunderous roar of your response. It is in that sacred pause, often lasting only two to three seconds, that you reclaim your power. This is where leadership is truly forged, not in the absence of challenge, but in your capacity to remain steady within it.

Adaptation is the essential, strategic work you do in the calm, safe harbor between the storms. It is the meticulous process of reinforcing the hull of your ship, mending your torn sails, restocking your depleted provisions, upgrading your navigation equipment, and charting a wiser, more sustainable course for the future based on the hard-won lessons of your past voyages. It is the conscious design of a life and a leadership practice that supports your well-being and amplifies your impact, rather than constantly testing your limits and depleting your reserves. This is not self-indulgence. This is strategic self-preservation in service of sustained excellence.

If you have truly engaged with this work, you now understand a set of profound and liberating truths. You understand that stress is an inevitable companion of a meaningful and ambitious life, but that burnout, its toxic, soul-crushing cousin, is optional. You understand that true, sustainable resilience is not about pushing harder, having more grit, or developing a thicker, more impenetrable skin; it is about leading smarter, with more compassion for your own very real human limits and more respect for the sophisticated operating system that keeps you alive. And you understand that the 3-A's are not a theory to be memorized for a test, but a set of practical, repeatable, and neuroscience-informed practices to be lived, embodied, and refined, one moment, one choice, and one conscious breath at a time. This is the new, upgraded operating system for your life and your leadership.

Beyond the Workplace: The Ripple Effect of a Resilient Life

While the primary context of this book has been the workplace, the principles and practices we have explored are not, and cannot be, confined to the hours between nine and five or the boundaries of your office walls. Your nervous system does not have a work setting and a home setting. It does not differentiate between a stressful board meeting and a stressful, emotionally charged conversation with your teenager. A hijacked amygdala feels the same whether the trigger is a looming project deadline or a difficult financial discussion with your partner. The physiological cascade of cortisol and adrenaline is identical. Your body doesn't care about your organizational chart.

The beautiful and profound truth is that when you learn to navigate stress in one area of your life, you are building a universal, transferable skill set that will inevitably and powerfully serve you in every other domain. The deep, intentional work you do to become a more resilient professional will, without any extra effort or separate practice, make you a more resilient, present, and compassionate human being in every relationship and role you inhabit.

In Your Relationships: Think about a recurring conflict you have with a loved one, the kind that follows the same tired script, produces the same painful outcome, and leaves both of you feeling disconnected and misunderstood. The old, reactive you, operating on autopilot, likely had a predictable pattern. Perhaps you would get defensive, your voice rising in pitch and volume as you interrupted to make your point heard (fight). Or maybe you would shut down completely, emotionally withdrawing behind a wall of silence to avoid the discomfort of conflict (flight). Neither response brought you closer. Neither response solved anything. Both left damage in their wake.

The new, regulated you has a radically different set of options. Imagine this: your partner brings up a sensitive topic, perhaps something about household responsibilities or financial decisions or how you spent your weekend. You feel the familiar heat of anger or the cold knot of anxiety rising in your chest, the old script queuing up in your mind (**Awareness**). But now, that sensation is your cue, your red flag, your moment of choice. Instead of launching into your old, well-worn script, you take one deep, grounding breath before you speak—a silent pause that lasts only two seconds but changes everything (**Regulated Action**). In that precious space, you access a new choice, a new response that wasn't available to you before.

You choose to say, "I can hear this is really important to you, and I want to understand your perspective fully. I can also feel myself getting defensive right now, and I know I won't be able to listen well from this activated place. Can we please take a 10-minute break and come back to this when I can give you my full, calm, undivided attention?" (**Adaptation**).

This single, advanced skill, the ability to notice your own activation in real-time and take responsibility for managing it, can transform the quality, safety, depth, and intimacy of your most important relationships. It is relationship intelligence in action.

In Your Parenting: Our children are absolute masters at triggering our deepest and most primal stress responses. They are experts at finding the frayed ends of our last nerves, especially at the end of a long, depleting workday when our regulatory reserves are already running on fumes. The old you might have come home, exhausted and empty, only to be met with a child's spilled juice all over the clean kitchen floor, homework still not started, sibling bickering escalating, dinner not even thought about yet. The internal monologue would be swift, harsh, and automatic: *"Are you kidding me? After the day I've had, this is the last thing I need! Why can't anyone in this house just keep it together?"* The reactive snap would be almost instantaneous, your tone sharp, your words regrettable the moment they left your mouth.

The new you has a different capacity, a different bandwidth. You walk in the door, feeling the heavy weight of the day's exhaustion settling in your shoulders and the tightness in your chest (**Awareness**). You see the spilled juice spreading across the counter. You feel the surge of irritability and frustration rising. But now, that feeling is your signal, not your sentence. You pause, close your eyes for a moment, place a hand on your heart, and take a single, deep, steadying breath (**Regulated Action**). From that more centered, more resourced place, you find the capacity to respond with a calm, reassuring tone: "Oops, accidents happen to all of us. Let's grab a towel together and clean it up. Then we can figure out dinner as a team" (**Adaptation**).

Your regulated presence, in that small but significant moment, does more than just clean up spilled juice. It communicates to your child that mistakes are part of being human, that you are a safe harbor even when you are tired and stretched thin, and that they are more important than a clean floor or a perfect evening. You are modeling for them, in real-time and in the most powerful way possible, what it looks like to be a resilient, self-aware, and compassionate human being. This is legacy leadership.

In Your Health and Well-being: Your fundamental relationship with your physical and mental health will also transform in profound ways. The old you might have treated your body like a workhorse to be driven, an inconvenient machine to be fueled with caffeine and adrenaline and sheer willpower, systematically ignoring its increasingly urgent signals of fatigue, pain, and depletion until it finally broke down and forced you to pay attention through illness, injury, or complete collapse. Rest was for the weak. Boundaries were for people who weren't serious about success. Self-care was a luxury you couldn't afford.

The new you understands that these signals, the persistent headaches, the disrupted sleep, the digestive issues, the inability to focus, the emotional volatility, are not an inconvenience to be medicated away or powered through. They are valuable, mission-critical data from an intelligent system trying desperately to keep you alive and functioning (**Awareness**). You learn to see rest not as a luxury or a sign of weakness, but as a non-negotiable and essential performance enhancer, as strategic as any business planning session (**Regulated Action**). You begin to intentionally and proactively build a lifestyle with sustainable rhythms of movement, nourishment, recovery, and genuine rest that support your well-being rather than constantly depleting it (**Adaptation**).

You move from a reactive relationship with your health, only paying attention when something is broken, only changing behavior when you receive a scary diagnosis, to a proactive, compassionate, and sustainable partnership with your body. You learn to see your body not as an enemy to be conquered or controlled, not as a machine to be optimized, but as a wise and trusted ally on your journey, providing you with constant, real-time feedback about what is and isn't sustainable.

This work is not about compartmentalizing your life into neat little boxes or wearing different masks for different audiences. It is about integrating all of who you are into a coherent, authentic, and resilient whole. The calm, centered, and powerful leader you are becoming at work is the very same calm, centered, and fully present partner, parent, friend, and human being you are becoming at home. There is no separation. There is only you, showing up more fully, more consciously, more humanly everywhere you go.

The Professional Platform: The Unexpected and Powerful Dividends of Resilience

While the primary motivation for embarking on this journey is often the deep, personal desire to reduce suffering and increase well-being, to simply feel better and function better in your own skin, the professional dividends of this work are immense, measurable, and far-reaching. In a world that is increasingly defined by what business leaders call the VUCA environment, Volatility, Uncertainty, Complexity, and Ambiguity, the ability to remain calm, clear, connected, and courageous under pressure is no longer a "soft skill" relegated to HR workshops and team-building retreats. It is the ultimate competitive advantage. It is the new currency of modern leadership.

It is what separates the leaders who thrive from the leaders who merely survive.

When you master the skills and embody the practices in this book, you are not just managing your stress or preventing your burnout. You are building a powerful, distinctive, and highly valuable professional platform that sets you apart in any organization, any industry, any market.

You Build Deep, Unshakeable Trust: People are instinctively and powerfully drawn to, and will place their deepest trust in, leaders who are steady in a storm. When your team knows, from direct and repeated experience, that you will not react with panic, blame, scapegoating, or explosive anger in the face of a crisis, an unexpected setback, or a significant failure, they will feel a profound and increasingly rare sense of psychological safety. They will be more willing to bring you bad news early, when it is still a manageable problem rather than a full-blown crisis, because they trust you will receive it with composure rather than punishment. They will be more willing to admit their own mistakes and ask for help when they need it, fostering a culture of accountability, learning, and continuous improvement rather than one of defensive posturing and blame-shifting. And they will be more willing to offer innovative, creative, but potentially risky ideas, which is the absolute lifeblood of any successful, adaptive, and future-ready organization. Your personal regulation becomes the bedrock, the foundation, the soil in which high-trust, high-performing, psychologically safe, and genuinely innovative teams can grow.

You Enhance Your Influence and Impact Exponentially: The person who can stay regulated in a tense, high-stakes negotiation, the one who doesn't take the bait when someone is trying to provoke a reaction, is the person who maintains the power position. The person who can listen with genuine, undefended curiosity instead of just waiting impatiently for their turn to talk is the person who actually understands what's really happening beneath the surface. The person who can communicate difficult news, deliver hard feedback, or navigate a sensitive conversation with clarity, compassion, and unwavering conviction is the person who holds the most influence in any room, any boardroom, any crucial conversation.

Your ability to manage your own internal state gives you a genuine superpower: the ability to more effectively read, understand, influence, and shape the external environment. You move from being a pawn of the emotional dynamics swirling in the room to being a skillful, respected, and trusted architect of them. People watch how you show up. They notice your steadiness. They feel your presence. And they are influenced by it, often without even realizing it.

You Create and Attract New Opportunities: As you become known in your organization, your industry, and your professional network as a resilient, steady, emotionally intelligent, and unflappable leader, new and exciting opportunities will naturally gravitate toward you like iron filings to a magnet. You will be the one senior leadership taps to lead the challenging but career-making new initiative. You will be the one asked to mentor the brilliant but struggling high-potential leader who is buckling under the pressure. You will be the one chosen to represent the company in a critical partnership negotiation or a sensitive client conversation. You will be the one invited to speak at industry conferences, to contribute thought leadership, to serve on advisory boards. Your resilience becomes a core and highly visible part of your professional brand, your reputation, and your value proposition, opening doors to career advancement, expanded influence, consulting engagements, board positions, and opportunities you may have never imagined possible.

Mastering these skills is not just about personal survival or avoiding burnout. It is about professional thrival. It is about becoming the kind of leader that the most talented people actively seek out and are desperate to work for, and the kind of colleague that everyone wants on their team when the pressure is at its highest and the stakes are at their most critical.

A Personal Message to You, From My Heart to Yours

As we prepare to close this chapter and this book, I want to speak to you directly, one human being to another, from my heart to yours. I want to speak to the part of you that may have picked up this book feeling exhausted, overwhelmed, cynical about whether real change is even possible, and perhaps even a little bit broken. I want to speak to the part of you that may have felt, for a very long time, that you are utterly alone in your struggle, that everyone else around you seems to be handling the relentless pressure with an ease and a grace that feels completely alien, completely unattainable to you. I want to speak to the part of you that wonders if you're just not cut out for this level of leadership, this level of responsibility, this level of demand.

I want you to hear me clearly, and I want you to let these words sink in past the armor of your intellect, past the defenses of your professionalism, and into the very core of your being: **You are not broken. You are not weak. You are not failing. You are human.**

You are a human being with a magnificent, ancient, and incredibly sophisticated nervous system that was brilliantly designed by millions of years of evolution to keep you safe in a world that no longer exists, a world of immediate, visible, physical threats that could be resolved by running or fighting. You are living and working in an unprecedented era of hyper-connectivity, relentless digital demands, perpetual availability, ambiguous threats, and systemic, unrelenting uncertainty. Your nervous system is doing exactly what it was designed to do. The fact that you are feeling the strain, the exhaustion, the sense of being constantly overwhelmed is not a sign of your personal weakness, your professional inadequacy, or your fundamental brokenness. It is a sign of your humanity. It is a testament to the fact that you are a caring, deeply committed, and conscientious person navigating a profoundly challenging, often unsustainable, and historically unique modern landscape.

Please, I invite you, I urge you, to consider letting go of the heavy, crushing burden of shame. Let go of the relentless, punishing internal self-criticism and the insidious, deeply internalized cultural story that you "should" be able to handle it all without breaking a sweat, without asking for help, without ever showing a crack in your armor. That story is a lie. It is a toxic, destructive myth that has been sold to us by a culture that often profits from our burnout, thrives on our overwork, and depends on our deeply ingrained belief that we are never quite enough.

My message to you is simple, and it is one I have had to learn the hard way, through my own painful, humbling, and ultimately liberating journey through burnout and back to wholeness: **Stress is a signal, not a sentence.** It is your body's intelligent, compassionate, and unwavering way of telling you that a boundary has been crossed, a core need has gone unmet, or a vital resource has been depleted. It is not a weakness. It is not a failure. It is information. It is an invitation to pause, to listen with a new level of respect and humility, and to respond to yourself with a new level of wisdom, skill, and genuine self-compassion.

With the right tools, with committed practice, and with the courage to challenge the narratives that no longer serve you, you can learn to navigate stress with skill and grace. You can transform your relationship with it from one of fear and avoidance to one of understanding and mastery. And you can come out stronger, wiser, clearer, and more whole on the other side.

The Journey Continues: Your Therapy Doctor™ and the "Talk to Me Nice" Series

This book, *Navigating Stress in the Workplace*, is a cornerstone of my work, but it is not the final destination. It is one essential part of a much larger, ongoing, and evolving conversation about the profound, transformative power of emotional intelligence in our lives, our leadership, and our organizations. It is a core pillar of my **"Talk to Me Nice"** series, a body of work dedicated to helping leaders and professionals master the art of healthy, effective, and compassionate communication. First, and most importantly, with themselves, that critical internal dialogue that shapes everything. And then, as a natural and powerful extension, with the people they lead, partner with, parent, and love.

My brand, **Your Therapy Doctor™**, is built on a simple but radical belief: that the core principles of good therapy, deep self-awareness, skillful emotional regulation, clear and boundaried communication, and the capacity for genuine, non-judgmental self-compassion, are not just for the therapy room or the coaching session. They are the essential, foundational, and most critical skills for effective leadership, sustainable high performance, and a well-lived, deeply meaningful life in the 21st century.

My work, through my speaking engagements, my organizational consulting partnerships, my executive coaching, and my writing, is to translate these powerful but often-inaccessible psychological concepts into practical, immediately applicable, and actionable tools that you can use every single day, in boardrooms and break rooms, in negotiations and difficult conversations, in moments of triumph and moments of crisis. I invite you to continue this journey with me. This is not the end of our conversation. It is just the beginning.

Your Call to Action: The First Step on Your New Path

A journey of a thousand miles, as the ancient proverb wisely reminds us, begins with a single step. You have done the hard, reflective, courageous work of reading this book, wrestling with uncomfortable truths, and building your personalized Stress Navigation Plan. Now, you are standing at the trailhead of a new path. The temptation, in this moment, can be overwhelming, to feel crushed by the scale of the journey ahead, paralyzed by all the things you "should" be doing perfectly starting immediately, anxious about whether you can really maintain all these new practices and habits. I want you to resist that temptation with everything you have. I want you to bring your focus back from the distant, intimidating mountain peak to the single, solid piece of ground directly beneath your feet right now.

Here is your call to action. It is simple, it is immediate, and it is powerful.

Open your notebook to the Personalized Stress Navigation Plan you created in the previous chapter.

Read it over with a sense of kindness, appreciation, and deep respect for the person who took the time, energy, and courage to create it.

Choose ONE thing. Not ten things. Not five things. Not even three things. Just one. Choose the single, smallest, most achievable, least intimidating, and most immediately accessible action or routine from your entire plan. Perhaps it's practicing your Box Breathing technique for just two minutes in the morning before you open your email or check your phone. Perhaps it's scheduling one 10-minute walk into your calendar for tomorrow afternoon and treating it as non-negotiable. Perhaps it's simply putting a sticky note with your chosen calming mantra on your computer monitor where you'll see it multiple times throughout the day.

Commit to that one thing for the next seven days. That is your only assignment. That is your entire goal.

That is all. Your goal is not to perfectly execute your entire, beautiful, comprehensive plan overnight. Your goal is not transformation by next Monday. Your goal is simply to take the first small, tangible, concrete step. It is to build a tiny, almost imperceptible bit of momentum, to create one small win. It is to prove to yourself, through direct, embodied experience rather than abstract hope, that change is possible, that you are capable of making a different choice, one small, regulated, intentional decision at a time.

You now have the map. You have the compass. You have the skills to read the weather patterns of your own nervous system and the strength to steer the ship even in choppy waters. The ocean ahead is vast and unpredictable, full of both inevitable challenge and breathtaking beauty, storms you cannot avoid and sunrises you cannot yet imagine. It is time to raise your anchor, to set your sails with intention, and to begin the magnificent, worthwhile, deeply human voyage of resilient leadership.

Final Reflection Questions:

Your Core Transformation: What is the single most important, most meaningful transformation you hope to experience as you begin to put your plan into practice? What would be different in your life, your leadership, your relationships if this transformation takes root?

Your First Step: What is the one small, achievable action you have chosen as your call to action? When, specifically, and how, specifically, will you implement it tomorrow?

Your Commitment: Who is one person you trust, a colleague, a mentor, a partner, a friend, who you can share your commitment with to increase your accountability, celebrate your progress, and receive support on your journey?

With All My Belief in You

You are standing at a threshold. Behind you lies the familiar but exhausting territory of reaction, depletion, and the quiet, resigned acceptance that "this is just how it has to be if I want to succeed." Before you lies something radically different, a life where you are no longer governed by the tyranny of your triggers, where your worth is not measured by your capacity to override and ignore your humanity, and where your leadership is defined not by how much pain you can endure in silence, but by how wisely, how skillfully, how compassionately you can respond to complexity.

This is not hyperbole. This is not motivational fluff. This is the lived reality of thousands of leaders who have chosen to do this work with commitment, courage, and consistency.

I believe in you. Not in some vague, platitudinal way, but with the deep, grounded, unshakeable conviction that comes from watching person after person, leaders just like you, perhaps even more skeptical than you, perhaps even more burned out than you, reclaim their power, rebuild their resilience, and redesign their lives through these practices. I believe in your capacity to transform not because you are exceptional in some rarified, superhuman way, but precisely because you are beautifully, imperfectly, magnificently human, equipped with the same nervous system, the same capacity for awareness, the same longing for a life that feels authentic, sustainable, and deeply meaningful.

The world desperately needs resilient leaders. Not the old, outdated definition of resilience, the grit-your-teeth, white-knuckle, martyr-yourself-on-the-altar-of-productivity, never-let-them-see-you-sweat version. The world needs the new kind, the evolved kind, the sustainable kind: leaders who know their limits and honor them without apology. Leaders who can hold space for tremendous complexity without collapsing into chaos or rigid control. Leaders who understand that their regulated presence, their emotional steadiness, their capacity to remain grounded in the storm is not a luxury, not a nice-to-have, not soft, it is the foundation upon which everything else is built. It is the platform from which all other leadership competencies emerge and become sustainable.

You are becoming that leader.

Not someday. Not when you finally have it all figured out. Not when life gets less complicated or the demands magically ease up or you finally feel ready.

Right now. With this next breath. With this next choice. With this next small, brave step forward.

Welcome home to yourself. Welcome to the helm of your own ship. Welcome to resilient leadership.

The ocean is calling. It's time to sail.

With profound respect for your journey and unwavering belief in your ca-
pacity,

Dr. Pauline Belton

Founder, Your Therapy Doctor™

Author, "The HEART of Resilient Leadership" Series

Business Integration

FROM PERSONAL RESILIENCE TO ORGANIZATIONAL THRIVAL

From Personal Resilience to Organizational Thrival

As we conclude this journey together, my deepest and most sincere hope is that the principles, frameworks, and practices within these pages have resonated with you not just as an individual seeking personal relief from the weight of chronic stress, but as a leader, a culture architect, and a conscious shaper of the human experience in your organization. The work of navigating stress and building genuine, sustainable resilience is, at its core, a deeply personal endeavor. It begins with the courageous inner work of turning on the lights of your own awareness, of learning to read your own internal weather patterns, of becoming the steady captain of your own ship. But its impact, its true transformative power, is profoundly collective and exponentially multiplicative.

A single resilient, regulated leader can stabilize an entire team in the midst of a crisis, becoming the eye of calm in the storm. A leadership team that has learned the shared language and embodied practices of resilience can transform the dynamics of an entire department, shifting it from reactive firefighting to strategic, intentional response. And a critical mass of resilient, self-aware, emotionally intelligent individuals throughout an organization can fundamentally and irrevocably shift the entire culture, moving it from a place of chronic stress, silent suffering, and mere survival to one of sustainable high performance, deep psychological safety, genuine innovation, and collective thrival.

This final chapter is a bridge. It is designed to take the concepts we have explored on a deeply personal level and translate them into the practical, real-world applications of organizational life. It is a comprehensive and strategic answer to the essential question that every forward-thinking, human-centered, and future-focused leader should be asking in today's volatile, uncertain, complex, and ambiguous world: **"How do we move beyond well-intentioned but superficial individual wellness initiatives and begin the deep, systemic, transformational work of building a truly resilient organization that can not only survive disruption but thrive within it?"**

The principles in this book are not abstract theories I have studied from a distance. They are the very foundation, the DNA, of the work I do every single day with organizations of all shapes, sizes, and sectors, from the hierarchical and often rigid structures of federal agencies and prestigious academic institutions to the fast-paced, agile, and relentlessly demanding environments of Fortune 500 companies and rapidly scaling startups. This book is not just a resource; it is an entry point. It is the beginning of a conversation and a potential partnership, an invitation to a deeper, more integrated, more effective, and more sustainable approach to leadership development, organizational health, and genuine culture transformation.

In this chapter, we will explore how these concepts translate into dynamic, experiential, and transformational training programs. We will examine the comprehensive, multi-layered approach of organizational consulting required to build a true culture of resilience from the inside out. We will look at specialized applications of this framework for different sectors with their unique challenges and stressors. And finally, we will explore the broader vision for this work, a powerful, positive ripple effect that flows from healthier workplaces to stronger families to more connected communities to a more sustainable, equitable, and fundamentally human-centered model of success.

Training Programs: Translating Concepts into Embodied Capabilities

Every single principle, every framework, every practice in this book directly translates into the live and virtual trainings I have developed, refined, and delivered over years of working with thousands of leaders and professionals across diverse industries. My approach to training is not about delivering a passive, information-heavy lecture on the neuroscience of stress or handing out yet another wellness checklist for people to ignore. It is about creating an immersive, engaging, psychologically safe, and deeply experiential learning environment where participants move from intellectually understanding a concept to building a tangible, embodied, immediately accessible capability.

The goal is not just for your people to *know* more when they walk out of the room. The goal is for them to be able to *do* more, to show up differently, more skillfully, more powerfully in the heat of a real-world, high-pressure moment. Knowledge without application is merely intellectual entertainment. Transformation requires experience, practice, and integration.

The Core Philosophy of My Trainings:

Practicality Over Theory: While all of my work is deeply grounded in the latest, peer-reviewed research from neuroscience, psychology, organizational behavior, and trauma-informed practice, the unwavering focus in the training room is always on practical, actionable, immediately applicable tools. The guiding question that shapes the design of every single training module, every exercise, every discussion is: **"What is the one small but powerful thing a person can do differently tomorrow morning, in their first meeting, in their first difficult conversation,**

in their first moment of feeling overwhelmed, that will make a meaningful, measurable difference in their day?"

Experience Over Explanation: Human beings do not fundamentally change by being told what to do or why we should do it. We change through direct, personal, visceral experience. My trainings are highly interactive and carefully scaffolded, incorporating confidential self-reflection exercises, vulnerable small-group discussions, and real-time guided practice of the core techniques, Box Breathing, the 5-4-3-2-1 Grounding technique, the 3-Minute Reset, the CLEAR™ Communication framework, the Positive No. The room is alive with energy, sometimes uncomfortable, always transformative, as people experience in their own bodies and in real-time their innate but often dormant ability to shift their physiological and emotional state with intention and skill.

Customization Over Generic Content: A training for a group of emergency room nurses facing life-and-death decisions every shift will look, feel, sound, and land very differently from a training for a team of financial analysts working on a critical merger deadline or a group of university faculty navigating the competing demands of research, teaching, and service. Before any engagement, I work closely and collaboratively with organizational leaders to understand their specific pain points, their unique cultural language and values, their most common and potent workplace stressors, and their strategic goals for the training. I then meticulously adapt the content, the case studies (using anonymized but recognizable scenarios), and the language to ensure the material feels immediate, relevant, resonant, and authentic to their lived experience.

Vulnerability Modeled from the Front: I don't stand at the front of the room as an expert who has transcended stress and achieved some enlightened state of permanent calm. I show up as a fellow human being who has walked through the fire of burnout, who has had to rebuild my own capacity for resilience from the ground up, and who practices these tools daily not because I have mastered them, but because I need them. This authenticity creates psychological safety and gives participants permission to be honest about their own struggles rather than performing competence.

A Glimpse into a "Navigating Stress" Workshop:

Whether it's a 90-minute keynote designed to inspire, disrupt conventional thinking, and plant seeds of possibility, or a full-day immersive intensive designed for deep skill-building and personal transformation, every session is structured around the proven architecture of the **3-A Approach™**:

The Awareness Module: Turning On the Navigation Lights

We begin by creating a psychologically safe, non-judgmental space for radical honesty and self-assessment. This is not about shame or comparison. This is about clarity. Participants are guided through a private, confidential **"Stress Signal Inventory"** where they identify and map their unique physiological, emotional, cognitive, and behavioral signatures of stress. We then move into a structured **"Lifestyle Audit"** where they examine the sustainability of their current rhythms, boundaries, and recovery practices with clear-eyed honesty.

The goal is to help participants see, often for the first time with startling clarity, their own personal, deeply ingrained, habitual patterns of stress and reactivity. This is frequently a profound "aha" moment for many attendees as they begin to connect the dots between their chronic physical symptoms, the persistent headaches, the digestive issues, the disrupted sleep, the constant fatigue, their emotional states, the hair-trigger irritability, the pervasive anxiety, the flattened affect, and their specific, predictable workplace triggers.

We name the patterns. We normalize the struggle. We remove the shame. And in doing so, we create the foundation for change.

The Regulated Action Module: Building Your In-the-Moment Toolkit

This is the most interactive, experiential, and often transformative part of the training. I don't just talk *about* nervous system regulation techniques; I lead the room *through* them, explaining the neuroscience behind why they work as we practice together in real-time.

We practice **Triangle Breathing** and **Box Breathing** as a group, with me guiding the rhythm and participants noticing the almost immediate physiological shift. I guide them through the **5-4-3-2-1 Grounding technique**, having them actively engage their senses and notice the real-time shift from internal chaos to external focus, from scattered to centered. We workshop the **"Positive No"**, that critical skill of setting a boundary without burning a bridge, by scripting and role-playing difficult but common workplace scenarios: the unreasonable deadline request, the meeting that should have been an email, the colleague who consistently oversteps.

We practice the **3-Minute Reset** between simulated back-to-back meetings. We explore **strategic disengagement,** the art of the intentional pause before responding to a triggering email or comment. The room is filled with energy, sometimes laughter, sometimes tears, and always a palpable sense of empowerment as people experience, in their own bodies, their capacity to shift their state not through willpower or positive thinking, but through specific, repeatable, evidence-based techniques.

The Adaptation Module: Building Sustainable Systems

In the final part of the workshop, we shift from individual, in-the-moment reactive tools to the essential, proactive work of building sustainable long-term systems and structures. This is where resilience moves from being an emergency response to becoming a way of life.

Participants begin to draft the first version of their own **Personalized Stress Navigation Plan**, identifying their specific high-risk situations, their go-to regulation tools, their non-negotiable recovery rituals, and their early warning systems. They work in small, confidential accountability groups to brainstorm implementation strategies, troubleshoot anticipated obstacles specific to their work environment, and identify their support systems.

We explore the **concept of micro-boundaries,** those small, strategic decisions about email hours, meeting schedules, and recovery time that accumulate into a sustainable rhythm. We discuss **strategic energy management,** the intentional design of your day around your natural energy cycles rather than just your calendar. We examine **the art of strategic disengagement,** knowing when to disconnect, when to delegate, when to decline.

Participants leave the session not just with a set of new tools sitting in a binder on a shelf, but with a clear, personalized, immediately actionable plan for how they will begin to integrate those tools into the fabric of their daily lives starting tomorrow morning.

The Impact:

The feedback from these sessions is consistently powerful and deeply moving. Participants often report a profound sense of relief, the relief of finally having language for their experience, of understanding that they are not weak or broken or alone, of being given a practical, non-pathologizing, neuroscience-based framework for addressing their challenges. They leave feeling not just temporarily inspired, but genuinely and practically empowered. They leave with tools they can use in the car on the way home. They leave feeling seen, understood, and equipped.

Organizational Consulting: Building a Culture of Resilience from the Inside Out

A single training workshop, no matter how powerful, can be a catalyst for change, a spark that ignites new awareness, disrupts old patterns, and opens new possibilities. But to create a truly resilient organization, one that can sustain high performance through inevitable disruption, the work must go deeper, wider, and longer. **A spark cannot catch fire on wet wood.**

Stress navigation, burnout prevention, and genuine organizational resilience are not just individual skill deficits to be addressed through training. They are deeply cultural issues, systemic issues, leadership issues. **A fish cannot thrive in toxic water, no matter how many swimming lessons it takes.** My organizational consulting work is about helping leaders to see, understand, honestly assess, and then intentionally transform the quality of the water, the culture, the norms, the unwritten rules, the reward systems, the communication patterns, the leadership behaviors that either support or undermine human well-being and sustainable performance.

I partner with organizations on a long-term, deeply collaborative basis to implement systemic resilience practices that move far beyond individual skill-building to address the underlying cultural dynamics, leadership behaviors, structural policies, and operational drivers of chronic stress and burnout. This is not a quick-fix program. This is a multi-phase, comprehensive, transformational engagement that typically includes four interconnected and essential components:

1. Leadership Coaching: Anchoring Transformation in the C-Suite

The journey always, without exception, begins at the top. Culture flows downhill. Leadership sets the emotional temperature. You cannot mandate a culture of well-being from leaders who are themselves burned out, reactive, and modeling unsustainable work practices. The transformation must begin with the senior leadership team.

Through a series of confidential one-on-one executive coaching sessions and facilitated leadership team workshops, we work on their personal resilience practices first, not as a nice-to-have or as a precursor to the "real work," but as the real work. They must learn to become the conscious, intentional, and authentic **"emotional thermostats"** for their teams and their organizations.

We work on deepening their **self-awareness,** their ability to recognize their own stress signals, their triggers, their reactive patterns, and their impact on others. We build their capacity for **self-regulation,** the ability to manage their own emotional state under pressure, to respond rather than react, to remain grounded when the ground is shaking. We examine their **communication style** under stress, do they become controlling or dismissive, do they withdraw or explode, do they blame or problem-solve? We strengthen their ability to **model the very behaviors of sustainable high performance** they want to see throughout the organization, taking breaks, setting boundaries, asking for help, admitting mistakes, prioritizing recovery.

A leader who is not personally and authentically embodying these principles, who talks about work-life balance while sending emails at midnight, who preaches boundaries while consistently overriding their team's capacity, who champions well-being while visibly running on empty, cannot lead a genuine culture change. Any attempt to do so will be immediately perceived as performative, hypocritical, and will ultimately fail. **Transformation begins with the person in the mirror.**

2. CLEAR™ Communication Training: Building Psychological Safety Through Skillful Dialogue

As we've explored throughout this book, unclear communication, lack of psychological safety, inability to navigate conflict constructively, and absence of skills for difficult conversations are massive, pervasive, and entirely preventable drivers of workplace stress, interpersonal conflict, and organizational dysfunction.

I lead teams, from the C-suite to middle management to front-line employees, through an intensive, experiential training on the **CLEAR™ Communication Framework**. This is not superficial training on how to craft better presentations or write more professional emails. This is advanced training on the essential, high-stakes skills of navigating conflict without destruction, giving and receiving feedback without defensiveness, building genuine trust and transparency, disagreeing respectfully, repairing ruptures, and creating the psychological safety that allows for robust debate, creative tension, and true innovation.

The **CLEAR™ model** stands for:

Center yourself first (emotional regulation before communication)

Listen without agenda (curiosity over defense)

Express with clarity and compassion (directness without brutality)

Align on shared values and goals (connection before correction)

Repair and strengthen the relationship (feedback as investment, not weapon)

This training is often the lynchpin, the turning point, of the entire culture transformation process. When people feel heard, when they can speak truth without fear of retaliation, when conflict becomes generative rather than destructive, everything shifts.

3. Policy and Process Review: The Organizational Resilience Audit

We then zoom out to examine the organization's systems, structures, policies, and unwritten rules through an entirely new lens. This is where we move from individual behavior change to systemic transformation. We ask the essential diagnostic question: **"Are your current policies and processes inadvertently creating stress, driving burnout, and undermining the very well-being and performance you say you value?"**

We conduct a comprehensive **"Resilience Audit"** of your key operational practices, cultural norms, and structural systems, examining them rigorously through the dual lens of human well-being and sustainable high performance. This audit typically includes:

Meeting Culture Analysis: Are your meetings productive, purposeful, inclusive, energizing, and time-bounded, or are they a primary source of dread, frustration, wasted time, and exhaustion? We analyze your meeting ecosystem, frequency, duration, purpose, facilitation, follow-through, and work to redesign meeting protocols and governance to be more focused, equitable, efficient, and respectful of people's finite attention and energy.

Communication Norms Assessment: What are the unspoken, unwritten, but powerfully felt expectations around email and Slack response times? Is there a culture of 24/7 availability and hyper-responsiveness? Are people praised for being "always on"? Are boundaries punished subtly or overtly? We work to create clear, explicit, leader-endorsed, and consistently modeled norms that protect employees' capacity for deep, focused work and their essential off-hours recovery time. We help organizations distinguish between urgency theater and actual emergencies.

Performance Management Redesign: Does your current performance review and feedback process foster psychological safety, continuous learning, growth, and development, or does it induce fear, anxiety, political posturing, and a sense of being judged rather than developed? We work to redesign feedback systems to be more frequent, more developmental, more balanced (strengths and growth edges), more future-focused, and less punitive. Performance management should develop capability, not create trauma.

Workload and Capacity Planning: Are you consistently under-resourced and over-committed? Is "do more with less" your unspoken operating principle? We help leadership teams conduct honest workload assessments, prioritization exercises, and capacity planning to ensure that expectations align with reality and that your people have the bandwidth to do excellent work rather than just survive.

4. Building Resilience Champions: Sustaining and Scaling the Transformation

To make cultural change sustainable, to ensure it permeates every level and every corner of the organization rather than remaining a top-down initiative that fades over time, the transformation must be embedded throughout the culture and owned by the people, not just mandated by leadership.

We work with the organization to identify, train, and support a diverse cohort of **"Resilience Champions"**, passionate, respected, credible informal leaders from across different departments, functions, and levels of the organization. These are not HR representatives or wellness coordinators. These are line leaders, individual contributors, and managers who are trained and equipped to:

Facilitate peer-led small-group discussions and workshops

Model the resilience practices authentically in their daily work and leadership

Serve as a grassroots support system, confidential resource, and safe sounding board for their colleagues

Provide real-time feedback to leadership about what's working and what's not in the transformation

Keep the conversation alive, visible, and normalized in the everyday flow of work

This creates a powerful, organic, self-sustaining network of support and cultural reinforcement. It ensures that the new norms, the new language, the new practices are reinforced from the bottom up and the middle out, not just cascaded from the top down. **Culture change that depends on a single charismatic leader or a single enthusiastic HR initiative will die the moment that leader leaves or that initiative loses funding. Culture change that is owned by the people is permanent.**

This kind of deep, comprehensive, systemic consulting work is not a quick fix or a one-time intervention. It is a long-term, courageous, and strategic commitment to building a healthier, more human, more psychologically safe, more innovative, more adaptive, and ultimately more successful organization. It is an investment in your most valuable and most vulnerable asset: your people.

Specialized Applications: Adapting the Framework for Unique and Demanding Environments

The core principles of the **3-A Approach™**, Awareness, Regulated Action, and Adaptation, are universal because they are grounded in the universal architecture and functioning of the human nervous system. Stress affects a federal employee's amygdala the same way it affects a software engineer's. Burnout destroys a university professor's capacity the same way it destroys a healthcare executive's. However, the language, the cultural entry points, the sector-specific stressors, and the practical applications must be thoughtfully and skillfully adapted to the unique context, constraints, and culture of each sector.

Federal Sector and Government Agencies: Leading with Integrity Under Constraint

Government employees and civil servants face a unique and often intensely frustrating constellation of stressors: the immense weight of public accountability and scrutiny, the ever-present tension of trying to serve the public good within the real-world constraints of limited resources and political interference, and the often soul-crushing reality of navigating rigid, hierarchical, slow-moving, and change-resistant bureaucratic structures.

In my work with federal agencies and government organizations, I adapt the frameworks to emphasize the critical importance and practical skills of maintaining internal regulation, clarity, and agency under external constraint and chaos. We focus heavily on building the psychological flexibility and emotional regulation skills to maintain personal integrity and sense of purpose when the external systems feel broken.

The practice of clearly distinguishing one's **"sphere of influence"** (what you can actually control and change) from one's **"sphere of concern"** (what matters to you but lies outside your direct control) becomes an essential daily tool for combating the feelings of powerlessness, futility, and moral injury that can lead to cynicism and burnout in this sector.

We also dedicate significant time to building strong, clear, unapologetic personal and professional **boundaries** as a necessary protective tool, not as selfishness, but as sustainability, for navigating rigid structures and competing demands without losing one's sense of self, one's values, and one's purpose in public service. **You cannot serve the mission if you sacrifice yourself.**

Higher Education: Transforming Academic Culture from Stress to Sustainable Excellence

The academic world is a complex, paradoxical, and often deeply dysfunctional ecosystem, simultaneously a place of profound intellectual inquiry, creative freedom, and transformative education, and a place of intense, chronic, and largely unspoken stress, exploitation, and burnout. The stressors are unique and multifaceted.

For Faculty: The relentless and often impossible demands of what is euphemistically called the "three-legged stool", teaching (including course prep, grading, student meetings, and the significant emotional labor of mentoring), research (including grant writing, data collection, publication, and the constant pressure to produce), and service (committee work, program coordination, community engagement). Add to this the precarity of contingent faculty positions, the hyper-competitive publish-or-perish culture, the lack of institutional support, and the expectation that passion for the work should somehow make exploitation acceptable.

For Students: The intense pressure of balancing newfound independence and self-direction with high-stakes academic performance, significant financial stress, the challenge of identity formation and belonging, pervasive imposter syndrome, and the mental health crisis that is epidemic on college campuses.

My trainings and consulting work in academic settings address both populations with customized, culturally resonant approaches:

For Faculty and Staff: We focus on ruthless prioritization and the courage to say no, on building micro-practices of regulation and recovery between classes or meetings, on developing sustainable strategies for managing the immense and chronically under-acknowledged emotional labor of mentoring students through crises, and on creating peer support networks that break the isolation of academic life. We also work on helping faculty reclaim their intrinsic motivation, reconnecting with why they entered academia in the first place, rather than being driven solely by external metrics and institutional demands.

For Students: We focus on building the foundational emotional intelligence skills of self-awareness and self-regulation to help them navigate the challenging developmental transition to adulthood, the intense pressures of academic performance, the complexity of relationships, and the reality of setbacks and failure as part of learning. We normalize struggle, challenge the myth of effortless perfection, and provide concrete tools for managing anxiety, building community, and asking for help.

The overarching goal is to transform academic culture from one that glorifies overwork and treats burnout as a badge of intellectual seriousness to one that recognizes sustainable well-being as essential to intellectual excellence, creativity, and genuine learning.

Corporate and Private Sector: Redefining High Performance

In corporate environments, from startups to Fortune 500 companies, the stressors often revolve around relentless speed, constant change, hyper-competition, unclear priorities, matrix reporting structures, and the glorification of hustle culture. The challenge here is often helping organizations see that resilience is not about working harder or having more grit, it's about working smarter, more sustainably, and more humanely.

We focus on helping organizations understand that **burned-out employees are not high performers,** they make more errors, have poorer judgment, struggle with innovation, damage relationships, and eventually exit.

We build the business case for resilience not as a feel-good HR initiative but as a strategic competitive advantage. We work on redesigning work to be sustainable at the pace of human beings, not machines.

Revenue Streams and Business Vision: A Ripple Effect of Well-Being

This book is more than a resource. It is more than content. It is an entry point, the beginning of a conversation, a relationship, and a potential partnership. The principles and practices detailed in these pages are the foundation for a comprehensive, integrated, multi-format ecosystem of services and offerings designed to create a powerful, positive, multiplicative ripple effect of transformation. The book feeds directly and strategically into:

Keynotes and Workshops for Organizations: Dynamic, disruptive, emotionally resonant, and highly customized 90-minute to full-day sessions that introduce the core concepts of the **3-A Approach™** and the **"Talk to Me Nice"** philosophy, challenge conventional wisdom about stress and performance, and provide teams with immediate, actionable, evidence-based tools to begin their resilience journey with momentum and confidence.

EQ-i 2.0 and 360 Assessment Integration: Comprehensive emotional intelligence assessment, interpretation, and development planning using the gold-standard **EQ-i 2.0** instrument, integrated seamlessly with the resilience framework to provide leaders with deep self-awareness and a personalized roadmap for growth across the five core pillars: self-perception, self-expression, interpersonal, decision-making, and stress management.

Certification Programs for Professionals: Multi-day intensive training and professional certification for HR leaders, organizational development practitioners, executive coaches, therapists, and consultants who want to become licensed facilitators of the **"Navigating Stress in the Workplace"** curriculum within their own organizations or with their own client base. This creates scalable, sustainable internal capacity for this transformational work and extends the reach and impact exponentially.

Digital Courses and Comprehensive Toolkits: Self-paced, multimedia online courses and downloadable workbooks that allow individuals, teams, and entire organizations to engage deeply with this work on their own timeline, complete with video teaching modules, interactive assessments, guided audio practices, implementation templates, and access to a supportive online community for accountability, troubleshooting, and peer learning.

Long-Term Consulting Partnerships for Culture Transformation: Six-month to multi-year, high-touch, deeply collaborative strategic partnerships with organizations that are genuinely ready to commit to the deep, systemic, often uncomfortable work of building a culture of resilience, psychological safety, and sustainable high performance from the inside out. This is for leaders who understand that real transformation takes time, requires investment, and demands courage.

University and College Partnerships: Customized, scalable programs designed specifically for higher education institutions, including faculty professional development, student wellness programming, leadership training for department chairs and deans, and institution-wide culture assessments and strategic planning for well-being integration.

Speaking and Thought Leadership: Keynote addresses at industry conferences, thought leadership contributions to professional publications, podcast interviews, and strategic positioning as a leading voice in the future of work, resilient leadership, and the integration of emotional intelligence into organizational strategy.

My Business Vision: Creating a Ripple Effect That Changes the World

My business vision is audaciously simple and profoundly ambitious: **I believe that the health of our workplaces is directly, inextricably, and causally linked to the health of our families, our communities, and our society.**

Workplaces characterized by chronic stress, fear-based leadership, toxic productivity culture, and normalized burnout send depleted, reactive, dysregulated, and disconnected human beings back into their families and communities at the end of each exhausting day. These individuals, good, caring people who are simply running on empty, have dramatically less capacity for patience with their children, for emotional presence with their partners, for generosity with their neighbors, and for active engagement in their communities. The stress doesn't stay at work. It metastasizes. It spreads. It damages everything it touches.

Conversely, workplaces characterized by genuine psychological safety, sustainable performance expectations, emotionally intelligent leadership, and a culture of well-being send energized, regulated, connected, and resourced human beings back into the world. These same individuals have significantly greater capacity for joy, creativity, patience, compassion, and contribution. They parent better. They partner better. They show up in their communities with more to give.

Therefore, the transformation of workplace culture is not just an organizational strategy, it is a social justice issue. It is a public health imperative. It is a moral obligation.

The more leaders, the more teams, the more organizations that adopt and embody these principles and practices, the greater and more powerful the ripple effect becomes. This work is about creating healthier, more human workplaces, which in turn create stronger, more emotionally connected families, more engaged and compassionate communities, more equitable and just institutions, and a more sustainable, regenerative, truly human-centered model of success and societal progress.

This is not just a business. This is not just a book. This is a movement. This is a mission. And I invite you to be part of it.

Your Personal Call to Action as a Leader

As you close this book and prepare to step back into the complexity and demands of your leadership role, I want to leave you with a final, powerful, and deeply personal call to action, not just for your own survival or well-being, but for your leadership legacy and the culture you have the power and the responsibility to create.

You hold within you a profound opportunity and a significant responsibility to be a force for positive, lasting, transformative change in the lives of the people you lead, the teams you build, and the organizational culture you shape every single day through your words, your decisions, your presence, and your example.

Start with Yourself, Always and Without Exception: Your first, most important, most non-negotiable step is to commit, with unwavering integrity and visible consistency, to your own practice. Build your **Personalized Stress Navigation Plan** and actually use it. Let your team see you taking your full lunch break away from your desk. Let them hear you setting clear, respectful, unapologetic boundaries with senior leadership. Let them witness you taking a visible breath and a strategic pause before responding in a tense, high-stakes meeting. Model the very behaviors, the self-awareness, the self-regulation, the self-compassion, the healthy boundaries, that you want to cultivate throughout your culture.

Your embodied, authentic example is the most powerful, most influential, and most credible leadership tool you possess. Your team doesn't listen to what you say about well-being. They watch what you do about your own.

Start a Conversation, Create Safety: Find one small, safe, low-risk way to start an honest, vulnerable conversation about stress, struggle, and well-being with your team. It could be as simple as sharing one concept from this book that deeply resonated with you or challenged you in your next team meeting. It could be introducing the **"One-Word Check-In"** at the start of your next one-on-one, simply asking "How are you, really, in one word?" and actually listening to the answer without trying to fix it.

You do not need to have all the answers. You do not need to be an expert. You do not need to solve everyone's problems. You simply need to have the courage to ask the questions, to name the elephant in the room, and to listen to the answers with an open heart, genuine curiosity, and without judgment. **Permission to be human starts with the leader.**

Take One Small, Systemic Step: Look honestly and critically at your team's current processes, meeting rituals, communication norms, and unwritten rules. What is one small but strategic systemic change you can make, not a one-time initiative, but a structural change, that would measurably reduce unnecessary stress and meaningfully increase collective well-being and sustainable performance?

Can you implement a **"no-meeting Friday afternoon"** policy to protect time for deep, focused work and planning? Can you create clearer, more explicit communication protocols and response-time expectations for your team's Slack or email channels? Can you build in a mandatory **5-minute buffer between all scheduled meetings** to allow for biological breaks, mental transitions, and brief resets? Can you redesign your team meetings to include a brief grounding practice at the beginning? Can you shift from praising overwork to celebrating sustainable excellence?

Small systemic changes, consistently applied and leader-modeled, create massive cultural shifts over time.

The journey to a more resilient, more human, more sustainable organization can feel overwhelming, even impossible, especially if you're looking at the mountain from the base. But like every meaningful journey, like every act of real leadership, it begins with a single, intentional, courageous step. My deepest hope is that this book has served as both a map for that journey and a source of courage, permission, and practical tools for you to take that first crucial step.

The world is in desperate need of a new model of leadership, one that is grounded not in the relentless, soul-crushing, ultimately unsustainable pursuit of more, but in the deep, quiet, revolutionary, and ultimately formidable power of resilience, wisdom, self-awareness, compassion, and full humanity.

Now, it is your turn to lead the way. The ocean is vast. The stakes are high. And you are ready.

Final Reflection Questions for Business Integration:

Your Leadership Anchor: As a leader, what is the single most important principle, practice, or mindset shift from this book that you want to anchor your leadership style in moving forward? What would be different if you led from that place consistently?

Your First Cultural Micro-Practice: What is one small, specific, low-risk micro-practice you can introduce to your team within the next 30 days to begin an authentic, ongoing conversation about well-being, sustainability, and resilience?

Your Ripple Effect Vision: What is your personal, compelling vision for the ripple effect you want to create, in your team, in your organization, in your industry, and ultimately in your community? What legacy do you want to leave? What is the very first, most courageous step on that path?

With deep respect for your leadership journey and unshakeable belief in your capacity to transform culture,

Dr. Pauline Belton
Founder, Your Therapy Doctor™
Creator, The 3-A Approach™
Author, "Talk to Me Nice" Series

Ready to bring this work into your organization?
Visit **YourTherapyDoctor.com** to explore keynotes, workshops, consulting partnerships, and certification programs designed to build resilient leaders and thriving organizational cultures.

www.ingramcontent.com/pod-product-compliance
Lightning Source LLC
Chambersburg PA
CBHW060406130626
46555CB00005B/1995